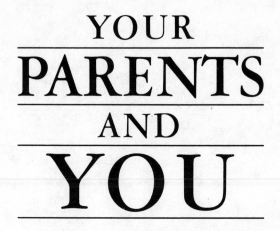

YOUR
PARENTS
AND
YOU

YOUR
PARENTS
AND
YOU

HOW OUR PARENTS SHAPE OUR SELF CONCEPT, OUR PERCEPTION OF GOD AND OUR RELATIONSHIPS WITH OTHERS

ROBERT S. McGEE / PAT SPRINGLE / JIM CRADDOCK

Rapha
PUBLISHING

Houston, Texas

WORD PUBLISHING
Dallas · London · Vancouver · Melbourne

Your Parents and You
by Robert S. McGee, Jim Craddock and Pat Springle

Revised Edition
Copyright © 1990 by Rapha Publishing

Originally published under the title:
The Parent Factor, by Robert S. McGee, Jim Craddock and Pat Springle
Copyright © 1989 by Rapha Publishing

Unless otherwise indicated, Scripture references in this volume are from the NEW AMERICAN STANDARD BIBLE, © The Lockman Foundation, 1960, 1962, 1963, 1968, 1971, 1972, 1973, 1975, 1977.

Scripture quotations noted NIV are taken from the HOLY BIBLE: NEW INTERNATIONAL VERSION. Copyright © 1973, 1978, 1984 International Bible Society. Used by permission of Zondervan Bible Publishers.

Portions of *The Search for Significance* book and workbook reprinted and adapted by permission. Robert S. McGee. (2nd ed. Copyright © 1990 by Robert S. McGee; Houston and Dallas, TX: Rapha Publishing/Word, Inc.)

Second Printing, Revised Edition, 1990
Printed in the United States of America

ISBN: 0-945276-13-3

*We dedicate this book to those who read it, with our sincere desire
that godly wisdom will be gained and lives will be blessed.*

Contents

Acknowledgments ix

Introduction xi

Section I THE PROBLEM: Our Perceptions of God, Self-Concepts and Relationships with Others Are Shaped by Our Relationships with Our Parents

1 *The Shaping of a Child* Jim Craddock 3

2 *Your Parents and You* Robert S. McGee 9

3 *Lookin' for Love* Jim Craddock 17

4 *Empty Solutions* Robert S. McGee 25

5 *Stages of Development* Robert S. McGee 29

6 *When Development Is Blocked* Robert S. McGee 37

7 *Emotional Healing and Development* Pat Springle 51

8 *The Role of Relationships* Pat Springle 61

9 *The Need to Forgive* Robert S. McGee 67

Section II THE SOLUTION: A Healthy Perception of God, Others and Ourselves

10 *Bonding with God* Jim Craddock 79

11 *God Wants Us to Know Him as Father*
         Robert S. McGee, Pat Springle 87

12 *The Names of God* Jim Craddock 99

Section III THE PROCESS: Changing Our Perceptions of God, Self-Concepts and Relationships with Others

13 *Metamorphosis* Jim Craddock 117

14 *"And You Shall Know the Truth..."* Robert S. McGee 123

15 *Dealing with Fears* Robert S. McGee 133

16 *"What Do I Do with My Emotions?"* Pat Springle 137

17 *Rivers in the Desert* Pat Springle 145

18 *Breaking the Cycle:*
         Modeling God's Character to Your Children Pat Springle 155

19 *Breaking the Cycle:*
         Responding to Your Parents Pat Springle 165

WORKBOOK SECTION

Introduction 175
Step 1   *The Nurturing Family: A Biblical Model*....................................177
Step 2   *Stages of Development* 181
Step 3   *Evaluating Your Relationships with Your Parents* 191
Step 4   *Evaluating Your Relationship with God* 199
Step 5   *Your Parents' Influence on Your Perception of God* 203
Step 6   *Analyzing Your Family*...211
Step 7   *The Names of God* 223
Step 8   *Learning More About God from Psalm 139* 231
Step 9   *Children of God* 237
Step 10   *Characteristics of Christ and Our Relationship with Him* 245
Step 11   *Motivations for Obedience* 273
Step 12   *Overcoming Emotional Roadblocks*...289
Step 13   *Forgiving Others* 317
Step 14   *Breaking the Cycle:*
            Modeling God's Character to Your Children 323
Step 15   *Breaking the Cycle: Responding to Your Parents*.....................331
Step 16   *Christ Repairs Damaged Lives* 337
Step 17   *A Twenty-Day Journal* 343

Acknowledgments

This book would not have been written without the support, encouragement and hard work of many people. Our thanks to...

...Brad Lewis, who promised to produce a beautiful manuscript, and did.

...Dan Sampson, who coordinated the publication of this manuscript.

...Dr. Ralph W. Neighbour, Jr., for his excellent work in getting this manuscript started.

... Dr. Steve Spotts, who gave us the benefit of his insights and wisdom.

... Susan Joiner, who edited the manuscript to give it clarity and a smooth flow.

...many of our friends who have struggled with their views of God and have seen genuine, life-changing progress.

... and to our families, who have loved us, encouraged us and modeled the character of God to us.

Introduction

A person's relationship with his parents is usually the most profound of his life. It shapes his self-concept, his hopes, his dreams, his perceptions, his relationship with God and his relationships with others.

Sadly, many of us come from homes where we did not feel the affection or receive the encouragement and patient correction that a child needs. Our perceptions of God may be colored and clouded by the neglect, abuse and manipulation of our parents. If so, we may assume that God is just like them—that He is neglectful, abusive and manipulative, too. If our perceptions of God are wrong, then our primary source of wisdom, love and strength is thwarted. We withdraw from Him. We don't trust Him. We are angry with Him. We feel alone and compelled to find fulfillment in other ways and through other relationships. But these alternatives only result in more pain and emptiness.

This book attempts to define and describe the way our perceptions of God have been shaped by our relationships with our parents. It shows how parental relationships affect our relationships with others and even with ourselves. But it doesn't stop there. It also identifies the truth of God's love and power, and suggests ways we can experience the reality of His character. It is through our true experience of Him that we can handle our other relationships correctly.

The workbook section of this book is designed to help you reflect on the pains and joys in your life and help you apply the truths of God's Word in your every emotion, dream and relationship.

Some of the discoveries you make may be difficult to handle alone. We suggest that you find a friend or a small group of friends to go through this material with you. Their wisdom, encouragement and affirmation will enhance your ability to make substantive and long-lasting changes in your life. And you will be able to help them, too.

It is our hope that you will experience the reality of God increasingly, and that this experience will enable you to enjoy more intimacy, love and acceptance than you have ever known!

Section I

THE PROBLEM: Our Perceptions of God, Self-Concepts and Relationships with Others Are Shaped by Our Relationships with Our Parents.

Chapter 1

The Shaping of a Child

Jim Craddock

Children are supremely moldable. They each have their own God-given personalities, and they each learn to make their own choices. But much like lumps of clay in a potter's hands, their confidence and self-concept are primarily shaped by their parents. If they feel loved, valued and protected, and if they are encouraged to try without the threat of condemnation when they fail, then they usually will be shaped into confident, secure people. If, however, children feel condemned by harsh, perfectionistic parents, or neglected by parents who are too preoccupied with their own selfish interests, then they usually will be shaped into adults who are plagued by insecurity, guilt, fear, anger, loneliness and withdrawal. They will likely be driven to accomplish goals and please others in an attempt to win the love and acceptance they crave. This, they hope, will fill the emptiness in their lives.

Parents play the critical role in shaping a child's life. In his book, *The First Three Years of Life,* Harvard physician Dr. Burton White says that a child desperately needs the unbounded love, affection and attention of his or her parents in order to develop emotional and relational health. Dr. White calls this "irrational love," and states that no one can take the place of parents in communicating this kind of love and in shaping and molding a child's life:

> *I have had the privilege of being able to compare the everyday experiences of very many children, from many kinds of families, and*

the evidence of my own observations is overwhelmingly that, all things
being equal, a baby's parents are far more likely to meet his most
important developmental needs than are any other people.[1]

The primary focus of this book is not on making you a better parent, though that is certainly one of its applications. Rather, this book is about you. It is designed to help you see how your life has been shaped by your parents. It focuses on your development—emotionally, relationally and spiritually—with the hope that such knowledge will enable you to experience more of God's freedom, grace and strength in each of these areas of your life. To understand this critical developmental process, let's look at the nature of children.

A young child (such as you when you were a child) forms his concept of reality by looking at his parents. By watching what they get excited or angry about, he learns what is important. By seeing how they relate to each other and to others, he learns about love and hate. By observing them, he learns about every significant issue in life. The child also ascribes godlike characteristics to his parents: what they say is Truth, what they demand is Law and how they treat him is Love. If their words and actions are loving, protective and compassionate, then the child is likely to experience good emotional, relational and spiritual health. But if their words and actions are harmful and confusing, his concept of life will be characterized by pain and distortion, too. The accuracy of these early concepts and the warmth of the family environment contribute significantly to a child's shaping in the critical areas of his self-concept, his relationships with others and his view of God.

The Child's Self-Esteem

If a child is affirmed consistently and disciplined in a loving way, he probably will grow up believing that he is valued and secure. He will be able to take appropriate social and business risks without the confining fear of failure, and he will have the potential to enjoy relationships without fearing intimacy.

If the child's needs for love and acceptance are not met because his parents are condemning or neglectful, he may conclude that something is wrong with him. (Like most children, he probably will think that his parents are always right, so the fault must be his, not theirs.) Consequently, he will learn to condemn himself for not being worthy of love, and will either deny his needs for love and acceptance, or try to win that love by his performance. If this self-condemnation is not arrested by consistent love, it can slowly evolve into a deeply-rooted self-hatred.

Relating to Others

In a secure and loving environment, a child learns to give and receive love. He learns to experience the deep joy and pain of intimate relationships with other people. In an environment characterized by severe criticism or manipulation, a child learns to condemn and manipulate others. He typically will whine until he gets his way. Even as an adult, he may whine and complain until people either give in to him or withdraw from him. He may become a master manipulator, subtly and intricately using praise and condemnation to change others' behavior to suit himself. People then become objects used to meet his needs instead of individuals to be loved.

We have a very strong tendency to emulate our parents' attitudes, behavior and relationships, good or bad. In other words, we tend to treat and relate to people the way our parents have treated and related to them (and us). Although it is true that some people attempt to be as unlike their parents as possible, this response is usually related to behavioral factors. For instance, a child of an alcoholic may refuse to touch alcohol. Even people who consciously choose to be different from their parents may discover, if they are able to be honest and objective, that they have assimilated the very personality traits in their parents which they despise. Parental modeling is a powerful, if sometimes complex, force in shaping children's lives.

The Child's View of God

For better or for worse, parents represent God to their children. A child's emotional and spiritual foundations are to be provided by them. Most important of all, parents are to model the love and strength of God to their children. They are responsible for portraying His reliability, His unconditional love, His acceptance and His purposeful discipline.

Though it obviously is impossible for parents to model the character of God perfectly, it is their responsibility to represent the Lord to their children. In the Scriptures, parents are instructed to have compassion for their children (Ps. 103:13), to train each child appropriately (Prov. 22:6), to discipline them firmly and lovingly (Prov. 23:13-14), to avoid provoking them to anger (Eph. 6:4), and to teach and model the character, purposes and instructions of God in what they say and do (Deut. 6:6-9). Clearly, it is God's design that parents reflect His love, protection and provision to their children so that they will be secure and learn to love, trust and serve Him wholeheartedly.

Parents may have the best of intentions and still fail to meet the nurturing needs of their children. Their own circumstances may be out of control. Perhaps severe health or financial problems are a continual source of preoccupation. Or, perhaps they are giving too much attention and authority to their children in an effort to provide a better home environment than they had. Most parents are doing the best they know how to do, attempting to survive and cope even though no one has ever shown them how to do so effectively.

Some parents, however, are simply too self-absorbed to give their children what they need. If they are "too busy," or if they are abusive, condemning or neglectful, their children will believe that God is condemning instead of forgiving, cruel instead of loving and neglectful instead of attentive.

When parents have unmet or unresolved needs, they generally are unable to meet their children's needs. This promotes at least two problems. One is that their distortions, hurts and needs will likely be passed from one generation to another. Secondly, and maybe more importantly, their children will lack the fundamental resources of perception, affirmation and strength necessary for coping with the many and varied problems in life. In healthy human development, parents normally impart these resources to their child. But when parents have unresolved issues from *their* childhood, their ability to impart these qualities to their children is hindered to one degree or another. Not only do children then develop distorted concepts of God, themselves and others, but the very mechanisms which enable them to conceptualize become distorted. Therefore, we can see that while teaching the truth is important, we also need to help people learn how to assimilate that truth so that they can apply it to their lives. Otherwise, desired growth and change probably will not occur. They may know a lot; they may even be excellent teachers of the truth, but deep changes in their hearts—those that would impact their lives—may still elude them. Real, substantive change can occur only when both the truth and the ability to perceive and apply that truth are firmly planted in a person's life. This is why it is so important for us to be involved in strong, vibrantly healthy relationships. In the context of loving relationships, we can learn to be honest with ourselves and others, we can learn to perceive life accurately, and we can receive comfort and encouragement in the slow and often painful process of growth. Perhaps a mature friend, pastor, counselor or a small group can provide an environment of affirmation for you as you seek to grow and change.

Although parents play a major role in shaping the identity of their children, a healthy home environment doesn't guarantee security and stability. One young woman from a stable, loving family was emotionally shattered by her peers in college. She became insecure and withdrawn. Conversely, poor parental modeling doesn't guarantee that children will be insecure. Two emotionally troubled young brothers from an abusive family were taken in by a foster family. They experienced deep healing as a result of the love and affirmation they received there, and grew to be fairly stable young men. These are exceptions. Parental influence is still a primary factor in shaping a child's identity.

Children are indeed like lumps of clay in a potter's hands. The kinds of relationships they have with their parents are central to the formation of their mental, emotional, spiritual and relational framework. Producing healthy children doesn't require parental perfection, but it does require a strong measure of love, affirmation, honesty, consistency and time (among other things).

Each of us is like a lump of clay that has been shaped and molded by our parents. The "parent factor" is therefore important to all of us. It is our hope that God will use this book profoundly in your life to give you:

1. An understanding about why you feel and respond the way you do. Quite often, developing this kind of understanding is painful, but objectivity is very important if one is to make substantial progress.

2. A process of change to improve your view of God, your self-concept and your relationships with others. The workbook section of this book is specifically designed to help you analyze these areas of your life, with Bible studies and questions to help you build a new and fresh belief system.

3. Tools for developing a strong, vibrant relationship with God. Such a relationship is the foundation for a life characterized by freedom, joyful obedience and deep relationships with others.

Chapter 2

Your Parents and You

Robert S. McGee

Your relationships with your parents have shaped your belief system and relational abilities significantly. If your parents were (and are) loving and supportive, then you probably believe that God is nurturing and affirming. You're probably a fairly secure and confident person who is able to relate easily to other people. But your parents may have had a tendency to treat you harshly, demanding a lot from you in exchange for their approval. If so, you probably believe that God is also that way and that you can never do enough to please Him. Feelings of insecurity resulting from that misconception may prompt you either to withdraw or be defensive in your relationships with others.

Whether they have been loving or aloof, kind or harsh, supportive or condemning, attentive or neglectful, your parents have played a major role in forming your concept of God, your self-concept and your ability to relate to others. The results can be wonderful or tragic.

Supportive, Accepting Parents

I was recently invited to a Bible study for young businessmen in Dallas. The group met at a restaurant in the morning before work. I don't want to say it was too early, but when we drove up, the other men were waiting in their cars because the restaurant hadn't opened yet! When we finally got inside, I wondered if I could get the waitress to give me coffee intravenously in both arms.

About halfway through the Bible study, I became relatively coherent. We were looking at passages of Scripture which describe evangelism and were talking about how to communicate the gospel in the marketplace. These men really wanted to serve the Lord, and it was a lively discussion.

After an hour or so, several of them needed to leave for work, and the group began to disband. One of them, Jim, who didn't have to go directly to his job, remained behind. He had been active in the discussion about evangelism, so I asked him some questions about his relationship with the Lord. It must be strong, I surmised, if he had the confidence to share his faith regularly.

Jim described how he had become a Christian and how the Bible study was helping him to be more effective in serving the Lord. I asked a question that I've learned to ask people like Jim: "The Lord said that those who are fruitful will be pruned so that they will bear more fruit. How do you respond when the Lord prunes you?"

He thought for a minute and said, "I assume the Lord knows what is best for me and what I need to serve Him more effectively."

I turned to Frank, the Bible study leader, who could tell I was impressed—delighted—by Jim's answer. Frank said, "He really means it. He has an excellent perspective on the character of God."

I asked Jim, "How did you develop your concept of God? It seems relatively positive and accurate from what I can tell."

"Well," he said, "my parents have always been really loving toward me. I always knew I could count on them when I was growing up, and they were fairly consistent in the way they disciplined me. I guess I got my impressions of God by watching my parents."

As I continued talking with Jim, I found that although he had to face tough issues with God as we all do, he seemed to have a peace about who he was. He knew he needed to make some changes in his performance, but he was content with the way he perceived that God had created him to be. Finally, I saw the influence of his early parent-child relationship by his openness in relating to others.

Verbally Abusive Parents

I asked Cheryl to describe her home life. "It was okay," she said, not exactly giving the kind of full description I was looking for.

I probed a bit. "Tell me how your parents got along."

"Well, they argued a lot. My father was a Sunday school teacher, but he was a bear at home."

"How did he treat you, Cheryl?"

Cheryl's head dropped slowly. "Okay, I guess."

"How did he show you that he loved you?"

"He didn't!" she exploded. "He doesn't love me. He always teased me and picked on me or let my brothers pick on me."

"How do you relate to him now?"

"As little as possible. I stay away from home unless I absolutely have to go there. When I do go, I stay for only a day or two. I can't stand any more than that."

Cheryl's difficulties were painfully obvious. Her parents had not communicated love and acceptance to her. They hadn't given her the freedom to fail when she was a child, so she withdrew from them, unwilling to risk possible rejection.

Her relationship with God mirrored her relationships with her parents. She felt that she could never do enough to please Him and yet she felt guilty if she didn't try. Her parents' belittling led her to feel God was doing the same. She had begun to put herself down and to fear relating to anyone.

In addition, Cheryl's focus was directed primarily toward herself: *Have I done enough today? What did my boss think of me when I said that? I wonder if I should have said no to Bill? Why do I feel this way? There must be something wrong with me!* Cheryl's introspection was morbid and paralyzing. Her immobility created tremendous guilt for her. She knew that God wanted her to be obedient to Him and felt that she knew what she should do, but a deeply rooted fear of rejection prevented her from doing it. As motivators for behavior, fear and guilt are a lethal combination!

Unaffectionate Parents

If you met Susan on the street, you might think that she sang in her church choir. In reality, she has slept with three different men this past week alone and has been with twelve others over the past month. How did she get into such a lifestyle? Her problem started a long time ago.

At the age of eight, Susan said to herself, *There must be something wrong with me. My Daddy won't hug me or touch me or spend time with me. I guess I'm not what I ought to be. If I were, Daddy would love me!*

Her father was a decent man, but he had grown up in a non-touching home. Such children, as they mature, often relate physical affection to sexual intimacy and will tend to be non-touchers as fathers, much to the detriment of their children.

By the time Susan was thirteen, she was trying to find in other men the love that her father had withheld from her. Her promiscuity caused her to be "popular" with older boys, even with older men.

She later married, not because she deeply loved her husband, but to get the affection she had always wanted but had never received from her father. As you can imagine, the couple had serious problems. After a while, one man couldn't meet Susan's insatiable desire for affection. There wasn't a chance for her marriage to succeed!

Susan realized something was wrong within her, but she couldn't pinpoint what it was. It was as though she looked at her conduct through a window and was shocked by it, but unable to change it. She stumbled through life confused, hurting and acting out her craving for fatherly love. Only through hours of counseling did Susan recognize that her life was a complex set of needs combined with problems that were created when those needs weren't met. She had a deep need to be loved and to love in return. Consequently, she had developed many behavioral patterns to try to gain that love from others—especially from men—but her behavior had led to complicated consequences and a lot of heartache.

As a result, Susan not only struggled with how she felt about herself, but with how she related to others, and especially to God. It was almost inconceivable to her that God could really comfort her or meet her emotional needs. Susan's situation at home typifies a relatively predictable phenomenon which we call "the absent-father syndrome."

The Absent-Father Syndrome

The absent-father syndrome is present in a large percentage of American homes. It is not a sickness, but a social disease which robs fathers of the enjoyment that should be theirs. Its effects are usually lifelong in duration, and are sometimes devastating for the children.

The syndrome occurs when the father is absent from home due to death, divorce, prolonged withdrawal or disinterest. The result is that he doesn't provide his children with the time and emotional support they need. Perhaps this is because he simply doesn't know how. Maybe his father didn't provide those needs for him. Or, perhaps divorce or any number of possible problems between his wife and himself prevent him from offering his children their emotional requirements.

Some fathers, after a divorce, feel it's no longer their place to act as "father." Some fathers simply perceive of the home as the wife's domain. Rather than provide any real input there, they withdraw to pursue other activities, like business, sports or the church, which enable them to feel more successful. In some cases, the climate may be more pleasant elsewhere. For whatever reason, the absent-father syndrome occurs when the father is physically and/or emotionally absent from his child's life. The child is the big loser; nobody can take the father's place in the family.

Results of the absent-father syndrome vary. The daughter whose father is absent may reject her appearance, and sometimes even her femininity. She may reason that if she can't attract her father, then she can't attract anyone. She may feel at a disadvantage with men, no matter how attractive she is. She will probably crave attention and affection, usually wanting to be held and never seeming to get enough. This may leave her vulnerable to sexual activity with young men, who will gladly exchange embraces for other pleasures. Many a father has been astounded to learn of his daughter's sexual activities, when in actuality he set her up for them. The exception to this is the woman who resents all men so deeply that she desires no attention from them whatsoever. She may become a "rejection sponge." The smallest inconsistency in her husband or friends will be taken as out-and-out rejection. She may not understand how someone could ever love her. This sensitivity to rejection may not be linked to just her husband, but have an influence on all of her relationships. She might find herself attracted to older men, looking for a "dad," and she may marry an older man. This may result in sexual dysfunction as she finds herself unable to "sleep with dad." Also, since her father was a passive figure, she may develop an attraction for passive men.

The woman who is a product of the absent-father syndrome will probably find it difficult to trust God. Her misconceptions about the father's role were made early, and she may experience a great deal of insecurity and aloneness as she is unable to trust even God the Father.

Sons also are affected by the absent-father syndrome. Having lost their male role model, they either depend on their mother or are forced to look to the world for a role model. In looking to the world, they will often attempt to be the "macho-man."

This is usually just an act to hide their insecurity in not being able to identify with men. Sons who look to the mother as the role model may adopt her mannerisms and pattern themselves after her. Like the daughters, the sons also find themselves craving masculine attention and affection, which can cause vulnerability to homosexual interaction. They will mistake sex for love, and like the daughters, become rejection sponges. Since mother was the dominant figure in the home, they too will have great difficulty trusting the heavenly Father.[1]

Emotionally Distant, Inactive Parents

Parents sometimes withdraw from their families when they feel overwhelmed by life's pressures and activities. Children then feel abandoned. Young children usually believe it must be their fault. This misperception is often confirmed by the withdrawing parent who feels guilty for not being loving and responsible, and so blames the child.

As the abandoned child enters other relationships, he tends to hold back, wanting to protect himself from being abandoned again. Unfortunately, this kind of "protection" actually results in more pain and a lack of intimacy in relationships due to his inability to commit himself to others.

People whose parents have been inactive or withdrawn usually find it difficult to accept love. They reason that because they could not provoke the love of their parents, there must be something really wrong with them. They resist accepting the love of others at face value. They feel lonely, guilty and condemned.

Finally, when it comes to God, they see Him as distant and uninvolved. When they hear of others' vibrant relationships with Him, they often conclude that God isn't like that with them because they're "such poor Christians."

Abusive Parents

Patricia volunteered to serve in a Christian organization. During her orientation, a speaker gave a series of lectures entitled, "God, Our Father."

Every time he started a lecture, Patricia got up and left the room. She had a problem! Her relationship with her father had been the opposite of what Susan (in the first case study) had experienced. Patricia's father had constantly molested and humiliated her during her childhood. She lived in constant dread of his presence in the home, particularly at night. She was afraid to tell her mother what was taking place. Consequently, Patricia lived in lonely, silent fear. Her childhood was a living hell.

She couldn't bear the suggestion that God was like a "father" to her! Her category for the word "father," shaped by her relationship with her dad, was too vile to be applied to God. As a result, she didn't have a positive concept of God as Father and the very mention of it created trauma within her.

She became physically ill during the lectures, and would have to go to bed. She explained to a friend, "I don't want a relationship with God the Father. I have one with Jesus and that's enough for me!

Since Patricia could not trust her own father, what sort of a relationship could she establish with her heavenly Father? For her, worshiping God was impersonal. There could be no emotion, no affection, no trust between her and God the Father.

Strange as it may seem, the reason she had chosen to enter a Christian vocation was directly related to her problem. You see, thinking of God as a person, a friend, was not possible for her. She followed a cold and impersonal set of rules and sought to relate to God by "serving" Him. She wanted to appease Him by living sacrificially as His volunteer in a religious organization. Intimate times of prayer with Him were impossible. The best she could attempt was to read from devotional books.

A young child who is abused will believe that something must be wrong with him. He reasons that even though his parent was wrong, he must have somehow provoked the situation. The shame is overwhelming and his ability to relate to others is severely disturbed.

Perfectionistic Parents

Perfectionistic people may make great employees, but they're lousy parents unless they can change their natural responses to their children. They have such high and rigid standards that even they cannot attain them. Neither can their children.

Often, perfectionistic parents rationalize that they are only pushing their child so that he might experience the most out of life, but they may be pushing him over the emotional edge. It is shattering for a child to feel that he can't measure up in his parents' eyes. The child will feel like a failure. He may try desperately to please them, and probably will fight the depression associated with repressed hurt and anger later in life. He may simply rebel. Rebellious children often have perfectionistic parents. The child may also avoid relating to peers who succeed. Instead, he will tend to run with those who are prone to failure and who therefore aren't threatening to him.

Whether they rebel or try to play the performance game, children of perfectionistic parents struggle with their perception of God. They just can't do enough for Him. Sometimes, they participate in ritualistic church activities. Sometimes, they drop out completely. In either case, they feel distant and condemned by God.

Objectivity and Loyalty

Some people feel guilty when they begin to evaluate their parents' lifestyles and influence. It's as though they were becoming disloyal, unloving children. That's just not the case! Taking an honest look at your heritage does not mean you must respond with vindictiveness, or harshly judge your father and mother. It simply means you recognize both that they have limitations and that they gave you the best they could give at the time! Whether their parenting was good or bad, they tried their best.

Be benevolent as you think about the way your parents raised you. At the same time, work to become the generation where the further passage of negative consequences is ended. In order to accomplish that, you'll need to develop some objectivity and understanding about what has taken place in your family.

Your story is being written as you read these pages! What will it be like? For Susan and Patricia, life was filled with confusion, pain and struggle. Yours can be different. The process may be painful and difficult but change is possible. As we continue, think about what your life would be like if it were included in this chapter!

Chapter 3

Lookin' for Love

Jim Craddock

The true stories in chapter 2 all demonstrate the powerful influence relationships have on us. Relationships, and especially our relationship with God, are the key to life. They are intended to be our foundation for stability and fulfillment. But those who have not experienced love and affirmation often turn to success and possessions for their security and significance.

What do these counterfeit goals look like? Here are a few quotes:

- "The good life is achieving one's goals."
- "It means having plenty of money to do whatever you wish."
- "A quality life requires you to have a good job, a good spouse and good health."
- "The best life? It begins when you can take long vacations, own your own business, live in a beautiful home and drive expensive cars."

According to John 8:44, Satan is *the father of lies;* his goal is to make us believe his lies. One of the myths he tells us is that success and possessions determine our quality of life. But that simply isn't true. God has made us in such a way that success, pleasure and possessions cannot ultimately satisfy us. Relationships (and especially our relationship with Him) provide our real fulfillment. Some of us may be more goal-oriented than others, but all of us are "lookin' for love."

Sarah: Enriched by Love

Sarah's father was a tailor and her mother was a Swedish immigrant. Her father had no money when the couple married in 1923. He worked eighteen-hour days to create enough savings to invest in his own business. In 1927, he finally reached his objective. He prospered, bought a home and hired several employees. Then, in 1931, the Great Depression wiped him out. There were no more rich men to buy his finely tailored suits. Unable to cope with the loss of all he had worked to create, he became severely depressed.

Sarah remembers her father during that bleak period. He slept on the couch while she tiptoed around the house, playing quietly with her dolls. She vividly remembers how their fine home was lost in a foreclosure and auctioned off for a fraction of what it had cost to build. They moved to a tiny apartment—and then to another—and another.

But there was love in that family, no matter where they lived! Sarah's two older brothers and mother constantly showed her affection. Even Sarah's father emerged from his depression and became very affirming of her. While she recognized that their food had become very plain, there was always enough to go around. A lengthy family time always followed the evening meal with open communication and laughter. Sarah particularly looked forward to the honest interaction that took place among her family then.

Sarah learned to love God in a poverty-filled house. Their finances had nothing to do with the amount of faith and trust in God which existed in her home. Love isn't expensive! Its value can't be weighed using the same scale for gold.

Today, Sarah is the wife of a pastor and the mother of three sons. Her oldest brother is the president of a seminary and her other brother is a missionary reaching teenagers in France. Her father died penniless, but he has enriched the world by introducing his three children to the Lord.

Eric: Material Wealth, Emotional Poverty

Eric was the product of a night of passion between a couple who enjoyed living on the fast track. They didn't want children, and they accepted his presence with thinly-veiled resentment.

His father was an attorney, his mother a designer. Their millions had been inherited. Their posh residences in New York and Palm Beach were designed for throwing parties.

During Eric's childhood, his parents shouted at him: "Don't touch that!" "Leave it alone!" "Be careful!" Each room was filled with expensive and fragile antiques that created endless reasons for Eric to feel out of place. When he was only three years old, he was severely beaten by his father for damaging a treasured vase. He was constantly reminded of his own worthlessness and the high value of things.

Eric's parents seldom told him they loved him. They rarely hugged him or encouraged him in his studies or sports. His "nannies" came and went, some trying harder than others to befriend him.

He still remembers the night he deliberately snapped off the hood ornament of his father's favorite Rolls Royce. He was eight years old at the time. He later said, "I enjoyed the beating I got. It was worth every bit of it to see his rage over that stupid thing being broken."

Eric became increasingly destructive. On one occasion, he deliberately poured black paint on his parents' expensive Persian rugs. His mother sent him to a psychiatrist for help with "his problem."

He spent his school years in private boarding schools, dreading holidays and vacation periods. When he was eighteen, he left the United States to roam around Europe. He sank into the drug scene, became evasive and withdrawn, and spent several months in prison cells.

When he was thirty years old, he encountered his first Christians in a free clinic on London's east side. It was several weeks before a trusting relationship developed between Eric and the workers there. Finally, Eric said, "My parents always told me that they didn't want a child. The last words I heard from my mother's lips were another reminder that I was an accident. I never want to see them again as long as I live."

Relationships Make the Difference

If a child is born into a family where affirmation and love are bountifully provided, he or she probably will develop a healthy self-image. If the family gives affirmation as a reward for success, and love becomes a reward for behaving properly, the child is likely to develop an insecure, competitive spirit. In each case, the child is shaped by the relationships within his or her home.

How does alcoholism affect the shaping of a child? What is the impact of a mother who doesn't want her child? What happens to a child thrust into a schoolroom with a neurotic teacher who ridicules his every mistake? What is the consequence of placing a teen in a drug-infested school, where violence in the hallways is a common occurrence?

A fractured childhood produces a variety of painful results. Some people experience intense guilt, anger and bitterness. They are driven to succeed to prove their worth, and are often thwarted in their close associations with others because they haven't been able to experience warm, affirming relationships.

Others respond differently. Instead of being driven to succeed, they try to avoid the pain of rejection and failure by withdrawing from risks—socially, professionally and in every other way.

Many of us are a combination of these two extremes. We are driven to succeed in those relationships and tasks where we are likely to do well, but we become passive when the risks seem to be too great.

On the Edge of Disaster

A few tortured souls leave family and friends behind in the hope of finding love and acceptance. It is a miserable search when they take the wrong path.

For example, the wife of a missionary and mother of three small children came to her counselor and declared, "God has told me to leave my husband and marry another person!" This young wife had been a committed Christian, who up to this point had seemed totally devoted to her husband and calling. What was it that made her willing to give up everything for another man?

She explained that this man had become her closest friend, that they could talk about anything and pray about everything together, and that life with him was an adventure she had never experienced with her spouse.

During counseling sessions, several things became apparent. She felt just as committed to Christ as she had before the affair began, and she didn't view her third-party involvement as being either sinful or immoral.

The counselor learned that her father had left the family when she was still a small child and that she had never established a close relationship with her stepfather. She married her husband, not because of her deep love for him, but because she felt "he would be good for her." In fact, she had been far more infatuated with another man prior to marrying her husband.

Problems of adjustment started immediately after the wedding. Instead of getting better they grew worse. She felt frustrated, angry, disillusioned. *Surely*, she thought, *marriage should be better than this.*

To her, it seemed as though her husband centered on their physical relationship. He always wanted to have sex—"as though that would make everything right." A strange feeling began to emerge within her. She tried to be a dutiful wife, but her feelings of revulsion toward sex grew stronger. As she described her feelings toward her husband to her counselor, he recognized that these same words are often used by little girls to describe sexually abusive fathers or stepfathers.

This woman was trying to make her husband meet her longing for a father's love. Her husband became confused and angry. Rather than admit that his marriage was failing, he tried to promote his masculinity through sexual aggression. This only increased the tension between them.

Then she met a man at church who treated her like a lady. She was attracted to him instantly, although he was almost fifteen years her senior. He not only showed her the attention and consideration she was seeking, but was understanding and sympathetic as well.

Their relationship started with conversation. Soon, she was sharing her frustrations and sadnesses with him, and he was confiding in her about his problems with his wife. Of course, as he understood her problems, she understood his. It felt so good just to be held. . . .

Divorce and Children

Consider the impact made upon a child in a home where divorce fractures the normal flow of life. Here is the true account of one victim. She said: "I grew up in a relatively happy, secure home. We lived in a lush, green valley in the middle of Washington State, with an icy-cold mountain river running through it. I had a really great childhood!

"Then I hit adolescence—that horrible time when you don't know if you're a child or an adult. It's an identity-building time. In the seventh grade, I was chosen to be an honor student. But in the eighth grade, I was flunking out!"

What could have happened to cause such a turnaround in a young girl? In this case, it was divorce, the hungry, vicious social disease that's eating away at many families today.

According to this young woman: "I never saw my parents fight. Later, I learned that this lack of fighting was their basic problem. They couldn't fight because they couldn't communicate at all. As the wall of bitterness grew, it became more impossible to overcome the problems in our home, and my parents' relationship became barren and empty. If only I could have seen what was going to happen.

"I vividly remember the day they told me they were going to get a divorce," she said. "It seemed like the only logical solution to them. I don't think they realized it would become an open sore that would never completely heal within me. There had been no warning, no fights, no screaming and yelling. I remember my heart pounding as sickening fear consumed me. It was like rolling toward a cliff in a car with no brakes, going faster and faster.

"At fourteen, just after the divorce, I began to make my own rules," she said. (Guilt-ridden parents often find it difficult to impose discipline, especially after a painful divorce.) "My anger and rebellion grew. I was a walking time bomb, filled with anger that would explode at the slightest bump.

"I chose friends who also were hurting and angry. I partied, drank, smoked, cussed, skipped school, harassed the teachers and police, shoplifted and much, much more."

The fracturing of her parents' relationship marked this girl's life indelibly. For all of us, relationships create our quality of life—healthy or unhealthy, bitter or sweet, secure or confused.

Biblical Examples and Admonition to Parents

In ancient Israel, a father's first responsibility was to guide his son. This awareness saturated the Jewish culture. The book of Proverbs, for example, contains potent teachings shared by King Solomon with his son. In praise of God, the prophet Isaiah wrote, "fathers tell their children about your faithfulness" (Is. 38:19). God intends for parents to experience His faithfulness and then communicate that faithfulness to their children.

In Deuteronomy, Moses talked to Israel's fathers about their earlier deliverance from Pharaoh's army at the Red Sea. He reminded them that their children were not present, and insisted that they share with them this experience of God's faithfulness.

Fix these words of mine in your hearts and minds; tie them as symbols on your hands and bind them on your foreheads.

Teach them to your children, talking about them when you sit at home and when you walk along the road, when you lie down and when you get up.

Write them on the doorframes of your houses and on your gates,

so that your days and the days of your children may be many in the land that the Lord swore to give your forefathers, as many as the days that the heavens are above the earth.

Deut. 11:18-21, NIV

Nothing has changed! A child's development in all areas—social, intellectual, physical, emotional, spiritual—is still the responsibility of the father and mother. Many factors affect a person's emotional health, including economics, extended family relationships, social context, physical health and peer relationships, but when parents offer their children a healthy balance of love and discipline, they usually produce healthy, well-balanced young adults. When parents are unattached to God and relate poorly to their offspring, their offspring generally create much pain and sadness for them.

Relationships Provide Our Role Models

From the first day of life, we pattern our actions after people who are close to us. Children instinctively copy the attitudes and actions of those they are exposed to most. It is God's design that they model themselves after loving and protective parents, but many parents don't cooperate with this plan.

Recently, a parent gave her three-year-old child a science fiction video movie to occupy him while she pursued her own interests. Unattended, the youngster watched it seven times.

In the movie, a man with a patch over one eye rode a motorcycle while killing and maiming several people per minute. The child later went into his bedroom and improvised a costume like the one worn by the man in the movie. He then began riding his tricycle around the neighborhood, wearing a patch over one eye and viciously clobbering all the little kids he met with a small baseball bat. Several were badly cut or bruised.

This child was simply copying his role model. He didn't have enough judgment to select a worthy model, so he copied what his own mother had endorsed when she gave him a videotape as an electronic baby-sitter.

We, too, unconsciously pattern ourselves after our role models, whether good or bad, and become like those whom we are exposed to most, even if those people are cruel to us. Almost invariably, husbands who batter their wives have come from homes where violence was commonplace.

On the other hand, positive role models provide powerfully positive results. Have you ever met a couple who has been happily married for years and now even look like brother and sister? Or, have you ever met a young man who walked, talked and spoke like an older person he admired?

How about you? Who is your role model? How powerfully has this individual influenced you? Do you talk, walk, think and reflect this person in your own mannerisms? What are you like today because of your father, your mother or the lack of one of them? We pick up our life patterns without thought, selecting from this person and that one ways to deal with life. Seldom is any of it intentional. It just. . . happens.

Chapter 4

Empty Solutions

Robert S. McGee

A person whose parents have given him affirmation, encouragement, protection, loving discipline and time probably will feel confident and secure as an adult. He probably will be able to relate well to the Lord and to other people, willing to try new things, take chances and even laugh at his mistakes.

Emotional, spiritual and relational health is greatly influenced by the degree of love and positive modeling one receives. A lack of these essentials for wholeness produces a vacuum within a person's life. When this is true, virtually everything he or she does is designed to meet his or her needs for approval and acceptance, and to avoid pain.

We come up with all kinds of ways to win approval and avoid pain. Let's examine a few of these alluring, but ultimately empty alternative solutions.

Looking for a White Knight

If only I had James (or whomever), *then I'd be really happy!* Some of us are waiting for someone to gallop into our lives on a handsome horse (or a new red Porsche!) and give us the attention and affection we want. We may be waiting for a spouse or friend to meet our deepest needs and make us really happy. Occasionally, someone comes along who seems to be "that special person." Our expectations (and demands) climb sky-high, but sooner or later, that person falls off his horse and we drop him like a lead balloon. Then we look for someone else to make us happy.

Many marriages begin this way. One partner expects the other to provide happiness, contentment and excitement. After a few weeks, a few months or a few years, these unrealistic expectations are shattered. In many cases, the couple divorces and the partners look for someone else to make them happy.

The Ostrich Syndrome

All of us have psychological defense mechanisms which we use to avoid pain and anxiety, but some of us use these mechanisms to an extreme. Like the proverbial ostrich with his head in the sand (ostriches don't really do that, you know!), we escape from reality by withdrawing, denying the truth in our lives, becoming passive, indecisive and numb. Avoiding emotional pain can have negative consequences, however. When we block out pain in this way we also block out intimacy, warmth and affection. Avoiding the pain of rejection causes us to miss the pleasures of relational involvement.

Denial, an unwillingness or inability to see problematic issues in one's life, can lead to either of two seemingly unrelated responses. Some people get clinically depressed as they suppress their pain and anger. Others become idealistic and say that everything is "just fine" and "getting better" without objectively seeing the good, the bad and the ugly in life. Such objectivity is too painful for them, so they hide behind their idealism.

The "Rambo" Defense

Some of us see others in one of two groups: *for me or against me.* Those who are for us can do no wrong, but those who disagree with us are branded as terrible, awful people. We may have a tendency to attack or criticize them for being stupid, narrow or mean.

These "Rambo" attacks are not reserved entirely for others, however. We may reserve our harshest attacks for ourselves, calling ourselves horrible names and berating ourselves terribly. This anger is a form of self-hatred.

The 007 Technique

Some of us attack others openly, but some of us attack in secret, behind another's back. We may covertly get others on our side, forming alliances and turning people against the object(s) of our scorn. Gossip is often the main weapon we use to secretly condemn others and elevate ourselves. It is a terribly destructive practice.

Rat on a Treadmill

Most of us are driven, racing to accomplish goals, trying to succeed, gain favorable attention and avoid any reflection on the emptiness in our lives. We are busy from the moment we get up until we go to bed. Even our devotions (if we have them) are characterized by this frantic pace. We read this chapter or that one, pray through our list, close our Bibles, check off "quiet time" and continue racing through our day.

Mary and Martha characterize the contrast between being reflective and driven. Jesus went to visit these women, and Mary...

> ...*was listening to the Lord's word, seated at His feet.*
>
> *But Martha was distracted with all her preparations; and she came up to Him, and said, "Lord, do You not care that my sister has left me to do all the serving alone? Then tell her to help me."*
>
> *But the Lord answered and said to her, "Martha, Martha, you are worried and bothered about so many things;*
>
> *but only a few things are necessary, really only one, for Mary has chosen the good part, which shall not be taken away from her."*
>
> Luke 10:39-42

Many of us are obsessive-compulsive about our schedules; that is, we're obsessed with thinking about all we "have to do" and compulsively driven to get it all done. Like rats on a treadmill, we are always running but never arriving.

Puppets

In both function and purpose, many of us are like puppets. We do whatever others want us to do, say what they want us to say and try to be what they want us to be. Our primary purpose in life is to please others, to impress them and to perform well enough to win their approval.

Some of us are fairly successful in this realm because we have a finely-tuned sense of perception. We are able to sense how our words, actions, attitudes and tone of voice will affect others. We then change our behavior to please them. We are like puppets, responding to every pull others make on our emotional strings.

Escapists

Relationships characterized by pain lead many to the numbing effects of alcohol and drugs. Many use these chemicals because they are effective and reliable, if only for a short time. The fact that people use this method repeatedly to numb themselves while aware of the chemical's destructiveness can only demonstrate how desperate some are to end their pain. Abusing chemical substances only compounds people's problems, adding another layer of "protection" that keeps them from seeing and dealing with reality in their lives.

Most of us demonstrate a combination of these empty solutions, orchestrating our lives for two primary purposes: to win approval and avoid pain. But no matter how hard we try, we experience only limited relief from the gnawing fear of rejection and failure.

We need to see the truth. Reality may be painful, but without it, we will never achieve growth and health in our lives. The other alternatives are not cute. They aren't clever. They are seductive and pathological. They rob us of intimacy, strength and hope. The sooner we begin to realize how empty these alternatives are, the sooner we will begin to experience the refreshment of God's truth, God's Spirit and God's people.

Chapter 5

Stages of Development

Robert S. McGee

Many educators and psychologists have observed patterns in human development, from birth to adulthood. Some of these authorities explain this developmental process in minute detail, especially as it concerns infants. Others define it more broadly.

A basic understanding of the stages of human development can help us gain valuable insight into our emotional, relational and spiritual progress—or lack of it. Four broad stages of development build upon one another. They are:

- Bonding (birth–two years old): the need to be loved
- Separateness (two–eleven years old): the need to set personal boundaries, including what one is and isn't responsible for
- Adolescence (twelve–eighteen years old): the need to develop adult relationships, gender behavior and identity
- Maturity (nineteen years of age and older): the need to continue growing in adult relationships, gender behavior and identity.

The ages given for each of the above stages are somewhat arbitrary because people develop at different rates for a wide variety of reasons. In fact, using only four stages to outline human development is a simplification of a very complex process. Each could be divided into many smaller, more defined stages which describe the subtle (and not-so-subtle) changes in a person's life as he grows and matures. Also, many aspects of development, such as bonding and separateness, are repeated again and again in different contexts and relationships throughout the growth process. The treatment of these stages here is only an introduction to the developmental process at the most rudimentary level. The basic concept, however, is that each stage serves as a foundation for the one after it.

Though the Scriptures do not outline stages of emotional, relational and spiritual development in a systematic way, they do speak clearly and strongly about the needs that comprise these stages. For example, our need for *bonding*, or attachment to another, is found in passages that portray love, compassion, value, warmth and affection (Gen. 21:15-16; 1 Sam. 2:19; Ps. 103:13; 127:3-5; Is. 49:15; Mark 5:23 and Luke 2:48 among others). The need for a child to have a sense of *separateness* (what he is and isn't responsible for) is described in passages about direction, discipline and instruction (Deut. 6:6-9; Prov. 22:6; 23:13-14). The need for a young person to *develop adult relationships, goals and behavior* is found in Ps. 119:9; 148:12-13; Prov. 1:1-7:27, and in many other passages, such as those in Proverbs which address "young men" and "my son." Finally, *the need to continue growing in one's relationships, goals and behavior* can be found in teachings like The Sermon on the Mount (Matthew 5-7), the instruction to the twelve (Matt. 10:5-42) and Christ's promise and commission to His disciples (Matt. 28:18-20).

A number of scriptural passages deal with adolescent and maturity issues like values, choices, goals, motives, handling conflict and spiritual warfare. (These issues are not encountered only in these stages, of course, but these passages are easier to understand and apply when one has developed a firm foundation of bonding and separateness.) All of the Scriptures are for all of God's people, and the distinctions between adolescence and maturity are often blurred. There does seem to be an observable flow, however, of building a strong foundation of emotional, spiritual and relational health so that a person can respond more freely and fully to the Lord.

In this chapter, we will examine each of these stages; in the next chapter, we will learn what happens when one's development is blocked at any one point in the growth process.

This chart gives an overview of the stages of development:

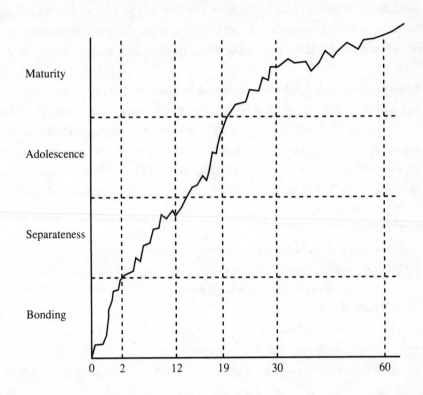

Bonding: The Need to Be Loved

From birth to one-and-a-half or two years of age, a child's greatest need is to *bond* with his parents. *Bonding* means forming an attachment. Its purpose is to convey feelings of warmth, love, value, worth, closeness, trust and specialness. Parents initiate this process by tenderly holding their baby, talking to him, making eye contact, playing with him, feeding him, changing his diapers and generally, by giving him a lot of time and attention.

The father of a three-year-old girl had made a habit of holding her often and talking to her softly since she was an infant. One day, as he held her in his lap, he told her, "I love you, honey."

She looked up at him and smiled and said, "I know that, Daddy."

"How do you know that?" he asked.

"'Cause you tell me that all the time!" was her reply.

Bonding—communicating warmth, affection and value to a child—takes time, attention and genuine love for the child. It can't be faked, and it can't be accomplished in a few hurried minutes from time to time. It is well worth the effort, however, because it forms a solid foundation for the second stage of development.

Separateness: The Need to Set Personal Boundaries

At about one-and-one-half years of age, a child learns a new word: "No!" He is learning to set limits and to assert his individuality. Bonding has to do with feeling loved; separateness has to do with healthy independence. For the next ten years or so, the child learns to be comfortable with his thoughts and desires. He learns who he is and who he's not. Here are some of the issues children begin to work through during this stage:

- *I am responsible for this. I'm not responsible for that.*
- *This is what I feel. I don't feel that way.*
- *This is who I am. That is who you are.*
- *I am in control of my life. You are in control of your life.*
- *I believe this. I don't believe that.*
- *I want to be this way. You can be that way.*
- *I can see both sides of an argument. I don't have to be one-sided in my opinions.*
- *I make my own choices. You make your own choices.*

It is during this second stage of development that the concept of one's "self" begins to emerge, laying the groundwork for the development of one's identity in later adolescence. If this budding concept of self is nourished and strengthened in a positive environment, a child will gradually learn to be perceptive, to think well, to experience his emotions and to relate to others.

Establishing boundaries during the separateness stage is much like setting physical boundaries on a piece of property, a concept illustrated in the book, *Codependency,* by Pat Springle.[1] The idea is that if each of us owned a ranch, we would individually be responsible for setting its boundaries, and then caring for it and protecting it. As caretakers, we also would be responsible for choosing whom to allow on our property. If invited to another person's ranch, we could go there for a visit. We would not, however, try to run anyone else's ranch; nor would we allow anyone else to run ours.

In the same way, we have individual personalities (thoughts, feelings and behavior), and we are responsible for setting our personal boundaries; that is, establishing what about ourselves we will share—and with whom. We may choose to allow certain others to share themselves with us. But we must avoid trying to run other people's lives, just as we should not allow others to run ours.

The desired result of bonding and separateness combined is a healthy independence of one's self, not selfishness; a recognition of one's individuality, not isolation or self-indulgence.

Unfortunately, a number of us are still struggling with our individuality, or separateness, from others. I recently had lunch with several couples, and during the conversation, I asked one of the men what he thought about a program we were working on. He expressed his ideas articulately. Then I asked his wife for her opinions. Her ideas were very different from her husband's. After she finished, he spoke again, changing his opinions to fit his wife's.

I spent a few minutes with this man the next day and asked him if he realized that he had changed his mind after his wife had expressed a dissenting opinion. He said, "Well, yeah. I guess I did."

"How often do you do that?" I asked him.

"Well...pretty often, I guess." This man was letting his wife's opinions and desires control him to a great degree. He had not learned to be separate, to have his own emotions, ideas and behavior. He was letting her run his "ranch."

Some people are able to maintain a healthy sense of separateness from others. One young man I know was working on a committee for a civic club. Another person, a friend who was also on the committee, said to him, "Dan, the project we're working on is really important to me. I need you to stay late tonight and finish it."

Dan had told his wife that he would take her out to dinner that night. What would he do? How would he respond to his friend? Would he give in? If he gave in, what would he say to his wife?

Dan was comfortable and confident about his decision. He calmly replied, "I'm sorry, I can't stay tonight. I already have something important planned. If you could let me know a little sooner next time, I could probably work it out."

Because he had learned to be separate and to set limits as he was growing up, Dan was calm and confident as he expressed his decision to his friend.

The stages of bonding and separateness lay a strong foundation for the development of an adult identity in adolescence.

Adolescence: The Need to Develop Adult Behavior and Identity

The years from twelve to eighteen are difficult and awkward for everyone, yet some are able to make the transition from childhood to young adulthood much more easily than others. Why is that? Among the many reasons is the degree to which a person has developed his sense of bonding and separateness. If he has a sense of inherent worth and believes he is loved and lovable, he is better able to reach out to others and build good relationships. Also, if he has learned to be comfortable with his own thoughts, feelings and behavior, he will be less influenced by the tremendous peer pressure all adolescents encounter during their teenage years.

On a firm foundation of love and limits, the adolescent can develop:

- An Adult identity: *What am I good at doing? What am I not good at doing? I accept my strengths without a sense of pride. I accept my weaknesses without a sense of shame.*

- Adult behavior: *What are good choices? What are unwise choices? How can I handle ambiguity and avoid being "black or white"? What risks should I take? What consequences am I willing to endure?*

- Adult goals: *What is worthy of my time and affection? What is really important to me? What is unimportant?*

- Adult relationships: *How can I experience both intimacy and separateness in relationships with others? What is real love? What is artificial or contrived love? How can I handle conflict? How can I let others fail and still love them?*

Resolving crucial questions like these begins in adolescence and continues for the rest of our lives as we mature in each of these areas.

Maturity: The Need to Continue Growing in Adult Behavior and Identity

No one ever "arrives" on this side of heaven. We all have a lot to learn about God, ourselves and others. In fact, one mark of maturity is realizing how little we really know and how much more we have to learn. As we mature, we gradually shed the cockiness of our youth and we develop a depth which doesn't have to have all the answers neatly packaged and expressed. With maturity comes more insight and less hurry; more honesty and less pretense; more real joy and fewer shallow substitutes; more genuine love and fewer hollow words. We can be assertive and still be submissive. We can be wise but not demanding. We can be strong but gentle; caring, and yet willing to let others fail so that they can learn their own lessons.

This kind of maturity is rare in our fast-paced, shallow culture, but some people do have it. Is there someone in your church who is compassionate but strong; someone who isn't in a hurry and isn't self-promoting, but who is willing to listen patiently, and to whom others go for wise counsel? Take time to look for a man or a woman like this; he or she may not stand out in a crowd. Then, spend some time asking questions and listening. Look into his eyes. Listen to the depth of her experience. You may hear of pain, loss and heartache, as well as hope, warmth and wisdom. It will be well worth your time. A relationship with a person like this could change your life.

What happens when a person doesn't progress through the four broad stages of human development? How is a person affected by abuse, divorce, neglect, alcoholism or other family disorders? The next chapter will examine blockages in our emotional, relational and spiritual development.

Chapter 6

When Development Is Blocked

Robert S. McGee

A person's emotional, relational and spiritual growth can be blocked at any point in the developmental process, but generally, the earlier it happens, the greater the damage. For example, if a person does not develop personal boundaries, he will almost certainly have problems in the adolescent and maturity stages. And a person who has had bonding problems will likely develop difficulties in all of the subsequent stages as well.

It is also possible for an emotional blow to be so severe that it not only blocks development, but actually reverses it, putting the person back at an earlier stage. An emotional blow of this nature might be suffering abuse from one's parent(s), sibling or spouse; the tragic loss of a parent, spouse, sibling or close friend; the commission of some act which is so shameful that it drastically alters one's life; involvement with the wrong crowd at school; deep hurt by a coach or teacher or any of a myriad of other possibilities.

It is not the isolated, traumatic incident that is usually the most detrimental to human development, however, but the consistently subtle, yet extremely powerful message that says, in effect, "You aren't loved." "You aren't good enough." "I'm ashamed of you." "I don't value your feelings or opinions." A person who is steeped in this environment not only believes that something is terribly wrong with himself, but that all of these hurtful communications are "normal" and will never be any different. It is an insidiously powerful situation which is, unfortunately, common to many. Parental modeling is among the most influential in human development. The way parents use their authority contributes either to a child's health and stability, or to his insecurity and instability. Here, it may be important to emphasize that our goal in presenting this material is not to blame others, but to understand how people develop healthy self-concepts and relationships, and what may have hindered this process in some of our lives. Understanding these issues may prove to be painful, and we may realize some unpleasant things about our parents, but understanding is not the same as condemnation. In a later chapter we will see how important it is to forgive those who have hurt us. At this point, we simply are trying to see if and how we have been hurt.

Let's examine the causes and symptoms of hindered or reversed growth in each of the developmental stages:

When Development Is Blocked in the Bonding Stage

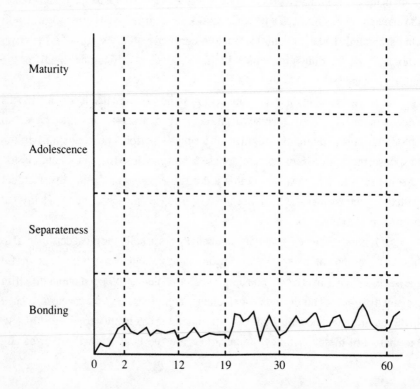

One of at least three significant events occurs in the life of a child during the bonding stage: he or she develops an attachment to a loving role model; he or she develops an attachment to an abusive role model; he or she is unable to form a significant bond with a role-model figure. The absence of bonding presents tremendous problems in every area of human development. One woman I counseled was raised by emotionally troubled parents. They became so absorbed in their own personal and relational problems that they had no time or energy left to give her. They lived together in the same house, but emotionally, her parents were absent.

A young man I know has an alcoholic father and a demanding, manipulative mother. His father spent very little time with the family, and his mother expected her young son to meet the emotional needs her husband failed to meet. In response to her demands, his primary concern became pleasing his mother and trying to win her approval. He consequently developed an unhealthy bond with his mother and had problems establishing limits, or a sense of separateness from her and others. The result was a rescuing, codependent relationship with his mother, which carried over into all of his relationships.

Bonding problems primarily result from abandonment (physical and/or emotional neglect) and abuse (emotional, physical, sexual, verbal, etc.).

The symptoms manifested by those who have not experienced a deep sense of being loved and valued are tragic, especially when contrasted with those which result from healthy bonding. Here are some of them:

Results of Healthy Bonding	Results of Bonding Problems
loved	shame, depression
lovable	self-hatred
value, worth	emptiness
special	often, addictions to drugs, alcohol, success, pleasing people, food, etc.
intimacy	fear of closeness, fear of being known
closeness	loneliness, denial, the inability to perceive and experience reality, feeling attacked (often because of the reality of being attacked), anxiety, fear

All of us exhibit some negative feelings and behaviors from time to time, but not to the extent that those with bonding difficulties do. As I explained these stages at a seminar, one woman commented, "I have felt lonely. Do I have bonding problems?" After more discussion, I explained that a person who is stuck in the bonding stage often has a pervasive and oppressive sense of loneliness (if he is in touch with his emotions). It is not a temporary feeling.

When a person's development is blocked in the bonding stage, it is often quite difficult for him to believe that God or anyone else could possibly love him. But a compounding problem is that he often doesn't even know what love is. He is then unaware of the nature and depth of both his need and the defense mechanisms he has unconsciously incorporated to block his pain.

When Development Is Blocked in the Separateness Stage

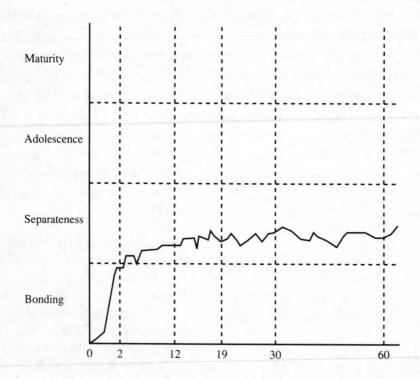

As Sharon described her present life and family background to me, I noticed that she seemed to have a problem in determining what her responsibilities were. She tried to take care of others' problems, but she didn't do a very good job of solving her own. In fact, she expected others to take care of her problems for her. When others wouldn't or couldn't do so, she thought they were being selfish. She spent her life fixing up other people's "ranches," and she expected others to take care of hers.

Some people come on our ranches to fix them up. They give us "helpful advice." They make our decisions for us. They "serve us" tirelessly. Some may say that they are "just trying to help" us, but they may condemn and belittle us in the process so that we will say and do what they want. Both kinds of people come on our ranches to manipulate and control us. One tries to control through kindness; the other, through condemnation.

Parents often are unable to find a healthy balance between advising and correcting their child, and giving him the freedom and affirmation he needs to assume his own thoughts, feelings and identity. They may offer the child a lot of nurturing as an infant, but by failing to teach him how to make his own decisions and take on those traits that are part of his unique personality, they fail to help him move from bonding to separateness. Their form of love is sustaining to the development of an infant, but smothering to a child in grade school, and even more harmful to the child who is growing into adolescence.

Most parents lean toward one end of a spectrum. Some are highly controlling, refusing to allow their children to work through the process of making their own decisions and developing their own thoughts and feelings. Other parents are relatively uninvolved in this important childhood process, so that their children have to try to figure things out entirely on their own. Both smothering and neglect create problems with the development of healthy independence for children. Some of these problems include:

- Feeling responsible for making others happy, successful and good.
- Assuming others' thoughts, feelings and behavior instead of developing one's own.
- Being unable to say no without feeling guilty.
- Saying yes to please others and win their approval.

- Being manipulated (controlled) by others.
- Trying to manipulate others.
- Being unable to make decisions because of a fear of rejection or failure.
- Having difficulty distinguishing between good and bad, acceptable or unacceptable behavior.
- Impulsively making decisions by perceiving different factors as "black or white," with very little ambiguity, or shades of gray. (People and situations are seen as all good or all bad.)
- Rescuing, fixing, enabling (codependency).
- Being overly responsible/competitive.
- Being irresponsible/passive.
- Frequently demonstrating anger, bitterness, resentment.
- Living in denial, unable to see one's problems with establishing limits.

Again, the ranch illustration can help us see some of these difficulties. A person who has problems with establishing limits goes onto other people's ranches and makes decisions for them, while he lets them come onto his ranch and make his decisions for him. He jumps his fences and lives on somebody else's ranch (telling others how to think, feel and act) while he lets others tell him how to do those things. He may get angry if they become too bossy or domineering, but he won't tell them to leave. After all, he's busy tending to somebody else's business.

Many people with separation difficulties actually have set limits—very rigid limits—in one or more specific areas of their lives. These might include raising their children or managing their job, their finances or certain relationships. They may let others tell them what to think, feel and do about many other parts of their lives, but not this one! If they feel threatened in this area (and they often do), they will defend it with tenacity and vengeance, often using either passive or aggressive behavior to do so.

John typifies many people who have problems with setting limits. John's father believed that raising children was a woman's job. He therefore poured most of his time and energy into his work, so that he had very little of either left to give to his son or his wife. John's mother was a domineering woman who was accustomed to getting her way in the home. She usually did so by alternately giving and withholding praise and approval, by feigning illness or by using sex as a tool for manipulation with her husband.

When John was growing up, he rarely was given opportunities to make his own decisions, and when he was, he often felt as though he'd been placed in a double bind. His mother might give him options, but she would withhold affection from him when he chose to do something that she really didn't want him to do. Rather than rebel, as some in similar situations do, John learned how to "read" his mother well and became devoted to making her happy in all that he said and did.

John was an exceptionally bright student who excelled in math and science. He made an independent decision to pursue a pre-med college program, and upon graduation, was accepted into medical school. He later started a private practice and married a woman much like his mother. When he married, John transferred his devotion and approval-seeking skills to his wife. He allowed her to run their home, to raise and discipline their kids, to tell him how to dress, how to drive, how he should feel and what he should think. But if she tried to give him any input on how to run his practice, like how he should deal with his patients or his secretary or nurse, or how he could arrange his furniture or his files, he became very agitated. His response was either to argue with her defensively or to act as if he'd listened to every word—and then dismiss all that she'd said.

Throughout his married years, John poured almost all of his available time and energy into his practice, working late and remaining on call on most weeknights and weekends. Helping his patients as he did gave John the feeling that he was a hero, despite the negative influence his wife's domination had on his sense of manliness.

John had allowed himself to be driven from most of his "ranch," but he was still clinging to a shed (his medical practice) in the "back forty." When he felt threatened by his wife's inquiries or suggestions about his work, he responded by being defensive or by withdrawing, pretending to hear her but shutting out her words.

Others who are defending an area of their lives may make demands, whine, complain, criticize or condemn the one(s) posing the perceived threat. Or, they may have a black-or-white response, believing that others are for them or against them, and try to get others on their "side" (against the perceived attackers). Again, it is common for those who have problems with establishing and maintaining limits to tell others how to run *their* lives, and then to be offended when the advice is not taken.

It is easy to be frustrated and angry with people who are so defensive, but we need to remember that the root of their defensiveness is hurt. Seeing them as hurting people who act defensively to avoid reinjury helps us to be compassionate toward them. If we also are defensive, it helps us understand why we feel and act the way we do.

When Development Is Blocked in the Adolescent Stage

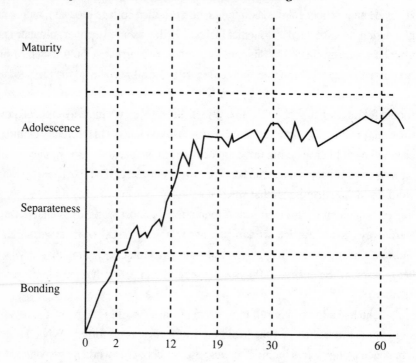

The most significant hindrances to development are in the bonding and limits stages. If growth occurs properly in these stages, the child will then be ready for the awkward stage of adolescence.

An emotionally strong and happy young man named Jim moved with his family when his father was transferred to a new job within his company. As Jim entered his new high school, he experienced all of the normal anxieties teenagers do when meeting people in a new school. He was tense and felt apprehensive.

His parents tried to encourage him. "Hang in there. Things will work out," they said. They were good about asking Jim questions and listening carefully when he talked, without always trying to change his negative feelings or provide answers to his problems.

Jim had played football at his previous high school, so he went out for the team. But instead of being a starter, he was placed on the second team. That was a disappointment. Then he learned that the girl he wanted to date was already going with another guy on the team. He was doing well in the classroom—until algebra came along. No matter how hard he tried, he could not seem to get the hang of it.

After a couple of months of this pressure, Jim's confidence and happiness slowly began to erode. There was no "turning point," just a number of seemingly minor tensions and setbacks. Jim began to doubt himself. He grew increasingly depressed and started spending time with some boys who weren't really bad—they were just sarcastic and cynical.

The next summer, Jim went with his family back to the town they had left almost a year before. Their neighbors and friends could hardly believe the changes they saw in Jim. The confident, happy boy they had known before had become a sullen, withdrawn and angry young man.

Problems in the adolescent stage of development may be caused by peer pressure, developing bad habits, or by making even a few bad choices which could lead to distortions in one's self-concept, a tendency to avoid risks because of the fears of failure and rejection, and a rigid performance motivation.

Some of the psychological symptoms of an arrested development at this stage are:

A poor self-concept
- uncertainty about one's personal strengths and weaknesses
- pride about strengths
- shame about weaknesses
- self-condemnation
- anger, bitterness

Making unwise choices
- unwilling to take risks
- taking impulsive risks
- unwilling to accept responsibility and consequences
- unable to make choices which are different from one's peer group

Immature relationships
- becoming too dependent on one person or group
- becoming isolated
- inability to handle conflict
- condemning others when they fail
- easily susceptible to peer pressure

When Development Is Blocked in the Maturity Stage

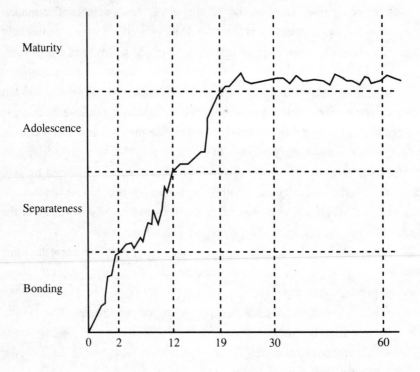

As is true of any stage, blockage in the maturity phase of growth can lead to regression. A classic example is the alcoholic who, after twenty years of sobriety, begins to neglect the basic principles of recovery and falls into relapse. Or the church pastor who becomes so involved in the needs of his congregation that he neglects his own needs and becomes enmeshed in sinful behavior.

Possible obstructions to growth in the maturity stage include a real or perceived sense of loss, burn-out, severe or repeated adversity, a deep hurt, harboring a grudge and experiencing loneliness, among others. Corresponding symptoms may include:

- Increasing anxiety about the future, resulting in sleeplessness, gastro-intestinal disorders, chest pains, muscular tension, twitching or profuse sweating.
- Increasing depression, and with it, lethargy, irregular eating and sleeping habits, boredom and/or an inability to concentrate.
- Being hurt and becoming preoccupied with revenge, or "getting even."
- Becoming increasingly isolated and withdrawn, sometimes by refusing to acknowledge and/or discuss negative feelings with others, or by developing an attitude of pride or exceptionalness. This attitude may be manifested by underlying beliefs such as: *I don't really need to. . . (pray, confess my sins, read my Bible, attend church, repent, become involved in caring relationships, avoid certain books or movies) because I basically have things together.* Or, *People need me; I just don't have time to. . . (pray, study my Bible, attend church, develop mutually caring relationships, take a vacation, spend time with my family, read a book, go to the movies).*

Stagnation in the maturity stage may bring with it an inability to continue growing in Christian virtues such as love, joy, wisdom, strength, faithfulness, gentleness and self-control (Gal. 5:22), or as I mentioned previously, it may lead one to regress to a previous stage of growth.

In some cases, a person may appear to be progressing well until hidden flaws in the developmental process are exposed by a tragic or painful event. Diagraming an experience like this is more difficult because the appearance of progress hides one's underlying weakness. From a distance, the person's life might resemble the graph on the following page.

Reversals

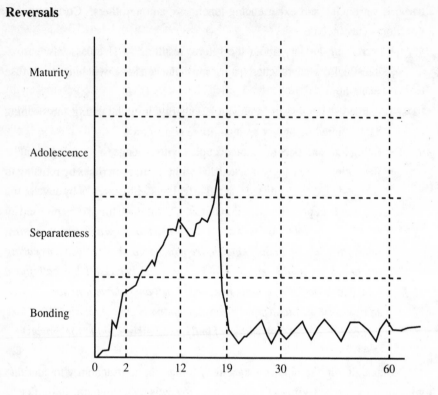

This diagram illustrates tragic consequences in a person's life. Unfortunately, it is not a rare thing.

A woman who seemed emotionally stable married a successful man whose propensity to alcoholism became apparent when his business went bankrupt. Unfortunately, this woman never had truly developed a healthy sense of separateness. If she had, she would have been able to be more honest with her husband in the early stages of his drinking. She might have told him that he had to take responsibility for his behavior, and that his increased irresponsibility was adversely affecting the family. Instead, she developed a habit of rescuing her husband: telling others that he was sick when he really was drunk, making excuses for him to their neighbors and friends, avoiding the real problem and only talking to him about peripheral concerns. After a year of living out these deceptions, she became unsure of herself. Her sense of stability and confidence collapsed. She no longer felt that she was special and lovable. Her husband's alcoholism revealed a flaw in her development, and her emotional, relational and spiritual health declined from apparent maturity to the point that she experienced problems with bonding.

A young man who seemed fairly confident and secure went out for the soccer team in high school. He was a good athlete, but his coach got upset with him on the first day of practice because he wasn't paying attention. Somebody else was talking to him and he didn't hear the coach's instructions. From that day on, the coach carried out a personal vendetta against the boy. He criticized him, ridiculed him, didn't let him play in games and tried his best to humiliate him. It worked. The boy was deeply hurt and lost confidence in himself. He became easily manipulated and indecisive. His apparent confidence and security had only covered a feeling of being unloved as a child. His athletic, academic and social excellence were attempts to block the pain of his parents' disapproval. The young man who had seemed to be progressing confidently through adolescence was now struggling with problems in separateness and bonding.

Understanding these stages of development has helped many people gain insights into why they think, feel and act the way they do. Realizing the extent of one's hurt and its consequences is often very painful. The next several chapters describe some solutions to these problems.

Chapter 7

Emotional Healing and Development

Pat Springle

As you have read through the first six chapters of this book, you may have gained insight into how you think, feel and act. You may have read an illustration or a characteristic and thought, *That's me! I do that, too!* You may be well along the path of understanding your needs for emotional, relational and spiritual health, or you may be taking your first faltering steps.

Perhaps you now are wondering, *How does a person experience emotional healing and growth? What encourages that kind of development? What hinders it?* In this chapter, we will attempt to answer those questions as we examine four important factors that affect healing and growth: courage, a deep understanding of why we are the way we are, taking appropriate steps toward change and having realistic expectations.

As you read this chapter, remember that this is only a book and that the factors discussed here will not produce life-changing results if they are applied only at the intellectual level. Rather, they need to be experienced in the give-and-take of meaningful relationships, possibly through the direction of a Christian therapist or counselor. For instance, learning to handle conflict requires both an understanding of the principles and the practical experience which allows us to go through the often difficult process of learning to apply those principles. As you read this chapter, consider also what environment and relationships will enable you to apply its principles at the "shoe leather" level of your life.

Being Courageous

It may seem strange to consider courage as an important factor in emotional health, but it is absolutely essential. The pain many people have repressed is so overwhelming and threatening that it takes a lot of guts to face it.

Two friends of mine illustrate the importance of courage. One man, Jeff, was neglected by his workaholic father, and was manipulated and smothered by his insecure mother. He grew up believing that nobody loved him and that nobody ever would. He learned to be socially skilled and professionally successful, and his prowess in these areas masked his pain and insecurity for a long time.

When he reached his mid-30's, however, Jeff started seeing some problems in his relationships with God and with others. He realized that he performed for everyone and yet felt accepted by no one. In some of our conversations together over a period of two years, he began to see the backlog of tremendous hurt and anger he had repressed. He also began to experience the emptiness and loneliness that he had hidden for almost his entire life.

In so doing, he realized that he had a choice: he could face the reality of his pain and work through it, or he could give up and deny it. The first route led to more pain, but also to the possibility of real health. The other led to immediate relief but long-term problems. Jeff determined to keep going.

One day I said to him, "Jeff, I admire you. You have tremendous courage. Many people would have quit if they had experienced the pain that you have, but you've kept going."

Russell was a different story. He talked to me about his family, but when I asked some probing questions, he said, "They did the best they could. They were fine. They loved me." I got the signal that he wasn't ready to talk about it.

A few months later, Russell and I met with each other again. His insecurities and people-pleasing tendencies were so evident I hoped he would be honest with me. But again when I probed, Russell became defensive and closed about himself.

We have had a lot of opportunities to visit since then, but Russell isn't open to even talking about the reality of pain in his life. What's the difference between Jeff and Russell? At least one factor is courage.

King David often experienced hopelessness, pain and depression. In Psalm 27, he described his trust in the Lord, in spite of seemingly overwhelming military, political and familial problems. At the end of this psalm, David expressed his hope and courage:

I would have despaired unless I had believed that I would see the goodness of the Lord in the land of the living.

Wait for the Lord; be strong, and let your heart take courage; yes, wait for the Lord.

Ps. 27:13-14

Having courage is an essential factor in facing the reality of hurt and anger in our lives.

Understanding Deeply

Someone may ask, "Why do I have to dredge up the negative events of my past and feel those awful feelings again? Can't I just pray for healing, and then trust God to make me whole?" The answers are no, you don't have to examine your past and feel repressed emotions; and sure, you should pray that the Lord will work in your life to bring emotional health. The principle, however, is that the more fully one understands the problem—whether it be a doctor accurately diagnosing a disease, a mathematician understanding a calculus problem or a person understanding the causes of his emotional, relational and spiritual difficulties—the more quickly and more probably he will find a workable solution.

In the same way, we can't know the experience of either God's comfort or healing until we are aware of our need for them. Such an awareness can enable us to apply His power to our lives deeply and specifically.

The process of analyzing pain and defensive behaviors can be grueling, however, especially for those whose development has been blocked in the bonding or separateness stages. These people usually are not very objective about repressed pain and anger, their causes, or their behavioral consequences. In fact, all of us usually drift toward one of two extremes. We lean toward either morbid introspection and self-condemnation, because we see ourselves as such bad people who have such bad problems, or we deny that we have any difficulties because we're afraid of facing pain. We may need to find an objective, affirming person who has been where we are now to help us avoid these extremes and move us along the right path. (The next chapter will focus on the role of relationships in this process.)

Taking Appropriate Steps

Progressing toward emotional health requires that we focus on two fronts: a deep level of growth, which includes understanding our concept of God and ourselves, and a more immediate, volitional level in which we actively put ourselves in environments and situations where we can learn and grow daily. By focusing on both of these growth levels, we will gain more insight and make more concrete progress as we take appropriate steps toward continued emotional development.

Some steps are appropriate for all of us, regardless of where we fall in the developmental process. All of us can learn to be courageous as we discover how to apply the Scriptures deeply and specifically to our lives. All of us need to be involved in healthy relationships and the study of God's Word. All of us can benefit from recognizing painful feelings, destructive behavior and wrong thinking. All of us are affected to some degree by the fears of rejection, failure, punishment, and feelings of shame, but some of us have been more deeply affected than others.

Let's look at specific steps we can take in each particular stage:

• *If You Are Blocked in the Bonding Stage:* Some people who have bonding difficulties have learned to be gregarious and socially adept as a way to win the approval they so desperately want from others. Others, however, are more obviously insecure and withdrawn. Both types of individuals are very lonely and empty; one simply has done a better job of fooling others—and maybe themselves—about their pain.

In a context of love and honesty, people whose growth has been blocked in the bonding stage need to:

- Understand why they feel, think and act the way they do. This involves an accurate analysis of the causes and consequences of the lack of parental bonding and/or severe emotional blow(s) they've experienced which reinforced a reversal later in their lives.
- Gain freedom and encouragement within a safe environment (where one can be genuinely honest and genuinely loved) to feel the hurt and anger of the past.
- Learn to forgive those who have hurt them.
- Deal with any addictions (to alcohol, drugs, sex, food, work, etc.) which are being used to dull feelings of pain and emptiness.

- Take the risks necessary to get involved in relationships, to get close to people, to be known by them, to develop feelings of dependency as a transition step toward independence and health, and to courageously face the prospect of rejection courageously again.

Those who have problems with bonding generally have difficulties with establishing limits and need to take steps in that stage after having developed some stability in the bonding stage. Many others have bonded fairly well. Their difficulties originate in the separateness stage.

- *If You Are Blocked in the Separateness Stage:* Those of us with separation problems have not been able to determine what we are responsible for and what we aren't. We think, feel and act the way we think others want us to, and we try to get others to respond the way we want them to. It is like being a puppet of others while also trying to get others to be our puppets.

We need to develop a mature, godly sense of independence through which we can appreciate and express our individuality, while giving others the freedom to do the same with theirs. Paul wrote the Galatian believers, *For each one shall bear his own load* (Gal. 6:5); that is, each of us is required to make his or her own choices and bear the consequences of those choices.

Others who have learned—or are learning—to experience healthy independence can be of great help to us as we take steps to:

- Understand why we are so overly responsible or irresponsible.
- Learn to feel our own hurt, anger and joy instead of feeling what others want us to feel.
- Learn to forgive those who have manipulated and hurt us.
- Think our own thoughts instead of adopting those of others.
- Do what we think is right instead of what others think we ought to do.
- Refuse to be manipulated and learn to say, *NO.*
- Let others be responsible for their lives and make their own choices without our interference.
- Avoid one-sided black-or-white extremes in our analyses and conversations about people, events or circumstances.
- Set limits about what we will be and do and what we won't be and do, so that we can respond to others calmly and confidently.

Each of us needs to learn to take care of his own ranch. We need to take responsibility for building strong fences and gates, and overseeing our own cattle, crops, home and family. We can then invite others to join us for a visit on our ranch, and we can go for a visit at theirs if we are invited. If they offend us, we can be honest with them about the hurt and consequences generated by their behavior. If necessary, we can ask them to leave our ranch.

With this kind of strength, we can be calm, secure and loving. We can then *choose* to give and serve rather than being compelled to do so in order to win someone else's approval.

A person with difficulties in this stage will almost certainly have difficulties with issues in the adolescence stage. Others, however, have bonded and separated quite well, yet they still seem to have problems which center on the adolescent stage of development.

• *Steps to Take if You Are Blocked in the Adolescent Stage:* In either physical or emotional adolescence, peer relationships seem to mean everything. If we find ourselves with people who are positive and encouraging, their attitudes rub off on us. In the same way, if we spend a lot of time with people who are negative, we usually become negative; if angry, we become angry; if violent, we tend toward violence. Adolescence is a very vulnerable stage of life; the strength that has been established in the bonding and limits years can be wasted by destructive peer relationships. The apostle Paul said it well: *Bad company corrupts good morals* (1 Cor. 15:33). In adolescence, we need to:

• Choose our friends wisely.
• Monitor our values, goals and relationships to see if they are going in the direction we want to go.
• Develop good habits—personally, relationally, professionally, etc.
• Identify our strengths and weaknesses, and learn to accept ourselves.
• Learn to forgive others and ourselves.
• Learn that we can't do everything and that we have to pace ourselves.

Someone who is learning and growing in these areas of life is well on the way toward maturity. It is possible, however, to be sidetracked in the maturation process.

• *Steps to Take if You Are Blocked in the Maturity Stage:* It is easy to think that someone who has reached the maturity stage is not vulnerable to being blocked in his or her development. But stagnation and reversal can occur here if one is not watchful and prepared. In fact, a person in this stage often experiences extreme spiritual battles because the forces of darkness want to thwart his or her effectiveness (see, for example, Eph. 6:10-13 and 1 Pet. 5:8-9).

Those of us in this stage who find ourselves stagnating, wandering or becoming embittered need to:

• Understand what is going on in our lives. Are the *worries of the world and the deceitfulness of riches* beginning to choke out growth (Matt. 13:22)? Are there signs of spiritual conflict and oppression? Is the Lord pruning us (John 15:1-11), or are we experiencing consequences of a rebellious attitude?

• Seek the counsel of mature, godly people.

• Be honest about any unresolved hurt or anger in our lives.

• Forgive those who have hurt us.

• Take time to replenish our emotional, relational and spiritual tanks. Read, pray, relax and laugh with friends.

• Determine what one thing we want to count for and accomplish instead of trying to do too many things well.

Another important factor in gaining emotional health is to be realistic about the process.

Having Realistic Expectations

Many people with the best of intentions communicate that a quick fix is available for virtually any problem, no matter how big that problem may be. All things are possible with God, but it is unreasonable to expect that a person will jump from deep bonding problems to maturity in a flash! Ultimately, the expectation of a quick fix can be very harmful. A person looking for relatively instantaneous results will often become disillusioned when the results don't happen overnight. He may give up the growth process entirely, and may condemn himself because he believes that his inability to respond in the prescribed, rapid way proves that something is wrong with him. Even worse, he may experience condemnation from the one who told him he could be healthy so quickly. That person may be threatened by the failure of his theory or system, and take out his fear and anger on the one who needs his love and patient encouragement most.

A very few people experience almost miraculous healing, but for most of us, growth tends to come through spurts of insight followed by long periods of consolidating and applying those insights in everyday life. Sometimes, those insights cause rapid growth; sometimes, it takes months or years to realize how those insights can affect our thoughts, emotions and actions.

One obvious principle is: The deeper the hurt, the longer it takes to heal. For the sake of illustration, consider four people involved in an auto accident (each in one of the four stages of development). The person in the maturity stage is alert and avoids the collision. He stops to help the others in the wreck. The person with problems in the adolescent stage has a cut on his arm. The bleeding is stopped and he is taken to the hospital for stitches. The fellow with limits difficulties has a broken arm, and the man with bonding problems has compound fractures in both legs.

The one with the broken arm will be in pain for a significant period of time, and will need several months to build up strength in that arm. The one with the broken legs will require surgery, and will endure weeks of pain, several months in casts and several more months of rehabilitation to regain his strength. It would be senseless and cruel to tell him that he will be able to run the next day. If he tried, he could cause himself further damage. In order to avoid reinjury and promote healing, each needs to give his wounds time and attention—the amount and length depending on the degree of the wound(s). All of them can, however, experience comfort, encouragement and love from others in the weeks and months following the accident.

The goal of the healing process is not self-improvement for selfish purposes, but freedom and health to love and serve Christ without being encumbered by the hurts and distorted thinking of the past. Just as medical illness and treatment require time and care for physical healing, tending to our emotional health will enable us to experience healing and move on to focus on Christ and others instead of ourselves.

Emotional healing and growth are difficult but possible for all of us. Since we have used charts to show both health and blockage, let's look at some graphs that might depict healing and further development, such as:

A person who has been blocked in the bonding stage, but who begins to heal and grow in his 30's.

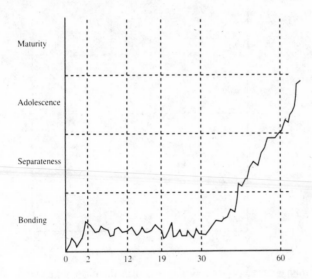

A person from an abusive home who finds people who love him and bond with him in high school or college, and who continues growing after that:

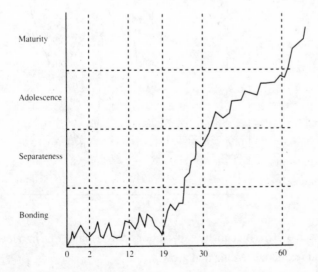

A person who has been stuck in the separateness stage, and who begins to grow in his 20's:

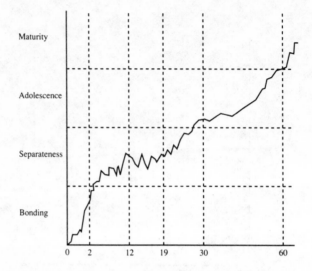

A woman who experienced a reversal in development when the man she married became obsessed with professional success, but who later began to experience hope and healing:

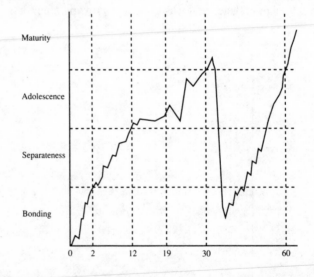

For each of us, too, realistic expectations play a major role in our emotional, spiritual and relational healing and growth.

Chapter 8

The Role of Relationships

Pat Springle

Intimacy and separateness. . . Healthy relationships are characterized by a blend of genuine love and the willingness to let another person have his own identity and make his own decisions. Many of us have experienced relationships characterized by a much different set of feelings and behaviors. Some of us have known only surface relationships. We have felt isolated and lonely, and have covered up our hurts and fears with humor, success, withdrawal, or with any number of other defense mechanisms. Some of us have had relationships in which we have been smothered, condemned, manipulated, hurt and angry. We in turn have often treated others in the same way, even though we've despised the way we have been treated.

The Lord created us as relational beings. It is His design that we find true meaning in life through the context of rich relationships. In this chapter, we will examine our relationships with other people; in the chapters following, we will look at our relationship with the Lord. Our relational needs are genuine. We need *both* a relationship with God and relationships with others if we are to become strong, healthy, loving people.

Let's look at some characteristics of healthy relationships, as well as how to develop these kinds of relationships:

Love

"I really care about you." "You are special to me." "I love you." All of us want to hear genuine expressions of warmth and acceptance. We want to feel valued. We want to feel loved. Yet some of us have difficulty accepting expressions of care and affirmation because we feel unworthy of being loved. We remain in our shell, afraid that if people really knew us, they wouldn't even like us, much less love us. We push people away through sarcasm, busyness or condemnation, and we remain isolated and empty. Or we may be addicted to pleasing people, trying to say and do what makes others happy so they will accept us. We may even seem to be very responsive to scriptural teaching—not because we are applying it deeply and experiencing the freedom and joy of being the independent, healthy people Christ wants us to be—but again, because we are trying to earn approval by being "good Christians."

It is difficult for the truth about God's love to take root within anyone who has never experienced genuine love. Some people are able to assimilate and apply God's Word with relative ease because they have a context for loving, affirming relationships. For others, however, the truth about God's love, forgiveness and acceptance seems to bounce off their hearts like a seed bouncing off of pavement. Many others, of course, are not in these extreme conditions but are nonetheless hindered in their experience of life because of deficiencies in their relationships.

In the sixteenth chapter of First Samuel, the prophet Samuel visited Jesse's family to anoint one of his sons as the new king of Israel. When Samuel told Jesse to bring his sons to a sacrifice, Jesse brought all of his sons—except David. Jesse did not value David enough to count him as one of his sons. David was a neglected child, yet God commanded Samuel to anoint him as Israel's new king.

The next chapter gives us another glimpse of David's relationships with members of his family. David's father sent him to take cuts of cheese to his brothers who had joined the army and to their commanders. When David saw that the giant Goliath taunted the army of Israel, he asked some questions.

His brother, Eliab, responded to David in bitterness and scorn: *Now Eliab his oldest brother heard when he spoke to the men; and Eliab's anger burned against David and he said, "Why have you come down? And with whom have you left those few sheep in the wilderness? I know your insolence and the wickedness of your heart; for you have come down in order to see the battle." But David said, "What have I done now? Was it not just a question?"* (1 Sam 17: 28-29).

From these two snapshots of David's life, we can see that he was devalued and neglected by his father and abused by his brother. Later, when King Saul threatened to kill David because the people loved the strong young man, Saul's son Jonathan became David's friend. The next several chapters of First Samuel describe how Jonathan risked his life to encourage David and help him escape his father's wrath. Though David's family had abandoned and abused him (see Ps. 27:10), Jonathan became a tangible example of God's love, acceptance and strength. Many of us also need to be involved with a caregiver like Jonathan who is equipped in some way to communicate the character of God to us.

A person usually begins making a transition from superficial or unhealthy relationships to a healthy sense of intimacy with others when he begins to receive persistent love from someone who cares about him. Often, this transition is long and awkward, and it can take some unusual steps. For instance, a person who has been neglected or abused usually has severely repressed emotions. When he begins to feel loved by a friend, pastor or counselor, and feels that he can trust that person, he may become dependent on him or her for a while. If handled properly, this transitional phase can lead to further progress and ultimately to a healthy independence where he can enjoy intimacy and individuality—with the caregiver and others.

Objectivity

One of the most common and pervasive defense mechanisms that blocks the pain (and growth) in our lives is denial. *Denial* is the inability or unwillingness to recognize truth or reality in one's life. Many of us have acted as though we don't feel hurt and anger from an early age. We may have learned this denial because our parents didn't acknowledge our feelings, or we may have experienced a severe emotional blow later in life and learned to deny our pain at that point. To use our medical illustration from the last chapter, we may act like someone trying to walk on a broken leg who says, "I'm okay. It's not bad at all."

Few of us learn to be objective about ourselves without help. Most of us learn to see reality more clearly only when someone loves us enough to *speak the truth in love* to us (Eph. 4:15). It also helps for someone to ask us questions and to affirm our fledgling feelings, especially when our emotions seem new to us.

Recently, I had an opportunity to sit in on a conversation between two friends. Randal had just finished talking to his father on the phone, and he was upset. During their conversation, Randal had explained that he and his family would not be able to see his parents at Christmas. His father had replied, "Then don't come! See if I care! Your mother and I have done so much for you, and you obviously don't appreciate us or what we've done. Well, that's fine!" And he hung up.

Dan asked Randal, "How do you feel about your conversation with your father?"

"I'm hurt!" Randal snapped.

"I don't doubt that," replied Dan, "but you also seem to be angry."

"Angry," Randal spoke softly. "Yeah, I guess I am. I guess it seems more palatable to be hurt than angry, but you're right. I am angry with my Dad."

This short conversation shows how one friend can help another to be more objective about his or her thoughts and feelings. A friend can be instrumental in helping a person set boundaries in the separateness stage, and in learning how to develop adult goals and relationships in the adolescent stage. He or she can ask lots of questions, as well as give objective counsel and feedback. He or she can affirm one's progress and correct errors in one's thinking and behavior.

As our objectivity progresses in an environment of love and acceptance, we are better able to come to terms with the depth of hurt that many of us have experienced. We can admit, *This is who I am. This is why I am the way I am. I'm not as healthy as I've tried to believe and portrayed myself to be, but it's better for me in the long run to be honest and feel pain than to be in denial.* A doctor can't treat a wound until the patient admits that he needs treatment. Similarly, a person usually sees little progress in his life until he's recognized his hurts and needs.

Hope

A relationship characterized by love and objectivity fosters hope. This is not a blind sort of hope based on unrealistic or fallacious expectations, but a hope that we will be able to shed our facades and defense mechanisms, receive comfort for our pain, and experience real love and purpose in life.

We often have superficial or false hopes. We hope that our pain will vanish magically. We hope that we can be successful enough for people to love us. We hope that we will find the "right person," someone who will meet our needs and make us happy. These hopes stimulate us and give us confidence for a while, but they leave us shattered and confused when they don't work out.

The only real hope we can count on is found in a Person, rather than circumstances, and deals with our most profound needs instead of those that are superficial. Christ Himself is our hope and in Him we find enduring love, comfort, forgiveness and strength. We hope that despite any sense of loneliness or isolation we may be feeling, He will become real to us, even though we may never have experienced the reality of His love and strength before. We hope that He will comfort us, and give us wisdom and courage about what we need to do.

Such hope doesn't just happen. Often it comes as a result of receiving His love through someone else, consistently and tenaciously over a period of time. It may first appear as a faint glimpse which only begins to grow as our relationship with Christ grows, as our concept of Him becomes more accurate and we slowly learn that we can trust Him to meet *all* of our needs. In all of this, we begin to learn that this kind of *hope does not disappoint* (Rom. 5:5).

Depth

As we grow and develop, our relationships will slowly acquire more depth. Whereas we now may be working to overcome the painful negatives in our lives, and deeply appreciate those who are loving and helping us through this process, we gradually will be able to move into more mature and healthy relationships with these people and others. We then can experience the adventure of developing adult relationships in which we can be free to be ourselves. In the process, we will learn to have a healthy give-and-take with others through which we can value their opinions even when we disagree. Our drive to succeed and to please people can be slowly replaced with the joy of loving and being loved. The shame and embarrassment that may have been characteristic of previous relationships can be replaced by honest interaction, openness and affirmation.

Every now and then, I see an elderly couple or some long-time friends whose relationship exceeds the superficial qualities which characterize most relationships. They understand each other. They no longer use facades to hide how they really feel; they don't just talk about politics or football or children. They relate on a deep level, reflecting a true sense of connectedness. These are the kinds of relationships in which one doesn't have to forgo individuality and autonomy for connection and intimacy. Nor do both partners always need to agree. The best relationships are usually those which are characterized by acceptance, honesty and understanding, even in the midst of conflict. These kinds of relationships aren't common, but they are possible. And the journey toward them can be a very positive and healthy experience.

Different people play different roles in our lives at different times. The Lord may use a caring and perceptive friend, pastor or counselor to get us started on the road to health. He may send others to take us the next step or two, and still others for another leg of our journey. In turn, He probably will use us in the lives of those who need to take steps we already have taken. Whether others are helping us or we are helping them, it is important that we not allow our relationships to become ingrown so that we are absorbed in one another. Instead, we need to point one another to the Lord, so that our human relationships and our relationship with Him can each enhance the other.

Chapter 9

The Need to Forgive

Robert S. McGee

One of the most significant hindrances to our emotional, relational and spiritual health is our failure to forgive others. Resentment and bitterness over another's offenses against us short-circuit our growth.

Sometimes we think we have forgiven others completely when we only have forgiven them partially.

After I talked to a church group about the need to forgive others, a woman approached me to pursue the topic further. We talked for a few minutes about her parents, her brothers and her husband, all of whom had hurt her deeply. "But I've already forgiven them," she stated emphatically.

"Yes," I replied, "you have forgiven them for the offenses you've seen and felt, but as your objectivity and perception about those events increase, you may find that you are more hurt than you have realized. If that is the case, then you will need to apply Christ's forgiveness to that level of hurt, too."

Forgiving others for past offenses against us often involves both a decision and a process. We make a choice to forgive another person when we realize that he or she has hurt us. As our understanding of the offense grows, we often realize that he or she has hurt us in ways we haven't seen previously. At each point in that process of growing objectivity, we can choose to forgive the person for the wounds he or she has inflicted on us.

Gary had demonstrated problems with his temper since childhood. As an adult, he became violently angry when his young children were not kind to each other. In talks with a perceptive friend, he realized that his brother had abused him when he was growing up. (Gary had always thought his brother's behavior was "normal," and that his own temper had resulted from his being such a "bad person.") He chose to forgive his brother for hurting him so deeply.

Several months later, Gary talked to his friend again about his relationship with his brother. As they talked about his brother's behavior over the years, Gary became furious! He realized for the first time that his brother didn't care that he had hurt Gary. Not only had he hurt him—he didn't even care! At that point Gary had another opportunity to extend forgiveness to his brother—this time for not caring that his destructive behavior had affected Gary.

Gary talked often with his friend about a number of things. During a visit together about a year later, they talked about Gary's parents. Again, Gary became livid. He realized that his parents could have protected him from his brother, but that they had chosen not to do so. He had asked them to intervene more than once, but they had refused to get involved. As Gary gained more perception, he became more hurt and angry, but after some thought about Christ's forgiveness for his sins, he again chose to forgive his family for hurting him.

Forgiveness means to remit or absolve a debt. When someone offends us, he or she creates a debt in the same way that our sins create a debt which can only be paid by Christ's substitutionary death for us. Forgiving others does not mean that we excuse them or say, "That's okay, it doesn't matter." Denial is not forgiveness. Extending true forgiveness means being honest and objective about the reality of another's offense, the hurt and the consequences caused by the offense, and then choosing not to hold that offense against the person's account with us.

Why Should We Forgive?

- *We have been forgiven by God through Jesus Christ.* "And be kind to one another, tender-hearted, forgiving each other, just as God in Christ also has forgiven you" (Eph. 4:32). See also Col. 2:13-14.
- *Christ has given us an example to follow.* "If I then, the Lord and the Teacher, washed your feet, you also ought to wash one another's feet. For I gave you an example that you also should do as I did to you" (John 13:14-15).

• *A spirit of unforgivingness will lead to spiritual oppression.* "And his lord, moved with anger, handed him over to the torturers until he should repay all that was owed him. So shall My heavenly Father also do to you, if each of you does not forgive his brother from your heart" (Matt. 18:34-35).

Unforgivingness is a sure way of cutting the flow of God's power in our lives. In fact, a number of negative consequences often result from a failure to forgive others. Before we examine these, let's look at some of the reasons why we may withhold forgiveness:[1]

Reasons for Not Forgiving

We often fail to forgive others (and ourselves) because we don't think it's possible. We forget how God has graciously forgiven all of our sins through Christ's death, and rationalize why we can't forgive. The following are among the countless excuses we make for our unwillingness to forgive ourselves and others:

• *The offense was too great.* Grant's wife had left him for another man, and he was bitter toward her. Her infidelity was too great a sin for him to forgive. But almost two years after the incident, God began to impress Grant with the idea that he should forgive his wife, *just as God in Christ also had forgiven him,* completely and willfully. When Grant finally did forgive her, his forgiveness was coupled with a commitment to rebuild his relationship with her so that she would not be compelled to repeat the incident with someone else.

Roger sat shaking with anger as he recalled his wife's rape. His anger was destroying his health and his relationship with his wife. *How can any man, who really is a man, forgive such an act?* he wondered. The transient who had raped his wife had moved on, and in his perversion, had probably forgotten the incident. He was never caught. Continuing to allow the offense to produce bitterness might ultimately do more harm to Roger and his family than the destructive act of the rape.

• *He(she) won't accept responsibility for the offense.* How many people have offended us, but won't agree that they were at fault? The offense might be something slight, such as being overlooked at a social event, or something major, such as being emotionally neglected as a child. Having others agree that they've offended us isn't necessary for us to respond properly to their offense.

- *He(she) isn't truly sorry.* John pulled a practical joke on you which caused you to be late for class, and your professor refused to accept your paper because you didn't have it in on time. John doesn't see anything wrong with a little joke— he's slightly sorry, but he still thinks it was hilarious. Even if John doesn't recognize the trouble he's caused you, you can still extend forgiveness to him through Christ, and refuse to hold the offense against him.

- *He(she) never asked to be forgiven.* For whatever reason, the offender never got around to asking you for forgiveness. Are you going to withhold forgiveness until it's requested? Who is suffering, you or the offender? What would God have you do? (Read 1 Cor. 13:5 and Eph. 4:32.)

- *He(she) will do it again.* Candy's husband had been out late every Friday night playing cards for three years. On some nights, he didn't come home. "Me? Forgive that jerk?" Candy asked. The Lord said that the number of times we're to forgive is seventy times seven . . . in other words, regardless of the number of offenses. However, forgiving doesn't mean condoning or accepting unacceptable behavior. Some situations calling for forgiveness also require confrontation and/or allowing the offender to experience the consequences of his or her behavior. For Candy, failing to both forgive and confront her husband will cause her to be the bitter loser.

- *He(she) did it again.* David had been a horrible husband to Mandy. However, after much effort, Mandy had forgiven him for his insensitivity, his greater concern for the guys on his softball team, his lack of affection for the children and his callous, domineering attitude. Then David saw how poor his behavior had become. He began to change. His relationship with Mandy started to improve—until he stayed out late again with the guys. He had done it again! One mistake set the whole conflict back in motion.

- *I don't like him(her).* Generally, we don't have a great deal of appreciation for those who have wronged us. In fact, every emotion within us may call for retaliation against the creep! Only when we realize that forgiveness is an act of the will, and not of the emotions, will we choose to forgive those who have hurt us.

• *He(she) did it deliberately.* "He knew what he was doing, and he did it anyway." George had been swindled out of $10,000 by his "best friend," Hal. It had been a complex scheme which had required precise timing over a period of several months. As George sat stunned, his mind raced through those times he had been generous to Hal. He thought of how much he had loved Hal and had repeatedly trusted him. The swindle had been completely deliberate, and Hal had used him. George had been played for a sucker. Hal must be laughing at him now. Whether the offense was deliberate or not, God still wants George to forgive Hal.

• *If I forgive the offense, I'll have to treat the offender well.* Ben excused his slander of Steve by pointing out how Steve had offended him. He felt justified in destroying Steve's reputation even though most of the things he had said about Steve were lies.

Shirley was cold to Greg, and had been for two weeks. It was her plan to punish him for two weeks because he had offended her. She would forgive him all right—as soon as she was through punishing him.

• *Someone has to punish him(her).* How often do we want God to be merciful to us and yet want Him to skin other people alive? When we don't see them suffer, we sometimes take it upon ourselves to be God's hand of vengeance.

Charles was their pastor, but according to Gloria, he had wasted the church's money. Gloria was in charge of the church women's group. She waited patiently for God to nail Charles, but when God didn't do what she thought He should, she just knew that she was to be the divining rod for Charlie's back. Soon the church had taken sides—pro-Charles or anti-Charles. The result was that the church disgraced itself by splitting in hatred.

• *Something keeps me from forgiving.* Satan actively promotes unforgivingness. When you attempt to deal with this problem honestly, you may be in for a tremendous spiritual battle, with both confusing and conflicting thoughts and emotions. Don't be surprised if you have to resist Satan at every turn in order to accomplish the task of forgiving the offender. Again, forgiveness is primarily an act of the will, not a warm feeling.

- *I'll be a hypocrite if I forgive because I don't feel like forgiving.* We often confuse hypocrisy with obedience. We are hypocritical only if we do something for selfish gain. For instance, a hypocrite might be a politician who comes to church in order to get its members to vote for him in the next election, but who despises the church and its people. To forgive as an act of the will in obedience to the Lord's command is true spirituality, not hypocrisy.

- *I'll forgive, but I won't ever forget.* If we continue to harbor the memory of an offense, we are only fooling ourselves in thinking that we have forgiven the offender, and we will not experience any freedom. In true forgiveness, we give up the right to remember an offense or to bring it up again during arguments. (Note: This doesn't mean that when we forgive a wrong, we'll never think of it again, but it does mean that we won't relish the memory. Choose to think about things that are true, honorable, right, pure and lovely [Phil. 4:8].)

- *I'll forgive because I have found an excuse for the offense.* Hank had been very irresponsible during the early years of his marriage. His wife Sally had always been able to forgive him by placing the blame on his mother, who had babied Hank even after he was grown. Yet Sally was continually angered by Hank and his mother. In fact, her volatile temper was destroying her marriage.

    Sally thought that she had forgiven Hank when she really had just excused him. By blaming Hank's mother for his immaturity, she had rationalized his behavior, and had reduced her perception of his offensive actions like this:

ORIGINAL OFFENSE   REDUCED OFFENSE

After reducing each offense, Sally then forgave it. The problem was that she did not deal with the real offense, but with a distortion of it. Therefore, the real offense remained intact in spite of her efforts at "forgiveness."

When you offend someone, or when someone offends you, do you immediately look for a "reason"? If you do, you may only be rationalizing. If you come up with an excuse to the question, *Why did I forgive him (or her)?* then you have not truly forgiven the offense. You have excused it.

Results of Not Forgiving

- *Stress:* Living with the high level of tension brought by an unforgiving attitude in a relationship can result in a weakening of one's mental resources, emotional difficulties, physical exhaustion and in some cases, illness.

- *Self-Inflicted Reinjury:* Robert recalled this incident: "As I drove home, flashing into my memory was a guy I played basketball with in college. He was a great antagonist of mine, and was one of the few people I have ever met whom I truly wanted to punch out. I began to remember the unkind things he had done to me. Soon, anger started creeping up inside me, and I realized that I had never forgiven him for what he had said and done those many years ago. Each time I thought of him, I would get a knot in my stomach and I'd be preoccupied with feelings of hurt and thoughts of revenge for hours, and sometimes, days."

  How many times are you reinjuring yourself because past offenses haunt you?

- *No More Love:* "I don't know if I can ever love someone again" is a frequent complaint from those offended by a lover. Our deepest hurts come from those we love. One way we deal with the pain of being offended is simply to withdraw, refusing to love anymore. We often make this unconscious decision when we have not adequately dealt with an offense. We may desperately want to love again, but feel that we are incapable of it. Refusing to experience love and feeling unable to love are both devastating conditions.

- *Bitterness:* Emotions trace their lines on our faces. We think others don't notice what's going on inside, but our anger can usually be detected by even the casual observer. One person recalled seeing a neighbor go through difficulties in her marriage. Hate created such an impression on her that her face became snarled. She still has an ugly look on her face. Unforgivingness produces ugliness of all sorts.

- *Perpetual Conflict:* A couple, both of whom had been previously married, received counseling several years ago. Having been hurt in their first marriage, they anticipated hurt from their present spouse. At the smallest offense, they would each react as if their spouse were about to deliver the final blow. They were constantly on the defensive, protecting themselves from the attacks they imagined their mate would deliver. Having been offended in the past, they anticipated more hurt in the present and future, and reacted in a way that perpetuated the conflict.

- *Walls That Keep Others Out:* Strangely, many of us refuse the love that others want to give us. We may feel anxious and threatened when personal intimacy becomes possible.

   Jane hoped and prayed that her husband Frank would come to know the Lord. This, she thought, would enable him to be more loving toward her and their children. One day Frank accepted Christ, and over time his life began to change. He became interested in Jane and started spending time with her and the children. He was sensitive and loving. Was it a dream come true? Instead of rejoicing, Jane deeply resented Frank for not changing sooner! *If Frank is able to love us like this now, then he's always had the ability,* she thought. She felt confused and guilty about her anger.

   Jane's anger was a defense mechanism to keep distance between Frank and her. The closer they might get, the more pain she might experience if he reverted to his old ways. She had never truly forgiven Frank, so the bricks of unforgivingness were stacked to form a wall that kept him from getting too close. Hiding behind a wall of unforgivingness is a lonely experience.

Forgiveness Is Not Erasure

   The modern idea of forgiveness is to approach an offense with a large eraser and wipe it off the books. God has never forgiven like this. He has demanded full payment for each offense. This is the reason for the cross. Beside every offense on our ledger is the blood of Christ, which has paid for our sins in full.

The Christian has a unique capacity to extend forgiveness because he or she can appropriate the forgiveness of the cross. God has forgiven us fully and completely. We of all people know what it is like to experience unconditional forgiveness. As a result, we can in turn forgive those around us. Think of it this way: *There is nothing that anyone can do to me (insult me, lie about me, annoy me, etc.) that can compare with what Christ has forgiven me for.* When we compare the offenses of others to our sin of rebellion that Christ has completely forgiven, it puts them in perspective. In Eph. 4:32, Paul writes, *And be kind to one another, tender-hearted, forgiving each other, just as God in Christ also has forgiven you.*

We will study more about biblical principles of forgiveness and how they apply to our relationships with others in the workbook section of this book.

SECTION II

THE SOLUTION: A Healthy Perception of God, Others and Our-selves

Chapter 10

Bonding with God

Jim Craddock

If we could go through a second childhood and there relate to someone who is consistently accepting and loving, we could find healing for much (if not all) of the damage we incurred then. But can we? We not only can, but this is exactly what begins to occur at the point of our salvation. We are reborn spiritually when we trust Christ as our Savior and Lord, and enter into a personal relationship with Him. We gain a new Father—the heavenly Father—who loves and cares for us completely. And we enter into Christ's body of believers, a new family that can provide us with warmth, affirmation, encouragement and hope.

Some of us were raised by parents who modeled God's love and reliability fairly consistently. However, we live in a fallen, sinful world; we all are fallen, sinful people. The role model which each of our parents provided for us has been tainted by that sin. As a result, even the best of parents can model only a distorted picture of God's perfect character. By the same token, even the worst of parents provide a glimmer of God's design for parenthood and familial relationships. Most, of course, are in the middle gray area: sinful (though perhaps redeemed) people in a sinful world, who are attempting to love and guide their children as best they can. We all receive strengths, weaknesses, benefits and liabilities from our parents. But upon reflection, many of us may find that the criticism, abuse, neglect and/or demands of our parents have produced painful emotions and destructive habits in our lives.

No matter how badly your parents modeled God's character, you can enjoy a healthy, intimate relationship with God and with others. God is a kind, patient Father who wants to demonstrate His love to His children. He has given us the truth of His Word, the power of His Spirit, and the warmth and encouragement of His people so that our self-concepts, relationships with Him and relationships with others can reflect His love.

Let God Be Your Model

Having received years of familial influence, and having developed a number of false conceptions and negative behavioral patterns, anyone desiring to change might wonder, *Is it possible for me to choose a new role model? Will it ever be possible for me to emulate someone who is infinitely loving, protective and giving?*

Yes! It is possible, but it doesn't happen by pressing a button. We can't rid ourselves of twenty to fifty years of negative input in an instant. In fact, though we may not always maintain a conscious awareness of our past, we will never be completely rid of its memories or influences. Childhood developmental patterns of thought, emotion and behavior are strongly entrenched in our lives, and even after we have begun to make real changes toward growth and health, certain difficulties can push us back into those older, more time-worn patterns. Our lives are complex and our growth is complex, too. Change is often long, slow and difficult. Developing behavioral patterns reflective of God's truth takes a commitment to honesty, a willingness to endure pain, understanding, obedience, perception and guts.

We need to start with a clear understanding of the character of God and the lies of Satan. The Lord has said, "Taste of Me, and see that I am good." He is a wonderful Father. According to the thirteenth chapter of First Corinthians, He is patient, kind and loving, not envious, boastful, arrogant or rude. He is never self-seeking. He is not quick to take offense. He keeps no score of wrongs. He does not gloat over men's sins. He knows no limit to His endurance and no end to His trust.

Perhaps you are thinking, *Choosing God for my role model is hard to consider as an option. I don't know Him well enough to know if I can be like Him, or even if I want to be like Him. And He is not tangible. How can I know what He's really like?*

Don't Let Satan Blind You to the Reality of God's Character

Have you been blinded by Satan about the reality of God's character? Satan has come *to steal, and kill and destroy* (John 10:10). He does not want us to experience God's love and forgiveness; instead, he wants to twist and distort our perception of Him. Satan has many negative and evil purposes for our lives, among them:

- Distorting God's character.
- Influencing us to believe that our relationships with the Lord are conditional, based on how good we can be.
- Wanting us to depend on people and things for our security and significance instead of depending on God.

Satan distorts our concepts of God's character. By so doing, he isolates us from God's help, strength and love.

Has he done this to you? Here's a test: To whom do you first turn when you have a problem? Do you turn to God first, or only when all else fails?

When our view of God is faulty we are not content to allow Him lordship of our lives. Rather, we see ourselves as victims of our circumstances and are thus more easily tormented by our failures and sins. If Satan can cause us pain and then cause us to associate it with the Father, he has succeeded in eroding our perception of a caring and compassionate God.

Because we haven't based our concepts of God the Father entirely on the inspired Word of God, all of us have faulty views of God as Father. Our concepts are based on the relationships we've had with our earthly fathers and other authority figures.

To a great many of us, the heavenly Father is a vague spiritual being, a cosmic policeman ten million light-years away. For all practical purposes, He is a stranger to us. And we don't trust strangers, much less love them. How can we put any confidence in someone we hardly know? We can't!

There's a clear connection between one's concept of God and one's emotional well-being. James 1:6 describes the consequences of not being able to trust God: *...for the one who doubts is like the surf of the sea driven and tossed by the wind.* Notice the contrast described in Is. 26:3: *The steadfast of mind Thou wilt keep in perfect peace, because he trusts in Thee.*

We tend to ascribe to God the characteristics of our fathers: good or bad, loving or cruel, protective or passive, gentle or aloof, etc. Some of us, therefore, have positive pictures of God because our fathers modeled His love and strength fairly consistently. But some of us have poor views of God because our fathers presented tyrannical or passive models to us.

What can change our faulty beliefs? The answer to this dilemma lies in the character of Jesus Christ. He has shown us the Father:

> *Philip said, "Lord, show us the Father and that will be enough for us."*
>
> *Jesus answered: "Don't you know me, Philip, even after I have been among you such a long time? Anyone who has seen me has seen the Father. How can you say, 'Show us the Father'?*
>
> *"Don't you believe that I am in the Father, and that the Father is in me? The words I say to you are not just my own. Rather, it is the Father, living in me, who is doing his work.*
>
> *"Believe me when I say that I am in the Father and the Father is in me; or at least believe on the evidence of the miracles themselves.*
>
> *"I tell you the truth, anyone who has faith in me will do what I have been doing. He will do even greater things than these, because I am going to the Father.*
>
> *"And I will do whatever you ask in my name, so that the Son may bring glory to the Father."*
>
> John 14:8-13, NIV

Even though the disciples had been with Jesus continually for three years, some of them seemed surprised to discover that He was God. They had not really understood that. Similarly, many of us haven't really understood that Jesus, the Father and the Holy Spirit are three different Persons, yet one essence.

All Jesus did, all He said and all the miracles He performed demonstrated His unity with the Father. The Father revealed Himself to us in the life, death and resurrection of Christ. Time and time again, Jesus reiterated this important truth. Here are some passages that describe the unity of the Father and the Son. Examine each one carefully:

Jesus gave them this answer: "I tell you the truth, the Son can do nothing by himself; he can do only what he sees his Father doing, because whatever the Father does the Son also does.

"For the Father loves the Son and shows him all he does. Yes, to your amazement he will show him even greater things than these.

"For just as the Father raises the dead and gives them life, even so the Son gives life to whom he is pleased to give it.

"Moreover, the Father judges no one, but has entrusted all judgment to the Son,

"that all may honor the Son just as they honor the Father. He who does not honor the Son does not honor the Father, who sent him.

"I tell you the truth, whoever hears my word and believes him who sent me has eternal life and will not be condemned; he has crossed over from death to life.

"I tell you the truth, a time is coming and has now come when the dead will hear the voice of the Son of God and those who hear will live.

"For as the Father has life in himself, so he has granted the Son to have life in himself.

"And he has given him authority to judge because he is the Son of Man."

John 5:19-27, NIV

I am one who testifies for myself; my other witness is the Father, who sent me.

John 8:18, NIV

The one who sent me is with me; he has not left me alone, for I always do what pleases him.

John 8:29, NIV

Jesus said to them, "If God were your Father, you would love me, for I came from God and now am here. I have not come on my own; but he sent me."

John 8:42, NIV

"I tell you the truth," Jesus answered, "before Abraham was born, I am!"

John 8:58, NIV

I and the Father are one.

John 10:30, NIV

"Do not let your hearts be troubled. Trust in God; trust also in me.

"In my Father's house are many rooms; if it were not so, I would have told you. I am going there to prepare a place for you.

"And if I go and prepare a place for you, I will come back and take you to be with me that you also may be where I am.

"You know the way to the place where I am going."

Thomas said to him, "Lord, we don't know where you are going, so how can we know the way?"

Jesus answered, "I am the way and the truth and the life. No one comes to the Father except through me.

"If you really knew me, you would know my Father as well. From now on, you do know him and have seen him."

John 14:1-7, NIV

. . . He (Jesus) *is the image of the invisible God, the firstborn over all creation.*

Col. 1:15, NIV

God, after He spoke long ago to the fathers in the prophets in many portions and in many ways,

in these last days has spoken to us in His Son, whom he appointed heir of all things, through whom also he made the world.

And He (Jesus) *is the radiance of His* (God's) *glory and the exact representation of His nature, and upholds all things by the word of His power. . . .*

Heb. 1:1-3

The Father, the Son and the Holy Spirit are one. God the Son stepped out of heaven and became a man so that God's love, forgiveness and care would be demonstrated in person to heal and comfort those who were hurting so desperately.

We must learn to see the Father in the character, words and actions of Jesus. The Holy Spirit will then begin to correct our erroneous concepts of the Father and provide all of the accompanying benefits.

Do you think God the Father would treat you differently than Jesus would? If so, reflect on the Scriptures given above and ask God to increase your understanding of who He is.

We tend to think God is so huge and impersonal that He doesn't feel pain. But He does! Christ endured the excruciating pain of being beaten, whipped and nailed to the cross. He endured the emotional pain of being deserted by His friends, spat on by His enemies and jeered at by the crowds who only days before had hailed Him as king. And He endured the humanly unimaginable spiritual pain of being completely separated from God the Father and taking on Himself the burden of every sin ever committed in the history of man, combined with the punishment for those sins: the righteous wrath of God. As the hymn writer expressed it:

> *Amazing love, how can it be*
> *That Christ my God should die for me?* [1]

Christ's sacrificial death paid fully for our sins which separated us from God. His atonement justified us—that is, it made us righteous in God's sight. His death propitiated, or averted, God's righteous wrath toward us. Among other incredible truths, His payment for our sins enabled us to be adopted as children of God. These two scriptural passages explain our adoption:

> *But when the time had fully come, God sent his Son, born of a woman, born under law,*
> *to redeem those under law, that we might receive the full rights of sons.*
> *Because you are sons, God sent the Spirit of his Son into our hearts, the Spirit who calls out, "Abba, Father."*
> *So you are no longer a slave, but a son; and since you are a son, God has made you also an heir.*
>
> Gal. 4:4-7, NIV

For you did not receive a spirit that makes you a slave again to fear, but you received the Spirit of sonship. And by him we cry, "Abba, Father."

Rom. 8:15, NIV

No matter how well or how poorly our fathers modeled the character of God, we can be convinced of our heavenly Father's love and power. Certainly it is to our advantage to have had good models in our parents, but for those of us who didn't, we have the clear and strong teaching of God's Word, the working of God's Spirit and the encouragement of God's people to help us understand His nature.

As we recognize how we have been deceived about who God is, it will be helpful to consider what it means to be a child of God. Consider these aspects of the parent-child relationship:

- A child gains a sense of security based on the trust he or she has in his or her parents.
- A child looks to his or her parents to see if they're calm in times of trouble. If the child believes the parents are upset, he or she will become upset.
- A child feels he will be okay if he just obeys his parents' instructions.
- A child believes that everything will be okay as long as his or her parents confidently convey that it will be.
- A child feels special because he or she is special to his or her parents.
- A child can be happy even without knowing all that's going on. He or she is then free to relax and enjoy life.
- A child can be honest about his or her positive and negative feelings.
- A child likes being around his or her parents.

Attitudes and behaviors like these are foreign to some of us in our relationships with our parents and, by extension, in our relationships with God. Our lack of trust and confidence in Him is due to our many faulty perceptions of His character. We may cognitively know certain truths about God and we may be able to articulate those truths, but learning how to live by that knowledge and base our actions upon it is much more difficult.

As you explore the rest of this book, pray that God will reveal to you which beliefs you have about Him that are wrong and ways by which you can experience your position as His beloved child more fully.

Chapter 11

God Wants Us to Know Him as Father

Robert S. McGee
Pat Springle

We have some friends who recently adopted a child after trying for years to have a baby. The little boy was only three days old when they took him home from the hospital, and though this couple was given only a few days notice from the adoption agency, they were thrilled beyond words! Their love for this adopted infant couldn't have been stronger if he had been of their own flesh and blood.

As Christians, we also have been adopted. The Scriptures teach us that we have been adopted by God into His family, but our adoption isn't quite like the one we've just described. We didn't come to God like infants with virtually blank slates. Much of our emotional and behavioral grid was firmly in place when we became Christians.

An illustration that better describes our situation is the story of a couple in Iowa who has adopted a house full of children between the ages of five and twelve. Each of these children was hurt deeply by neglect, abuse or the sudden loss of both parents. Nobody else wanted these misfits, these "problem children," but the Iowa couple gave them a home and a name. Several children were more emotionally stable than the others, and they responded relatively quickly to the couple's love and care. Most of them, however, didn't respond well when they first entered the family. They didn't trust their new parents.

It was only after months of consistent, patient affirmation and correction, after months of wiping up spills without condemning words, after months of reading to them and playing with them that the message started to sink into these children's hearts and minds one by one. They could trust their new parents. Each could have a new identity.

We are like these children. Some of us can respond to our adopted Father fairly easily. Some of us need a little more time to understand His love and care so that we can trust Him, feel close to Him and obey Him. How we think about God and about ourselves determines virtually every attitude and action in our lives. Until we are convinced that our new Father is loving and strong, we will continue to be bitter and self-reliant or fearful and withdrawn. We desperately need to comprehend the meaning of our new identities as God's adopted children.

Sometimes even people who are deeply loved and thoroughly cared for have poor perceptions of God. The story of the prodigal son in the fifteenth chapter of Luke serves as an illustration of this dilemma. The younger of two sons asked for his share of an inheritance, and after receiving it, wasted it in an immoral lifestyle. When he found himself totally destitute, he realized that he could ask his father to let him be a lowly hired hand. Instead, when he went to his home, his father lovingly forgave him and reinstated him to the full privileges of sonship. End of story? Not quite.

The older son was in the field when he heard the sound of music and dancing. A celebration of some kind was taking place. When a servant reported that the festivities were in honor of his wayward younger brother who had selfishly wasted part of the family fortune, and that his father had forgiven him and received him back into the family, he was furious!

The father begged him to come join the party, but the older brother retorted:

> . . . *Look! For so many years I have been serving you, and I have never neglected a command of yours; and yet you have never given me a kid, that I might be merry with my friends;*
>
> *but when this son of yours came, who has devoured your wealth with harlots, you killed the fattened calf for him.*
>
> Luke 15:29-30

He had worked hard all his life and had never been given a party like his degenerate brother had received. He was bitter and jealous. The father responded gently:

> . . . *My child, you have always been with me, and all that is mine is yours. But we had to be merry and rejoice, for this brother of yours was dead and has begun to live, and was lost and has been found.*
>
> Luke 15:31-32

The father was obviously kind and generous to both sons, but the older one had never noticed. His younger brother, who had come home expecting to be a field hand, was experiencing the blessings of a beloved son. In contrast, the older brother, who had been around his loving father all of his life, saw himself as only a field hand. His false perception of his father had cost him dearly!

We use the term "child of God" quite often, but what does it mean? What difference does it make? How can a person experience the intimacy and blessing of being God's child?

John Stott capsulized the New Testament's teaching on adoption:

> . . . *it was Jesus himself who always addressed God intimately as "Abba, Father," who gave us permission to do the same, approaching Him as "our Father in heaven." The apostles enlarged on it. John, who attributes our being children of God to our being born of God, expresses his sense of wonder that the Father should have loved us enough to call us, and indeed make us, His children. Paul, on the other hand, traces our status as God's children rather to our adoption than to our new birth, and emphasizes the privilege we have in being sons instead of slaves, and therefore heirs as well.* [1]

God Himself initiated our adoption as His sons and daughters; therefore, we are secure in our relationship with Him (Gal. 4:4-6). We are the recipients of the spirit of adoption which overcomes and casts out the fearful spirit of slavery (Rom. 8:15). Our status as God's children is made possible entirely by His grace so that our security is based on His strong love and power, not on our self-righteous efforts and fickle emotions. (See Titus 3:3-7.)

Through our adoption, we have more than legal standing with God (wonderful as that is!). We have intimacy with Him. In the Old Testament, the mighty character of God produced a sense of fear and dread in men. The New Testament also portrays the awesomeness of God, but it adds the truth that this mighty God is the Father of believers. Instead of shrinking back in terror or dread, we are encouraged to *draw near with confidence to the throne of grace, that we may receive mercy and may find grace to help in time of need* (Heb. 4:16). Though God is the majestic, sovereign, omnipotent Creator, we can actually have an intimate relationship with Him. We are assured of this by the inner witness of the Spirit (Rom. 8:16) as He communicates both His love and His direction to us (Rom. 8:14). Paul gives us the overwhelming reason why God wants us to experience this intimacy with Him. It is because of *the kind intention of His will, to the praise of the glory of His grace, which He freely bestowed on us in the Beloved* (Eph. 1:5-6). What a statement of the Lord's strong affection toward us!

When He adopted us as His children, the Lord pledged Himself to provide for us. Jesus assured us of the Father's generous response to our needs:

> *Ask, and it shall be given to you; seek, and you shall find; knock, and it shall be opened to you.*
>
> *For everyone who asks receives, and he who seeks finds, and to him who knocks it shall be opened.*
>
> *Or what man is there among you, when his son shall ask him for a loaf, will give him a stone?*
>
> *Or if he shall ask for a fish, he will not give him a snake, will he?*
>
> *If you then, being evil, know how to give good gifts to your children, how much more shall your Father who is in heaven give what is good to those who ask Him!*
>
> Matt. 7:7-11

God has granted to His children the status of being heirs of His promises, purposes and provisions. Our response to this kind of relationship is fairly predictable. As we begin to understand the fatherhood of God and our identities as His sons and daughters, we respond in affection by calling Him, *Abba, Father*

(Rom. 8:15, Gal. 4:4-7). This is not an arms-length relationship; rather, it is one of depth, honest expression and intimacy. We respond to His love by taking steps to purify our motives and actions (2 Cor. 6:14-7:1 and 1 John 3:3). We want to honor the One who is our Father. The intensity of our desire to honor Him enables us to suffer rejection and deprivation for His sake (Rom. 8:17), and to love other members of His family even if they are radically different from us (Eph. 2:11-22).

The more that we understand our identities as God's sons and daughters, the more we will sense the tremendous privilege it is to be children of God. We will begin wanting to honor Him. Instead of having a foot-dragging "have-to" attitude about obeying and serving God, we will begin to develop a "want-to" attitude.

How can we change our sense of identity to reflect what Scripture says is true of us?

Some people have had parents who did a good job of modeling the character of God. Assuming identities as loved and accepted children of God is fairly easy for them. But those whose earthly parents neglected, abused or manipulated them begin to assume their true identities by *contrasting* God the Father with their earthly parents instead of *equating* Him with them. Each can say, *Even though my parents neglected me, the Lord never does. He cares for me and provides for me. Even though my parents didn't give me much attention, the Lord is always thinking about me. He knows my every thought, feeling and need.*

A person's identity changes as his perception of God and of himself changes. This usually requires a blend of three elements: cognitive, volitional and relational. Studying God's Word gives him basic truths needed for meditation and incorporation into his life. Then, there are specific instances each day which call for making choices: *Will I respond like an unloved, cast-off orphan, or like a loved and accepted child of the Almighty God?* Third, he needs the modeling and affirmation of other members of God's family to help him understand and grow in his new identity.

When a young child is adopted, his new identity will grow and develop if these three elements are present. But another element is needed to help him assume his new identity: the active and specific involvement of the parent. If the child is struggling with his identity and asks the loving parents, "Will you help me?" they will respond with compassion and strong action.

It is the same with our adopted Father. If we are struggling to understand and apply our new identities as His children, we can ask Him for help. The Holy Spirit is our helper, and He will give us the wisdom and courage we need to live according to our new identities.

There are many ways to describe the characteristics of a child of God. God's initiative to provide for His children yields an affectionate and deep response. Let's look at five characteristics we share as God's children:

God Is Our Refuge

Are you fearful? Does an unexplainable dread prevail upon your thinking, or do you experience a peace that surpasses your normal response to stress?

When we experience difficulties, we are quick to look for solutions. Usually we try to solve our problems by using our own wisdom and strength, or by using the resources of another person or organization, but the Lord's abilities far exceed those of the world combined. He may use the resources He has given to us or others to meet our needs, but He is our refuge, the source of all wisdom, strength and peace. Three classic passages communicate this truth:

> *God is our refuge and strength, a very present help in trouble.*
> *Therefore we will not fear, though the earth should change, and though the mountains slip into the heart of the sea;*
> *Though its waters roar and foam, though the mountains quake at its swelling pride. [Selah.]*
>
> Ps. 46:1-3

> *Trust in the Lord with all your heart, and do not lean on your own understanding.*
> *In all your ways acknowledge Him, and He will make your paths straight.*
>
> Prov. 3:5-6

> *Peace I leave with you; My peace I give to you: not as the world gives, do I give to you. Let not your heart be troubled, nor let it be fearful.*
>
> John 14:27

In any and all circumstances, remember, God is our refuge.

God Is Our Source of Supply

Often in our daydreams we wish we had someone who would supply us with all our needs. We do! Our heavenly Father can—and will—supply them. It is because we do not understand His character and have developed alternate supply lines that we fail to believe God will meet our needs.

Here's a painful test: Think about all the things you own. Who supplied them? When we think of our possessions as being supplied without God's intervention, we reveal our true belief system.

One Christian honestly confessed: "When I think about my house and car, I believe they resulted from my job. Actually, when I look around my house, I think of each bit of furniture as being supplied by a source other than God. My parents gave me the living room furniture for a wedding present. My wife bought me my favorite chair. Many other items were bought on an installment plan with the help of my bank. In all honesty, I don't really think much at all about God being my Provider."

It takes some serious thinking to recognize that we can and must look to our Father as our Provider. In fact, our jobs and possessions are really not ours. They were provided by God and they belong to Him at all times.

We Are Precious to God

Our Father is so concerned about us that He knows when we lose a hair from our heads (Matt. 10:30). He never ceases to love, to nurture, to care for and protect us. We are very special to Him!

The apostle Peter wrote to comfort and encourage the Christian Jews who had been scattered because of persecution:

> And coming to Him as to a living stone, rejected by men, but choice and precious in the sight of God,
> you also, as living stones, are being built up as a spiritual house for a holy priesthood, to offer up spiritual sacrifices acceptable to God through Jesus Christ.
>
> 1 Pet. 2:4-5

In this passage, Peter explains that Christ is a *living stone* rejected by men and that He is *choice and precious in the sight of God*. Then Peter identifies us with

Christ and says that we, too, are living stones, choice and precious in the sight of God. Peter doesn't stop there. He then describes the results of understanding this wonderful identity. Those who realize that they are precious to God learn to abhor sin the way God does. Their passion in life is to honor the Lord through love, obedience and service.

Our status before God is one of great security and significance. Peter goes on to capsulize our position in Christ and our subsequent response in verse nine:

> *But you are a chosen race, a royal priesthood, a holy nation, a people for God's own possession, that you may proclaim the excellencies of Him who has called you out of darkness into His marvelous light.*
>
> 1 Pet. 2:9

We have great worth because of our relationship with God. As we are increasingly convinced of our new worth and identity, we will want to honor Him more and more.

We Worship God

Consider the emotions of a young man or woman who has fallen in love. He or she will experience tremendous joy and excitement when it is time for the loved one to arrive.

What about your emotions when it's time for your personal Bible study and devotions? Does worship bore you, or do you get excited when you prepare to meet with God?

If we really see Him as our Father, we will recognize that God is both loving and majestic. He delights in being worshipped! And He is worthy of our praise and obedience.

At the same time, we would do well to remember that worship is not based just on an emotion; it is an act of the will. No matter what our emotions are like (happy or sad, glad or angry, thankful or sullen), we *choose* to reflect on God's character. Perhaps thinking about His faithfulness will encourage us when we are depressed, or perhaps as we think about His love, we will realize that we haven't been loving to someone in particular. If that's the case, we can confess our sin to God (and perhaps to that person!) and then rejoice in His grace and faithfulness more fully.

God Reigns over Us

Our world has the mistaken opinion that man can dictate his terms to God and tell Him how we will relate to Him. The apostle Paul wrote about the rebellious spirit of the human race:

> *For although they knew God, they neither glorified him as God nor gave thanks to him, but their thinking became futile and their foolish hearts were darkened.*
>
> *Although they claimed to be wise, they became fools*
> *and exchanged the glory of the immortal God for images made to look like mortal man and birds and animals and reptiles.*
>
> *Therefore God gave them over in the sinful desires of their hearts to sexual impurity for the degrading of their bodies with one another.*
>
> *They exchanged the truth of God for a lie, and worshipped and served created things rather than the Creator—who is forever praised. Amen.*
>
> Rom. 1:21-25, NIV

Many of us have fallen into the trap of trying to make God our servant instead of allowing Him to be our ruler. When God does not respond as we want Him to, we often become angry with Him. But God relates to us on the basis of who He truly is, not as we think Him to be.

At the time of our conversion, we are rescued from eternal condemnation, granted status as children of God and given a sense of purpose. At that point we are to surrender our lives to Him. We are not to withhold any area of our lives from His right to reign over it. The Holy Spirit will later reveal areas in our lives which are not under the total lordship of Christ. We are to then yield those areas as He makes us aware of them.

It is imperative that we have a clear understanding of the nature and character of Christ. As our Savior, He rescues us from selfish and ultimately empty lifestyles. As our Lord, He is our acknowledged owner and master. We are His bond-servants, delighting to do the will of the One who loved us enough to rescue us from hell and give us peace and purpose.

Scripture is our final authority. The Bible is the inspired Word of God. If we believe the Bible is God's message to us, we will not use it as just an ornament to carry in and out of church services. Reading it will have a daily, vital priority in our lives because we will see our need to draw on its insight, wisdom, strength and comfort.

If the Lord is to rule over us on a moment-by-moment basis, we must look toward Him and let His Word speak to us. Memorizing verses, "hiding them in our hearts," is an excellent way to remember His lordship over us. In reading the gospels, note how many times the writers quote Scripture from the Old Testament. Before they could do that, they had to know the Scriptures intimately.

Knowing God's Word was no more important for them than it is for us. We cannot interpret the life around us accurately unless we do so in light of the Scriptures. And we cannot know the Scriptures unless we spend time studying them.

In addition, we are the Lord's *bondslaves*. Being a bondslave is a deliberate choice. The term comes from the Old Testament:

> But if the servant declares, "I love my master and my wife and children and do not want to go free,"
> then his master must take him before the judges [or before God]. He shall take him to the door or the doorpost and pierce his ear with an awl.
> Then he will be his servant for life.
>
> Ex. 21:5-6, NIV

The voluntary commitment of the servant to his master is a deliberate one with far-reaching consequences. Paul often referred to himself as a bondslave of Jesus Christ. The deliberate surrender of his life was total.

God is our loving and powerful Father. The more accurately we perceive His character, the more we will believe that we can count on Him. We will learn to depend on His constancy even when our feelings and circumstances change. For instance, when a child goes through the "terrible two's," a dependably loving parent doesn't react to the child's tantrums in anger and condemnation. He or she isn't manipulated or controlled by the child's anger but instead maintains a calm and nurturing environment. The parent serves as a container for the child's anger while helping the child come to grips with the fact that the world is a hostile place where things will not always go his way. In the same way, we can learn that God provides a constant and loving environment for us as we learn to cope with the problems we face. Our emotions will change. Our circumstances may fall apart. But He remains loving and strong on our behalf. He is worthy of our affection, obedience and service.

Chapter 12

The Names of God

Jim Craddock

It is vitally important that we create a mental category for the Lord based upon the truth of Scripture. As we do, we will form a new foundation for our lives—a new source of love, faith and obedience. By changing our understanding of who He is, we will draw closer to Him.

What's in a Name?

Scripture gives many descriptive names for God. Most of them today are translated as "God," or "Lord," or "Lord God," but in the original Hebrew text, every name given for God reveals something special about His character. None of these names has been given to Him by man. His names are His own selection, used to reveal Himself in all His fullness. So sacred are the names presented in this chapter that one-third of the Ten Commandments forbids their use in any flippant manner. Aspects of His nature revealed through His names should not be regarded frivolously.

In ancient times, names did more than identify people and their family relationships. They were used to designate a particular characteristic of the person named. An example of this is found in the name *Jacob*, which means "Supplanter." He was a crafty, self-seeking person until he met God. After his encounter with the angel of the Lord, his name was changed to Israel, meaning, "He struggles with God."

In the third chapter of Exodus, God commissioned Moses to free the Israelites from Egyptian bondage. In verses thirteen and fourteen, Moses said to God:

> *"Suppose I go to the Israelites and say to them, 'The God of your fathers has sent me to you,' and they ask me, 'What is his name?' Then what shall I tell them?"*
>
> *God said to Moses, "I AM WHO I AM* [JEHOVAH]. *This is what you are to say to the Israelites: 'I AM has sent me to you'"* (NIV).

JEHOVAH is a very significant name for God because it means that He is eternal and self-existent. This name gave new credibility to Moses, the man identified with it. Throughout the difficulties of his confrontations with Pharaoh, the Exodus and the forty years in the wilderness, Moses knew he could trust JEHOVAH.

By examining some of God's other names, we can learn more about His character.

Three Primary Names for God

ELOHIM (God)

This Hebrew word is a combination of two words: EL, meaning "unlimited strength, energy, might and power" and ALAH, meaning "to swear, declare or make a covenant." Together, they describe God as One of infinite strength and faithfulness.

The first mention of God in Gen. 1:1 refers to Him as ELOHIM: *In the beginning God created the heavens and the earth.* Jesus used this term in Matt. 19:26 when He said, *With man this is impossible, but with God* (ELOHIM) *all things are possible.*   In this case, His endless power is revealed by the use of His name.

ELOHIM is a plural word. Although God is a single deity, His trinitarian nature is clearly stated by the plural use of the word. For example, Deut. 4:35 emphasizes the *unity* of the Godhead:

> *You were shown these things so that you might know that the Lord is God* [ELOHIM]; *besides him there is no other* (NIV).

Genesis 1:26, on the other hand, emphasizes the *plurality* within the Godhead: *Let us make man in our image, in our likeness. . . .* This passage is our first introduction to the Trinity: the Father, Son and Holy Spirit.

In Heb. 1:3, we are told:

> *The Son is the radiance of* [ELOHIM'S] *glory and the exact representation of his being, sustaining all things by his powerful word* (NIV).

Jesus Christ has revealed to us the One who always keeps His covenant with man. He will do what He has sworn to do. His power is constant. It doesn't waver. James 1:17 says: *Every good and perfect gift is from above, coming down from the Father of the heavenly lights, who does not change like shifting shadows* (NIV).

We can know and depend on God's covenant promises, sure that He will not change His mind. He has sufficient power to create all things and to sustain them. He never becomes too busy to keep His promises. He is totally dependable.

Perhaps your father often promised to do things for you or with you and then didn't follow through. If your "father category" has been shaped by an undependable parent, and if you now find it difficult to trust God, then this name for God will be important to you. By His very nature, God cannot break His covenant promises with us!

ELOHIM is a name for God which will enrich your prayer life. It will continually remind you that His power is limitless and that He always, always keeps His promises. Think about this name when you are claiming His promises to you as recorded in His Word.

JEHOVAH (Lord God)

Meaning "He who is truly present," JEHOVAH describes God as the dependable and faithful God who can be fully trusted. It can also mean, "I will always be what I have always been."

JEHOVAH is the personal name for God. While ELOHIM speaks of His power, JEHOVAH speaks of His intimate relationship with us. God took the initiative with Moses and the Israelites, and stepped deliberately into the lives of people who were slaves.

When you feel that God isn't really interested in you and your problems, remember the meaning of God's name, JEHOVAH! This name is connected with His mighty acts of setting people free, of redeeming them from bondage. It assures you that God is personally and vitally interested in every single thing about you, and that He is committed to leading you to a solution for your difficulties. As a Father who cares, He is not bored by your difficulties, even when they are repetitious.

Jesus referred to Himself in John 8:58 by saying, *I tell you the truth, before Abraham was born, I am!* He did not say "I was," but "I am," using the word JEHOVAH. Once again, we are reminded that Christ has fully revealed the Father to us.

By studying passages where JEHOVAH is used, we learn that God existed before anything had been created, that He is holy, that He hates and judges sin and that He loves and saves sinners. In all cases where it is used, His deeply personal relationship with us is the focus of the name.

In reading the first five books of the Bible, it is fascinating to note how the writer sometimes refers to God as ELOHIM and at other times as JEHOVAH. In each case, a different emphasis is being made about His character. The powerful One is also the personal One who numbers every hair on our heads and who sees every tiny sparrow that falls to the ground. In fact, an entire series of descriptive words are attached to this name so that we can understand more about God's character. We will review these later in this chapter.

ADONAI (Lord)

In Josh. 3:11, God is called *Lord* [ADONAI] *of all the earth.* As with ELOHIM, this word for God is in the plural, again pointing to the Trinity. It refers to God as One high and above all things, the ruler of all there is.

The name ADONAI is often coupled with JEHOVAH to remind us that although we have an intimate relationship with God, we are not to view Him as a human counterpart.

ADONAI emphasizes that God is Lord and Master, "One who exercises rule and authority." The emphasis is on a relationship between a master and a servant. Our Master has the right to expect absolute obedience from us. In return, we have the right to expect provision and direction from our benevolent Master.

Being a servant to ADONAI is a fantastic arrangement! We have the privilege of representing the God of the universe. What could bring greater meaning to our activities? In return, He provides all the resources we need to do His will.

When you see yourself as a servant of ADONAI, you will be thankful that He will provide for all of your needs. You also will recognize the necessity of being obedient to His guidance because He knows best and has your welfare in mind.

Scholars have discovered that the word ADONAI was not used by any other ancient civilization—only Israel! It's a special word, used to reveal a special relationship between God and those who are closely related to Him.

If you sometimes use "Master" or "Lord" in your prayers, remember the One who exercises all rule and authority, and then respond in faith, obedience and glad service to Him.

Compound Names for God

In addition to the three primary names for God, four names combine with the word EL to describe His character:

EL SHADDAI (God Almighty)

The Scriptures emphasize the Lord's nature as the giver and sustainer of life in the name EL SHADDAI. SHADDAI is taken from the Hebrew word SHAD, meaning "breast." Even as a mother breast-feeds her child, so God is described as One who feeds and nurtures His own. The term is used in Gen. 17:1; 28:1-4; Ps. 91:1, as well as in other intimate and personal circumstances in the Old Testament. For example, God was called by this name in reference to the birth of Isaac—the miracle child born to a man and woman too old to expect a baby. EL SHADDAI was the One who made provisions for poor Hagar and her son, Ishmael, when Sarah demanded that Abraham evict them from their household. He is the One who today cares for the fatherless and the homeless.

The name was used again when circumcision was instituted as a covenant sign between God and Israel. This rite, performed on every Israelite male, was a symbol of the special covenant relationship between God and His people.

You will want to use this name when you need God's care and provision.

EL ELYON (Most High God)

This name reminds us that the Father is the possessor of heaven and earth. He is the omnipotent, Almighty God. This description is found in Gen. 14:18-23; Dan. 5:18; and Ps. 83:18.

EL ELYON demonstrates God's supremacy over all pagan deities. It literally means "the strongest strong one." This does not suggest that there are any other gods in the universe who are less powerful than EL ELYON. The pagan notion that He is the highest among a huge community of gods is absurd, because there is only one God. All others are myths or demons. Nevertheless, there are still tens of thousands of so-called "gods" worshipped by Orientals, Asians, Africans and Indians. In reality, the power usually attributed to them is the activity of Satan, who attempts to counterfeit the acts of God.

In Abidjan, the capital of the Ivory Coast in West Africa, the Christians fervently sing, "Jesus is higher! Satan is lower! Jesus is higher! Satan is erased!" Like the Christians in Abidjan, we can trust and triumphantly announce that our God is Most High. . . EL ELYON. As we encounter resistance in following God's will, either within or outside ourselves, we need to call upon EL ELYON.

EL OLAM (The Everlasting God)

OLAM means "eternal duration, everlasting, evermore; something secret, hidden or concealed." This name directs our attention to God's timelessness, His vast knowledge and His constancy. The term is used, among other places, in Gen. 21:33; Deut. 33:27 and Ps. 90:1-2.

In Gen. 21:22-31, the patriarch Abraham had a confrontation with King Abimelech and Phicol, commander of the Philistine forces. When a treaty between them had been completed, Abraham planted a tree as a monument and called upon the name of EL OLAM (Gen. 21:33). He knew that these two men were as changeable as the weather, and that the treaty would be worthless apart from God's unchanging nature. In the next verse we are told, *And Abraham stayed in the land of the Philistines for a long time.* EL OLAM was his security!

Moses is the author of Psalm 90. In it, he meditates on the eternal presence of God. He refers to EL OLAM in verses one and two when he says:

> *Lord, you have been our dwelling place throughout all genera-*
> *ions.*
>
> *Before the mountains were born or you brought forth the earth and*
> *the world, from everlasting to everlasting you are God* [EL OLAM]
> (NIV).

These verses transcend time and space, causing us to recall that our heavenly Father is unlimited by conditions which restrict and inhibit us.

In Deut. 33:27, Moses again uses this word for God in his final address to his people: *The eternal God* [EL OLAM] *is your refuge, and underneath are the everlasting arms* (NIV). How comforting it must have been to Moses to entrust his beloved Israel to such a God!

The nature of God as revealed in the name EL OLAM will be very important to you when you must trust God and God alone with situations where His stability is all you have to depend on.

One couple found themselves in such a situation when their teenage son ran away from home. For several days, they suffered the agony of not knowing if he was alive or dead, or whether they would ever see him again. As they prayed, they called upon EL OLAM and He gave them His peace which surpasses understanding.

He will do the same for you. When conditions get stormy, speak His name with peace in your heart.

EL ROI (The God Who Sees)

The Hebrew name ROI means "the one who sees." Our God is revealed to be One who watches over us, concerning Himself with our needs. He sees that our needs are met. He also sees our every thought, word and deed. Passages using this term include Gen. 16:13-14 and Heb. 4:13.

Hagar's condition was miserable. First, her mistress Sarah called upon her to become pregnant by her husband. Then, in a fit of jealousy, Sarah threw her out of the house while she was carrying the unborn child. Without a destination, Hagar found herself alone by a spring in the desert. Her loneliness and feelings of rejection were intense. God appeared to her in Gen. 16:7-12, advising her to return to Sarah. He then told her he would increase her descendants through Ishmael. In verse thirteen we read,

> She gave this name to the Lord who spoke to her: "You are the God [EL ROI] who sees me," for she said, "I have now seen the One who sees me" (NIV).

Does God know your condition? Of course He does! He is EL ROI. Here again we see the constant theme in all of these names for God: His awareness of everything about us.

If your earthly father failed to mirror this understanding and awareness of your needs, you will want to reflect on the truth that God is with you constantly, understanding all your circumstances and able to meet all your needs.

These marvelous names are only the beginning of God's revelation about Himself. We shall now consider eight compound names related to the name JEHOVAH.

JEHOVAH-JIREH (The Lord Will Provide)

The name JIREH means "to see to it or to provide." The use of the term involves references to God's testing after He has prepared us to meet and pass the test. This concept appears in Gen. 22:8 and again in Phil. 4:19, where He promises to *meet all your needs according to His glorious riches in Christ Jesus.*

In Gen. 22:1-19, Abraham's relationship with God and with his son Isaac is severely tested. He faces the important question of which one is most precious to him. Obeying God completely, he plans to sacrifice his child as requested. As they climb together to the altar site, Isaac asks, *"Where is the lamb for the burnt offering?"* Abraham responds, *"God Himself* [JEHOVAH-JIREH] *will provide the lamb. . . ."*

It's hard to imagine a better way to illustrate the significance of this word than through this story. God never intended for Abraham to kill Isaac. He wanted Abraham to demonstrate that his love for God was greater than his love for his son. Abraham prepared to follow through with God's demand, but the Lord stopped him. His provision was a ram, a substitute sacrifice for Isaac.

JEHOVAH-JIREH presented a substitute for us, too. The Lamb of God was Jesus Christ. He came "to provide for" our sin problem by offering us the only possible solution to our separation from God. If He cared enough to go to the cross to provide for our most fundamental spiritual need, then we may be certain that He will not stop there. He provided a dry path through the Red Sea for Israel. He provided release from a prison cell for Peter. He still provides all we need to walk with Him. Paul states in Rom. 8:32: *He who did not spare His own Son, but delivered*

Him up for us all, how will He not also with Him freely give us all things? (NIV).

The Lord is gracious and generous, but don't use this name to manipulate Him to get your selfish wants. Those who have tried to manipulate God have been disillusioned by His lack of cooperation. As a perfect Father, He knows what we need, and He knows when we need it. Understanding His will and His purpose will save us a lot of frustration in expecting His provisions to be what we want when we want them.

JEHOVAH-NISSI (The Lord My Banner)

The word NISSI refers to a banner, an emblem, a war flag. This description of God's character refers to men entering conflict. Flying as a banner before them is JEHOVAH-NISSI. This wonderful name reminds us that all power is with Him and all strength for battle comes from Him. He will lead us to victory. In Ex. 17:15, after Moses won a victory over Amalek, he built a memorial altar and called it "The Lord Is My Banner."

This term is also found in the fifty-ninth chapter of Isaiah. Isaiah saw the corruption in Israel. In verse fourteen, he wrote: *justice is driven back...truth has stumbled in the streets, honesty cannot enter* (NIV).

When God saw this lack of justice, He was *appalled that there was no one to intervene* (Is. 59:16, NIV). Who would care for the helpless ones who were prey for the greedy? The answer is given in verse nineteen:

From the west, men will fear the name of the Lord, and from the rising of the sun, they will revere his glory. For he will come like a pent-up flood that the breath of the Lord [JEHOVAH-NISSI] *drives along* (NIV).

They were not alone in their struggle. JEHOVAH flew over them like a victory banner, like a mighty tidal wave of judgment blown along by the wind of His Spirit.

Sometimes we, too, find ourselves seemingly helpless before circumstances. In those cases, we can raise our Banner high and remember that JEHOVAH-NISSI is our strength and shield for our every battle.

JEHOVA-TSIDKENU (The Lord Our Righteousness)

TSIDKENU, added to JEHOVAH, reminds us that God is the only truly righteous One. He Himself is the absolute, impeccable standard. Perfect righteousness is the natural attribute of God; it cannot be found elsewhere. This name is a reminder that the only righteousness we ever will have is His righteousness.

In Ex. 9:27, the term is used by Pharaoh. Plague upon plague had caused him to see the mighty power of God until he finally understood the contrast between himself and Israel's deity:

> *Then Pharaoh summoned Moses and Aaron. "This time I have sinned," he said to them. "The Lord* [JEHOVAH-TSIDKENU] *is in the right, and I and my people are in the wrong"* (NIV).

In the twenty-third chapter of Jeremiah, the Lord reveals His disgust with those who were supposed to care for Israel. In verse one, they are described as unrighteous *shepherds who are destroying and scattering the sheep.* It is then that the prophecy is given in verses five and six:

> *"The days are coming," declares the Lord, "when I will raise up to David* [or up from David's line] *a righteous Branch, a King who will reign wisely and do what is just and right in the land.*
>
> *In his days Judah will be saved and Israel will live in safety. This is the name by which he will be called: The Lord Our Righteousness* [JEHOVAH-TSIDKENU]" (NIV).

Our right standing before God is not based on how good we are. (If it were, we would be in big trouble!) It is based on the greatest swap in history: the Lord's exchange of His righteousness for our sins. Paul describes this exchange in his second letter to the believers in Corinth:

> *For God took the sinless Christ and poured into him our sins. Then, in exchange, he poured God's goodness into us!*
>
> 2 Cor. 5:21, TLB

We can also take comfort from Paul's comment in 2 Tim. 4:8:

Now there is in store for me the crown of righteousness, which the Lord, the righteous Judge, will award to me on that day—and not only to me, but also to all who have longed for his appearing (NIV).

The Lord is a righteous judge and He will give eternal rewards to those who love, honor and obey Him.

JEHOVAH-RAAH (The Lord My Shepherd)

God's role as our shepherd is revealed in this compound name. He is seen as One tending, pasturing, leading, feeding and protecting His flock. As His sheep, we are completely dependent upon our Good Shepherd. His compassion for us is so complete that He laid down His life for us, and He will gather us as a flock when He returns to the earth. Examples of this concept are found in Num. 27:16-17; Psalm 23; Ezek. 34:23; Matt. 9:36 and Rev. 7:16-17.

Interestingly, this name for God communicates our status as sheep. Of all God's creatures none has a poorer sense of direction. Sheep also are among the few animals that have no means of protecting themselves. When wolves attack them, they simply panic and run around until they're killed. They must be watched and protected constantly, and found when they've strayed.

Reflect on this name for God the next time you face a decision and don't know what choice to make. Think about it when you are under attack and can't defend yourself. Remember it when you feel that your life has just fallen off a cliff and you are clinging, helpless and frightened, to the last limb you can reach. He is JEHOVAH-RAAH at such times for you.

JEHOVAH-RAPHA (The Lord That Heals)

The Hebrew word RAPHA means "to cure, to heal, to restore." Our Lord is described as the One who will heal the physical, moral and spiritual illnesses of His children. While in His sovereignty He does not always choose to heal our physical ailments, He has the power to do so. This lovely name is found in Ex. 15:26:

*He said, "If you listen carefully to the voice of the Lord your God
and do what is right in his eyes, if you pay attention to his commands and
keep all his decrees, I will not bring on you any of the diseases I brought
on the Egyptians, for I am the Lord* [JEHOVAH-RAPHA], *who heals
you"* (NIV).

In Matt. 9:12, Jesus spoke of spiritual healing as He said, *It is not the healthy
who need a doctor, but the sick.* Peter reminds us that JEHOVAH-RAPHA *bore our
sins in his body on the tree...by his wounds you have been healed* (1 Pet. 2:24, NIV).

Today, a ministry called RAPHA cares for those who suffer from emotional
distress and/or substance abuse. This organization takes literally the promise that
God is our healer and applies sound, biblical principles to bring JEHOVAH-
RAPHA to hurting lives.

Call upon God by this name when you need healing. His power can heal
shattered marriages and ugly memories of past events. He can restore children who
have become rebellious. He can touch physical illnesses and change destructive
habits.

JEHOVAH-SHALOM (The Lord My Peace)

Most of us are familiar with the Hebrew word, SHALOM, meaning "peace."
This term describes the end of all strife and conflict, the removal of everything that
causes division or destroys harmony. Other concepts that describe its meaning
include wholeness, completeness, being well or perfect, harmony of relationships
with God and reconciliation based on a completed transaction. You will find this
concept used as the basis for Eph. 2:14-17 and Col. 1:20.

Don't miss the important fact that we find peace in a Person, not a condition.
Jesus said He would bring a special kind of peace that the world couldn't give or take
away. He is our peace.

Although Sharon worked in a church office, her work was emotionally
draining. There always seemed to be too many phone calls, too many deadlines, too
many interruptions. She developed severe tension headaches.

Sensing her unrest, the church pastor began to be concerned about her. He
asked her, "Sharon, are you allowing your circumstances to control your life or are
you allowing God to be in control?" She resented the question at first, but as they

talked about her past, she began to realize that her relationship with her father was a great part of her difficulty.

He was a drifter who frequently moved his family from town to town. By the time she entered the tenth grade, Sharon had attended eleven schools. She married when she was seventeen to get away from home.

Sharon continued to talk to her pastor over a period of several weeks. Finally, she was able to say, "I have been controlled by the circumstances of my life for as long as I can remember. I've never been able to trust God as Father."

Like others, she had used her "father category," based upon her experiences, to define God's character. As JEHOVAH-SHALOM slowly became more real to her, a new lifestyle developed. Even in the midst of phone calls, deadlines and interruptions, Sharon began to experience God's peace. As time passed, she began to influence all who related to her. The attitudes resulting from her previous circumstances were slowly being replaced by a new perspective and understanding of God's character. Her tranquility was the result of her newfound relationship with the heavenly Father.

JEHOVAH-SABBAOTH (The Lord of Hosts)

SABBAOTH means "to mass together, to assemble for warfare." This is God's fighting name as the Lord of hosts. He is the leader, the all-conquering Savior, the guide and guardian of His people. He is the commander of invisible armies.

Jerusalem had been reduced to a pile of rubble, and the temple was totally demolished. The people of Judah lived as prisoners in Babylonia for many years. When Zechariah and Zerubbabel returned to Jerusalem, God told them to rebuild the temple, an overwhelming request! It had taken all the wealth and influence of David and Solomon to build it the first time. They had all the resources of a healthy nation and almost unlimited manpower. Sister kingdoms had donated cedar and other building materials. How could these powerless men do so great a task? We see the answer in Zech. 4:6-10:

> So he said to me, "This is the word of the Lord to Zerubbabel: 'Not by might nor by power, but by my Spirit,' says the Lord Almighty [JEHOVAH-SABBAOTH].

"What are you, O mighty mountain? Before Zerubbabel you will become level ground. Then he will bring out the capstone to shouts of 'God bless it! God bless it!'"

Then the word of the Lord came to me:

"The hands of Zerubbabel have laid the foundation of this temple; his hands will also complete it. Then you will know that the Lord Almighty [JEHOVAH-SABBAOTH] has sent me to you.

"Who despises the day of small things? Men will rejoice when they see the plumb line in the hand of Zerubbabel. . . "

What battle do you face? Is God the commander-in-chief of your conflict? If so, you cannot lose even though the struggle may be long and the battle fierce! With JEHOVAH-SABBAOTH all things are possible.

JEHOVAH-SHAMMAH (The Lord Is Present)

SHAMMAH means "is present." With this beautiful term, God pledges His presence to us. Further, the name reminds us that we cannot escape His presence. The term is found in Gen. 31:3; Ps. 68:16 and Ezek. 48:35, and in the New Testament, this idea is communicated in Matt. 28:19-20.

Corrie ten Boom, author of *The Hiding Place,* had a habit some people found irritating. As she visited with someone, her lips often shaped words which could not be heard. On one occasion, a person talking to her stopped in the middle of a sentence and said, "Miss ten Boom, are you saying something to me? I didn't catch it." She replied, "You must excuse an old woman. I was just talking to our Lord about what we are saying to each other." For her, JEHOVAH-SHAMMAH was a participant in her every conversation. His presence was her joy, His companionship as real as the presence of the people around her.

You, too, can delight in His constant presence. One man decided to turn off the radio in his car and use his commute to work each morning to communicate with the Lord. A mother chose to arise each morning one hour before the family to enjoy her morning coffee with JEHOVAH-SHAMMAH.

Generations ago, Brother Lawrence wrote a book on this subject that is still in print, a classic of Christian literature called *Practicing the Presence of God.* Perhaps it's time for you to discover what thousands of others have known: the Lord is never absent from you.

In a very real sense, the name JEHOVAH-SHAMMAH is a summary of all the other names of God. Whether your condition requires Him to provide, protect, defend, comfort or guide, He is present with you and He will be what you need.

Meditate on these names of God. You will profit greatly by committing them to memory. For a few days, deliberately use them in the place of "Father" or "Lord" when you pray. Find peace, strength and wisdom in your new knowledge of His character.

Section III

THE PROCESS: Changing Our Perceptions of God, Self-Concepts and Relationships with Others

Chapter 13

Metamorphosis

Jim Craddock

Sam grew up in a home where his performance was highly scrutinized, but he was rarely affirmed. He was always encouraged to do better. His father was too involved with his own business to spend time with Sam. His mother was a perfectionist; nothing he did was ever quite enough to please her. More than anything, Sam wanted to make his parents happy so that he could win their love. But they used this eagerness to manipulate him to do what they wanted him to, seldom giving him the reward of their praise and approval.

When I met Sam, he was a highly successful young man, but he also was driven—driven to perform to earn the approval of others. No matter how well he did, he felt a nagging sense of condemnation. We visited casually a few times, and I learned more about his family. Then one day he called to ask me how he could cope with his parents.

As we talked, he realized that he had been manipulated by his parents all his life. They had withheld their love and affirmation so that he would feel compelled to do what they wanted him to. The need for approval is compelling! But this realization was a new revelation to Sam. He had never understood that the way he had been treated by his parents wasn't God's design for families. After years of conditioning, he thought manipulation was normal.

Sam's view of God was based on his relationships with his parents. He saw God as aloof and demanding and tried to win His approval by performing for Him just as he had for his parents, but the results were the same. He felt that he never could do enough for God. In fact, Sam's erroneous perceptions of God led him to believe that God condemned and criticized him. Years of parental modeling had strongly influenced Sam's view of God. What could change it?

At least four principles are central to a metamorphosis in one's perspective of God. These principles define and describe a process of change, giving us hope for progress when "quick fixes" don't provide the help we need:

1. Recognize the contrast between the character of God and that of your parents.
2. Choose God as your source of security and significance.
3. Dwell on God's love, forgiveness and power at any and every given moment.
4. Be patient; develop a "siege" mentality.

These principles are very difficult to apply by ourselves. Most of us need the encouragement, accountability, insight and honesty that a friend or a group of friends can give us. Even in the context of affirming relationships, growth isn't easy, but it can be an adventure. Let's examine each of these principles:

• *Contrast God's character with that of your parents.* No parent is perfect; none perfectly communicates the loving and powerful character of God. But some do quite well. Some parents give love unconditionally. They protect and provide for their children. They correct poor behavior with loving discipline.

Some parents, on the other hand, are guilty of neglect, condemnation, manipulation and other forms of abuse. They effectively destroy their children, who, apart from the grace and power of God, will reproduce the same patterns for generations to come.

The vast majority of parents fall between these extremes. We may think that Christian parents are always good models while unbelievers are always poor models, but that isn't the case. Some parents who are unbelievers model the love, protection and provision of God while, in some cases, Christian parents don't.

Both Christian and non-Christian parents are likely to model some aspects of God's character well at some points in their lives and poorly at others. It's a mixed bag of signals, but remember, they're probably doing the best they know how to do based on the imperfect modeling they received!

As we begin to recognize the contrast between God's character and that of our parents, we may respond in any number of ways. If the contrast isn't too great, we may better understand God's love and rejoice in that new understanding. But if the contrast is great, we may experience an initial stage of anger and resentment. Feelings like these are not wrong and should not be repressed. Tuning into your emotions is a part of the healing process. (For a better understanding of how to handle your emotions, see chapter 16.)

• *Choose God as your source of security and significance.* The process of correcting our misperceptions of God involves making some monumental decisions: to see the difference between our parents and God; to feel the pain of our losses and enter the process of healing; to take time to study God's Word and to pray.

But our conceptual metamorphosis also involves a multitude of daily decisions to choose God as our source of security and significance. The shift from getting our sense of self-worth from our parents to getting it from the Lord is difficult but necessary. The Lord is loving and faithful. We can trust Him completely. David wrote: *For my father and my mother have forsaken me, but the Lord will take me up* (Ps. 27:10).

Isaiah also wrote that the Lord's love far surpasses even that of a mother's: *Can a woman forget her nursing child, and have no compassion on the son of her womb? Even these may forget, but I will not forget you* (Is. 49:15).

When a farmer's well runs dry, he digs a new one to meet the needs of his family and farm. When an army runs out of supplies, they do whatever it takes to provide for the needs of the soldiers. When we realize that no human being can meet our needs for security and significance, we must go to the source of abundant affirmation and purpose: Jesus Christ. We can (we must!) cling to Him. He is worthy of our affection and obedience.

A commitment to radical thankfulness is helpful in enabling us to make these daily choices. When someone's disapproval threatens to crush you, when you fail in an important task, when you don't feel like you look your best, when you are feeling introspective and depressed or when you are angry. . . be honest about how you feel and choose to give thanks for God's love, purpose and power.

Notice that I didn't say you need to *feel* thankful. You can't control your feelings, but you can choose—as an act of your will—to dwell on God's character.

You can thank Him for His compassion for you and His direction for your life, knowing that He can use any situation for good.

Radical thankfulness rivets our attention on the Lord, not on the fickle approval of others or the often distressing circumstances of life. It is often helpful to have the encouragement of a support group as you learn to make these choices. Most people learn best with a combination of cognitive teaching and relational reinforcement. You may want to find a friend or a small group to go through this book and workbook with you. It can be a rich time of interaction, and can facilitate the process of change a great deal.

• *Dwell on God's love, forgiveness and power.* After you recognize the contrast between God's character and that of your parents, spend time studying the love, forgiveness and power of God portrayed in Scripture. He is the source of our security and significance. Only He loves us perfectly. The famous French philosopher and physicist, Blaise Paschal, said of Christ's exclusive ability to meet our needs:

> *There is a God-shaped vacuum in the heart of each man which cannot be filled by any created thing, but by God the Creator, made known through Jesus Christ.*

Even if no one else loves you, Christ loves you deeply. Even if no one else accepts you, the Lord accepts you unconditionally. Even if no one else will forgive you, Christ's death is the payment and the proof of His complete forgiveness. We need to dwell on these powerful and transforming truths day after day.

"A chapter a day keeps the Devil away" may be a cute saying for vacation Bible school, but it takes concerted effort, study and focused prayer to transform our minds and change our perspective of God. The modeling of a lifetime doesn't change easily. We would do well to plan regular times to study, think, pray and memorize God's Word so that His truth can fill our minds and change our hearts.

• *Be patient; develop a "siege" mentality.* Quick fixes sound great, but they seldom work. For most of us, deep change takes time. Avoid looking for an instant way to transform your misperceptions of God. It took time to develop these misconceptions; it will take time to change them. It is a process.

When a Roman army attacked a fortified city, the commander didn't shoot a couple of arrows and expect the city to fall. The army spent months and sometimes years in siege warfare. It was slow and tedious, but it was usually successful.

Our warfare against our inaccurate perceptions of God is like siege warfare. It is slow and tedious, but if we stay with it, there's great hope for success. Paul wrote of this warfare to the believers in Corinth:

> *For though we walk in the flesh, we do not war according to the flesh,*
> *for the weapons of our warfare are not of the flesh, but divinely powerful for the destruction of fortresses.*
> *We are destroying speculations and every lofty thing raised up against the knowledge of God, and we are taking every thought captive to the obedience of Christ. . . .*
>
> 2 Cor. 10:3-5

The misconceptions we have about God are speculations. Our wrong perceptions are *lofty things raised up against the knowledge of God.* These are fortresses that require a siege mentality, patience and endurance. In the end, the walls will fall and the captives will be released.

You may gain a flash of insight and experience a surge of change at the beginning of your metamorphosis, but don't be discouraged if you don't experience deep emotional healing and transformation overnight. Realize that it takes time to change fundamental perceptions about God and ourselves. Realize that the Word of God and the power of His Spirit are a powerful combination. The process may be slow and painful, but it's worth it.

As you work through the principles outlined in this chapter, remember to be kind to your parents. No, they weren't perfect, and yes, they may have harmed you terribly. But they were probably doing the best they knew how to do. Even if they weren't, you can extend God's love and forgiveness to them as you learn to experience it yourself.

This chapter has explained the process of change. The next one identifies what is needed for effective change to occur.

The workbook section of this book is designed to facilitate your study and application of God's truth. This chapter will become more significant to you as you spend time on the exercises and studies in the workbook.

Chapter 14

"And You Shall Know the Truth. . . "

Robert S. McGee

In reading the previous chapters of this book, you probably have recognized how significantly your perception of God has been shaped by your parents. You may have enjoyed reliving some of the pleasant memories associated with a loving and protective family, or you may have discovered that your memories are quite painful. Hopefully, you have realized that no one's parents are perfect; all fall short of God's grace. For that reason, I've written this chapter to answer the question: *How can our perception of God more exactly represent who He truly is?*

Take a moment to consider your present relationship with God. The apostle John tells us that to all who have received Jesus as Lord and Savior, He . . . *gave the right to become children of God—children born not of natural descent, nor of human decision or a husband's will, but born of God* (John 1:12-13).

The new life we receive as God's children is not the result of good works or penance. It is a gift, paid for at the cross by Jesus. Through the Father's grace, we were adopted as fellow heirs with Christ and given all the rights and privileges of sonship at the moment of our conversion.

The Lord has reserved many blessings for us. We will recognize and experience these increasingly as we gain a more accurate understanding of who He is. Paul tells us in Rom. 12:2:

Do not conform any longer to the pattern of this world, but be transformed by the renewing of your mind. Then you will be able to test and approve what God's will is—his good, pleasing and perfect will (NIV).

To change our relationship with God, we must replace our wrong perceptions with truth. This is vitally important because the way we think usually affects the way we feel, and the way we feel often determines the way we act. Therefore, we must reject any lies that Satan has planted in our minds about the nature and character of God.

The following illustrations may help us to see the process for changing incorrect perceptions of God to those that are true and accurate:

The Way You May Have Perceived God

Situations: Various interactions with your father

Category: Your beliefs about all fathers

Thoughts: *God is like my father; therefore, I will relate to Him in the same way that I relate to my father.*

Emotions: Depending on your relationship with your father, emotions about God may be love or fear, dependence or distrust, affection or anger

Actions: Depending on your relationship with your father, either obedience, trust and service, or anger, rebellion and withdrawal

An Accurate Perception of God

Situations: Truths and biblical accounts about God and His activities

Category: Beliefs about God

Thoughts: *God is loving, kind and powerful. I can relate to Him knowing that He is glad I am His child.*

Emotions: Comfort, thankfulness, joy, security, significance, contrition, humility, freedom, zeal, etc.

Actions: Obedience, trust, seeking His will, service, loving others, evangelism, discipleship, etc.

Aspects of a person's poor relationship with God can be traced to his false beliefs. For example:

Situation:	*I have been released by my employer.*
False Belief:	*God punishes people by making bad things happen to them.*
Thoughts:	*God has decided I need to be punished. There's no way to please or understand Him. He's just like my father. I could never please him either! I've just got to have someone hold me and tell me I'm loved...or...I've got to prove myself in my next job...or...I need to escape this pain.*
Emotions:	Fear associated with loss of income; anger and shame resulting from loss of job
Actions:	*Told no one, including my wife; cleaned out my desk, went to favorite bar and got drunk*

Do you see how our beliefs are embedded in our thoughts and how they control our emotions? In turn, our emotions direct us to act in certain ways. If Satan has convinced us to believe his lies about God, we will be imprisoned by them, acting as though they were true.

Faith in the character of God enables us to live above the crises caused by circumstances. Identifying our false beliefs about God's character is, therefore, our first step toward new freedom in Christ Jesus.

Most of our painful emotions are actually signals which help us uncover deceptions in our belief system. Fear, anger, depression and stress are some of the results of believing Satan's lies. When we begin to feel these emotions, we must learn to ask ourselves, *What lie am I believing in this situation?*

In my book, *The Search for Significance,* I've explained that we can almost always trace painful emotions back to one of four false beliefs. These deceptions distort our perceptions of the intimate love, forgiveness and power of God, and keep us in a constant state of insecurity and turmoil.

The chart on the following pages contains not only the four foundational lies (or false beliefs), but also a list of some of the consequences of believing those lies. The chart then gives the contrast to the lies: God's specific scriptural solutions and some of the results of living by these truths. [1]

FALSE BELIEFS	CONSEQUENCES OF FALSE BELIEFS
I must meet certain standards in order to feel good about myself.	The fear of failure; perfectionism; being driven to succeed; manipulating others to achieve success; withdrawing from healthy risks
I must have the approval of certain others to feel good about myself.	The fear of rejection; attempting to please others at any cost; being overly sensitive to criticism; withdrawing from others to avoid disapproval
Those who fail (including myself) are unworthy of love and deserve to be punished.	The fear of punishment; propensity to punish others; blaming self and others for personal failure; withdrawing from God and fellow believers; being driven to avoid punishment
I am what I am. I cannot change. I am hopeless.	Feelings of shame, hopelessness, inferiority; passivity; loss of creativity; isolation, withdrawing from others

GOD'S SPECIFIC SOLUTION	RESULTS OF GOD'S SOLUTION
Because of justification, *I am completely forgiven and fully pleasing to God. I no longer have to fear failure.*	Increasing freedom from the fear of failure; desire to pursue the right things: Christ and His kingdom; love for Christ
Because of reconciliation, *I am totally accepted by God. I no longer have to fear rejection.*	Increasing freedom from the fear of rejection; willingness to be open and vulnerable; able to relax around others; willingness to take criticism; desire to please God no matter what others think
Because of propitiation, *I am deeply loved by God. I no longer have to fear punishment or punish others.*	Increasing freedom from the fear of punishment; patience and kindness toward others; being quick to apply forgiveness; deep love for Christ
Because of regeneration, *I have been made brand new, complete in Christ. I no longer need to experience the pain of shame.*	Christ-centered self-confidence; joy, courage, peace; desire to know Christ

Why do we so easily believe lies about God? Why can't we recognize them for what they are? The reason may be that our beliefs are a mixture of both truth and deception, and until we see the contrast between them, we can't separate the two. In the previous example of being released by an employer, it is true that the person was fired, but to believe that the employer's decision was caused by God's cruelty is a wrong perception. Therefore, the person was believing both truth and deception at the same time.

False beliefs are not benign. They result in depression, fear, anger or hopelessness. As a corollary to presenting us with false beliefs, Satan also encourages us to question God's intentions for our lives. Here are some of his distortions of God's desires for us:

Distortion: Evil Comes from God

We hear that a good, righteous man has been brutally murdered and we ask, *God, why did you let this happen?* Does God care that this tragedy happened? Yes! But God did not cause the murder. Someone who was out of control caused it. In a fallen world, many tragic—even evil—things happen. This is the nature of sin. It always produces heartache and pain. God does not snatch people from the fallen world the moment they become Christians. He leaves us here in the midst of pain and suffering to be light and salt to the rest of the fallen race.

Does God know about such suffering? Does He care? How does He react? We need only think of Jesus on the mount overlooking Jerusalem, weeping over the result of evil in that city. Or we may watch Him weeping at the tomb of His dear friend Lazarus. Our God is One of compassion. His heart breaks when sin smashes lives.

How deceitful Satan is! First Peter 5:8 tells us that he goes about *like a roaring lion, seeking someone to devour.* At the very moment he infests men with murderous intent, he tries to make us think God is the cause! Satan wants us to blame God when we hear about a tragic accident or the serious illness of a child. What does Scripture say about blaming God?

> *When tempted, no one should say, "God is tempting me." For God cannot be tempted by evil, nor does he tempt anyone;*
> > *but each one is tempted when, by his own evil desire, he is dragged away and enticed.*

Then, after desire has conceived, it gives birth to sin; and sin, when it is full-grown, gives birth to death.

Don't be deceived, my dear brothers.

Every good and perfect gift is from above, coming down from the Father of the heavenly lights, who does not change like shifting shadows.

He chose to give us birth through the word of truth, that we might be a kind of first fruits of all he created.

James 1:13-18, NIV

God may test us to strengthen our faith, but He never tempts us, because the goal of temptation is to cause a person to sin. God gives good and perfect gifts. He not only prospers us in tangible ways, but He gives us the strength and wisdom to endure difficulties. These, too, are good gifts!

What will we believe, Satan's lie or the Bible's clear explanation? If we believe that God is responsible for evil, we are distorting the truth. Who could trust a God like that? The Scriptures teach us that God is sovereign. That doesn't mean He always intervenes in negative circumstances. It does mean that He has a purpose and that He will fulfill it, despite the evil of our fallen world.

We must always remember that God is a Person, not a powerful machine. Scripture repeatedly portrays Him as One who loves, who cares, who sorrows, who listens attentively. There is no evil in Him.

Distortion: God Doesn't Care About Me

God is rarely praised for anything and often blamed for everything. We make prayerless choices, sometimes knowing they are not what He wants for us. Yet, when things turn out badly, we wonder, *God, if you really loved me, why didn't You keep me from doing that?*

The obvious solution is to recognize that God does not force us to follow Him, but He has built natural consequences into the spiritual realm, even as He has built physical laws into the universe. As certain as the law of gravity is the spiritual law that says, *Whatever a man sows, this he will also reap* (Gal. 6:7).

With open arms, He reaches out to us. He offers us full access to His wisdom and power if we will follow Him. At the same time, He is not a vending machine to supply all of our whims and wants. As a Father, He knows when it is best to say no to His children, and when to say wait. Regardless of His response, we can be assured that we will always receive His best when we leave those choices up to Him!

Perhaps a passive or absent or insensitive father modeled to you the idea that fathers don't really care about their children, and that children just need to do the best they can on their own. But our heavenly Father isn't like that! The Scriptures teach that He is loving, compassionate and protective of His children.

Distortion: My Trials Don't Benefit Me

Romans 8:28 is familiar to many of us: *God causes all things to work together for good to those who love God, to those who are called according to His purpose.* This promise is often misunderstood to say that we will be perfectly happy with the outcome of our difficulties, but it doesn't say that. The verse talks about *God's* purpose, not ours. Often, our purposes are self-serving. God's design is to wean us from our self-centeredness to a life of devotion and service to Him. Our trials may not benefit us in the way we want, but in the way He wants.

Distortion: God Won't Meet Our Needs

Satan whispers in our ear, *No wonder God has so few friends; He treats the ones He has so shabbily.* With His complete knowledge of the present and future, the Lord often acts in ways we don't understand. We fail to remember that our knowledge is limited. Our lack of information often prompts us to question God's care and provision.

Paul had a physical malady which caused him much distress. Three times he asked God to remove it, but the Lord had other plans. Paul recounted: *And He said to me, "My grace is sufficient for you, for power is perfected in weakness." Most gladly, therefore, I will rather boast about my weaknesses, that the power of Christ may dwell in me* (2 Cor. 12:9).

The Lord didn't do what Paul expected, but He met Paul's need nonetheless. And Paul responded with contentment and faith: *Therefore I am well content with weaknesses, with insults, with distresses, with persecutions, with difficulties, for Christ's sake; for when I am weak, then I am strong* (2 Cor. 12:10).

The Lord is powerful and compassionate. He can meet our needs, but sometimes His perception of our needs is different from ours. He may know that we need courage, wisdom and faith more than money, praise and health. He will provide what we need when we need it.

Distortion: God Should Have Made Me More Attractive

We ask, *How can I trust God when He has created me with this body and face?*
Madison Avenue would have us believe that our appearance must be perfect if we
are to experience true happiness and fulfillment. But comparison does not breed
contentment, only pain and emptiness. Paul warned the Corinthians not to play that
destructive game:

> *We do not dare to classify or compare ourselves with some who*
> *commend themselves. When they measure themselves by themselves*
> *and compare themselves with themselves, they are not wise.*
>
> 2 Cor. 10:12, NIV

When we compare our appearance to someone else's, we forget that our worth
is not based on how we look, but on the love, forgiveness and acceptance of God.
We need to accept who we are as a gift from the Lord and let Him show us how our
appearance fits into His overall plan for our lives.

If we allow the Holy Spirit to replace lies and distortions with the truth about
the character of God and our new identity in Christ, we will discover that we no
longer need to be controlled by circumstances. Further, these circumstances will
have less influence on our emotions. Our emotions are usually based on our *beliefs*
about a situation, not the situation itself.

Jim, for example, broke his engagement with his fiance, Susan. Susan became
deeply depressed. Her emotions were a direct result of her beliefs about the
situation, not the situation itself. Let's consider two ways she might respond. First,
a pattern that is based on a distorted view of God and herself:

Situation:	Jim has broken their engagement.
Belief:	*God didn't create me as a beautiful woman; He created me to be ugly.*
Thoughts:	*I'm not capable of attracting a husband. My mother always made fun of the way I looked. I guess she was right.*
Emotions:	Anger with her mother as she remembers the ridicule; anger with Jim for destroying her dreams of being loved and accepted; anger with God because He (supposedly) made her with "such an ugly appearance."
Actions:	Repressed anger, depression, withdrawal, self-condemnation.

Susan doesn't have to come to these conclusions! She has a distorted view of God and blames Him for the breakup. She has isolated herself from the One who should be her greatest comfort and her closest companion. Her problem is not really the situation. Instead, it's the way she is perceiving it and responding to it. She believes that God deliberately chooses "ugliness" for some people and forces them to be unattractive. But she can respond with faith and hope if she believes the truth about God's character:

Situation: Jim has broken their engagement.

Belief: *Even though this hurts, I know that God loves me and gives His best to me.*

Thought: *I can learn to be content in the Lord as a single adult, or, I'm being guided to the husband He has for me.*

Emotion: *Oh God, this hurts so much! I really wanted to marry Jim and have a loving and affirming husband, but thank You, Lord, for keeping me from marrying the wrong person. Thank You for being my constant companion.*

Actions: Honest expression of emotions to the Lord. Appropriate expression of emotions to other people. Developing and enjoying other friendships. Behavior characterized by thankfulness.

Susan can be objective and honest, and she can experience inner peace by trusting in the character of God instead of living in anxiety and nursing her hurt. Satan's lies bring depression, but God's truths produce rest! She can experience what matters most in life: she is deeply loved by God, completely forgiven, fully pleasing, totally accepted and complete in Christ. She can live a life of love and depth and meaning.

As we learn to identify the deceptions in our belief system and discover in Scripture who God truly is, we can move into a totally new lifestyle. He has given us His Word, His Holy Spirit and loving, mature believers to guide us on our journey. All that we need has been provided.

Chapter 15

Dealing with Fears

Robert S. McGee

Learning facts in a classroom seldom does as much good as learning them in real-life situations. Just as you learned about your earthly father by watching him and interacting with him in different circumstances, so you can learn about your heavenly Father by spending time with Him and watching Him work in your daily situations. Many of life's circumstances produce anxiety, a form of fear. Such moments are the best times to discover why you are fearful. You can then learn to replace those fears with an understanding of God's character, as well as faith, obedience and peace.

We learned about four false beliefs in chapter 14. Let's take another look at their consequences:

The Fear of Failure

Are you overly sensitive to criticism? Are you compelled to justify and explain your mistakes? Do you become depressed when you fail? Do you get angry with people who interfere with your attempts to succeed and then make you feel incompetent? Traits like these are characteristic of a fear of failure, which is rooted in the false belief: *I must meet certain standards in order to feel good about myself.*

The Fear of Rejection

Do you go out of your way to be liked by people, even when you must compromise your convictions to earn their approval? Do you avoid certain people? Are you devastated when someone else gets more attention than you do? Do you daydream a lot about promotions or compliments? Do you compare your looks, possessions, status, prestige or abilities with others? Actions like these are typical of those who fear rejection. A fear of rejection results from the false belief: *I must be approved by certain others to feel good about myself.*

The Fear of Punishment and the Propensity to Punish Others

Are you afraid to make a mistake because you fear that someone will criticize you? Do you fear what God might do to you? After you fail, do you feel like God is disgusted or angry with you? Do you condemn yourself when you fail as a type of self-punishment? How do you respond when others fail, especially when you are depending on them? Are you generally accepting or critical of others? Guilt and condemnation are consequences of the false belief: *Those who fail (including me) are unworthy of love and deserve to be punished.*

The Feeling of Shame

Do you dislike the way you look? Do you feel past experiences have ruined your life? Do you see yourself as a "loser," and often feel inferior when you are with a group of friends? This leads to the false belief: *I am what I am. I cannot change. I am hopeless.*

Confronting Your Fears with the Truth of God's Word

I've wrestled with a sense of failure, rejection and worthlessness throughout my life. I've tried to overcome these negative feelings about myself by working hard, by trying to please others and by avoiding those feelings of hurt and anger that are often generated by experiences of failure and rejection. But over time, I've discovered that repressed hurt and anger ultimately build and, at some point, begin to surface in inappropriate ways: being sarcastic with my wife, for example, or exploding at my kids.

Doing away with this kind of behavior has required my becoming more sensitive to painful feelings. Over time, I've gained an increasing awareness of the depth of hurt and anger in my life. Working through the issues surrounding these emotions often has been unpleasant, but I'm pleased to be developing a greater capacity for complete honesty about the realities of my life.

I recently had an encounter with a longtime friend. Several years ago I helped him when he felt insecure about his job and some central relationships in his life. I had been vulnerable with him, hoping that some transparency on my part would help him to be more honest about his fears and hurts. Not long ago, however, I learned that he had told several people some things about me that weren't true. In the past I would have felt angry, but I wouldn't have admitted that my anger was the result of feeling deeply hurt. I would have excused the offense by saying, "That's okay. It doesn't matter. I don't really care." But excusing someone isn't the same as forgiving him or her.

This time I wanted to be more honest with myself, with the Lord and with my friend. First, I realized that I had experienced not only a *fear* of rejection, but actual rejection. I admitted that my friend's offense both hurt and angered me. Then I reflected on the incident by asking myself a few questions, such as, *What is true here? How would I usually respond? How does the Lord want me to respond this time?* I looked up several passages in Scripture about the unconditional love and acceptance of God, and the true nature of forgiveness.

Then I went to see my friend. I told him what I had heard, and that I was deeply hurt and angry with him. Although it was hard to be so honest, I knew that I needed to be. The results were mixed. I felt that I had achieved my goal of being completely honest and knew that I had chosen to forgive him., but my friend didn't respond as I'd hoped he would. He apologized to me when we met, but I've since learned that he has told yet another person some untrue things about me.

I may need to confront him again, but at least I'm being more honest about my emotions, and am learning to apply the Scriptures more deeply in my life.

Other people's offenses often play on our insecurities: our fears of failure, rejection and/or punishment, as well as our sense of shame. We need to learn how to detach from our hurt long enough to determine which fears someone else has triggered, the lie behind those fears and the truth of God's Word. We also need to forgive anyone who has offended us—past or present. Jesus said: *But I say to you who hear, love your enemies, do good to those who hate you, bless those who curse you, pray for those who mistreat you* (Luke 6:27-28). Paul wrote the Colossians...*put on a heart of compassion, kindness, humility, gentleness and patience; bearing with one another, and forgiving each other, whoever has a complaint against anyone; just as the Lord forgave you, so also should you* (Col. 3:12-13).

Forgiveness does not mean submitting to someone else's abuse, whether verbal or physical, nor does it mean that we are to rescue others from the consequences of their harmful behavior. It does mean that after being completely honest about the gravity of another's offense and the hurt it has caused us, we choose to release the offender from any debt we perceive he or she owes us as a result of the offense. Forgiveness replaces the motive for revenge with compassion.

Try using the following plan the next time you need to tackle negative feelings generated by people or circumstances:

1. *Realize* that you are experiencing anger, fear or anxiety. Also realize which lie you are believing (see the chart in chapter 14).

2. *Reject* the lie because it distorts your perception of God and produces painful consequences in your life.

3. *Replace* the deception with the truth of God's Word. Then reflect on these truths to see how they apply in your present situation. And finally, praise the Lord for His love, forgiveness and power.

Using a plan like this can help you defeat the harmful effects of hurt, anger and fear by confronting those emotions with the truth of God's Word. Over time, you'll discover that situations you might normally run from can be used as opportunities for reflection, growth, prayer and praise.

Chapter 16

"What Do I Do with My Emotions?"

Pat Springle

When some people first analyze the difference between the character of God and their parents, they experience immediate insight and relief: *Oh, so that's why I've felt distant from the Lord! Now I understand.* For them, the transition to a deep and fresh experience with the Lord is fairly easy. But for others, this catharsis comes later. When they begin to recognize the contrast between the unconditional love of God and the neglect, abuse or manipulation of their parents, they go through a period of great pain before they can experience relief. Years of repressed emotions can't be brushed aside or solved easily and quickly.

Several years ago I met a conscientious, hard-working pastor named Chris. He was bright and athletic, but also very shy. I wondered why he seemed to feel ill at ease in social situations. When we had an opportunity to visit at length, I asked him a few questions about his background.

"Chris, what are your parents like?"

"They're okay. Dad's an engineer and Mom's a high school English teacher."

"How did you get along with them when you were growing up?"

"Fine, I guess."

"How did they treat you? Did you feel loved and accepted?"

After a long pause, Chris looked down and said, "I guess I was kind of the ugly duckling in the family. My brothers and my sister were smart and did well in sports, but I came along last and, well, I guess I didn't do as well as they wanted me to."

"How do you know that, Chris?"

"No matter how hard I tried, they never seemed to be satisfied. They always said things that implied I should have done better." His voice got lower. "I just wasn't the son that I should have been."

"Did you think it was up to you to make your parents happy?"

"Of course! Had I been the kind of son I should have been—like my brothers were—they would have been happy with me."

"How did they show you that they loved you?"

"My father, well. . . he. . . I don't think he did very much. He provided for me, but he isn't a very loving man—at least not to me. My mother would occasionally tell me that I'd done well in sports or in school, but when my father shouted at me, she never defended me or anything." He concluded, "It's my fault. I just wasn't the kind of son they could be proud of."

I spent the next half-hour explaining to Chris that it wasn't his fault. It wasn't up to him to make his parents happy. That responsibility belongs to parents, not children. Parents have the God-given responsibility of loving and protecting their children. But Chris wouldn't buy it. His sense of guilt and responsibility prevented him from seeing that he was a victim of a form of abuse. He showed no emotion at all during our conversation. He was numb.

Chris and I had several opportunities to visit more about his family. Gradually, he started to see the light. "You mean. . . they were supposed to love me unconditionally. . . and it's not up to me to make them happy?" He raised his arm and slammed his fist on the desk! His eyes widened and then he glared in anger. "I can't believe they did that to me! What would my life be like now if they had loved me?"

The story about Chris is not an isolated incident, even among pastors. When we get in touch with our past, we sometimes open a Pandora's box of painful emotions, such as anger, fear, anxiety, shame, guilt, sadness and bitterness.

Anger may take the form of mild frustration, but if repressed over a period of time, it festers into resentment and bitterness. These feelings often find their outlet and expression in revenge. Or, a person may try to compensate by being driven as a workaholic, or by escaping through substance abuse or other compulsive behaviors.

Fear is less volatile, but just as damaging. It promotes the kind of numbness and withdrawal that can amount to emotional, spiritual and social paralysis. Most people who have repressed their emotions have repressed some combination of anger and fear. The fears of rejection and failure can cause a myriad of painful symptoms.

Three principles can help us to experience and express our emotions, whether they are mild or the product of years of repression. These principles are:

1. Be honest with yourself.
2. Be honest with God.
3. Be honest with others.

Be Honest with Yourself

The first step toward coping with repressed emotions is, of course, to recognize that they are there. When one woman began to understand how her father's outbursts of anger had driven her into an emotional shell, she became angry with him. But she caught herself. "I can't be angry. I'm a Christian." She started to confess her anger to the Lord.

Had she stopped there, she never would have been able to deal effectively with her past. She would have continued to repress her emotions.

After some encouragement and patient instruction, she realized that Christians don't just have happy feelings. They get angry, too! An emotion like anger isn't always the result of sin. It may be a response to the neglect or abuse inflicted by others. Willful disobedience is sin, but emotions are products of many factors including our sins, the sins of others, circumstances, our backgrounds, hormones, etc. Emotions, in and of themselves, are not sinful.

When we realize that we are angry or fearful, the correct response is to be honest about those feelings, try to understand their root cause and then choose to act in a way that honors the Lord.

Sometimes I hear Christians say, "I'm really frustrated!" A statement like this is often another way to avoid saying that we are angry because anger seems less acceptable to us than frustration. It is an attempt to downplay our emotions and rationalize their severity. A friend of mine used to say "I'm frustrated!" fairly often. When I realized that there was more emotion than mild frustration behind his words, I decided to ask him, "Rick, aren't you a little more than 'frustrated'? Aren't you really angry?"

He looked at me for a moment, then a big smile spread across his face. "Yes, you're right. I guess I *am* mad. It just doesn't sound spiritual for me to say I'm angry."

We rationalize a lot of anger by saying that we're "frustrated." We need to be honest so that we can analyze the source of our anger and find a healing solution from the Lord.

Be Honest with God

The Lord is never surprised by our emotions. He is *omniscient*, or all-knowing. He knew everything about us before the world was created, and He is our understanding, loving and trustworthy confidant. We can tell Him everything about how we think and feel—and we should tell Him.

David wrote this admonition to us:

> *Trust in Him at all times, O people; pour out your heart before Him; God is a refuge for us.*
>
> Ps. 62:8

Pour out your heart to the Lord. One man I know is deeply emotional. When he feels something, he feels it deeply! On a few occasions, when he has been really upset, he has gotten into his car and driven down the highway screaming at the top of his lungs! I'm not sure what other motorists have thought, but he says that this enables him to tell the Lord how angry he feels without any inhibitions.

Few of us will go to this extreme (The highways are crazy enough as it is!), but all of us need to express our thoughts and emotions to the Lord. That takes time. A couple of minutes won't do it. We need to get into the habit of both instant honesty and quiet, prolonged communication with the Lord so that we can reflect on our feelings and situations and His truth about them.

David was an excellent model of *pouring out one's heart to the Lord.* The Psalms reflect his deeply personal relationship with God, and include a full range of emotions. Let's take a look at a small sample of David's honest expressions to the Lord:

• **Anger**

Ps. 139:19-22: *O that Thou wouldst slay the wicked, O God; depart from me, therefore, men of bloodshed. For they speak against Thee wickedly, and Thine enemies take Thy name in vain. Do I not hate those who hate Thee, O Lord? And do I not loathe those who rise up against Thee? I hate them with the utmost hatred; they have become my enemies.*

• **Fear**

Ps. 140:1-4: *Rescue me, O Lord, from evil men; preserve me from violent men, who devise evil things in their hearts; they continually stir up wars. They sharpen their tongues as a serpent; poison of a viper is under their lips. Keep me, O Lord, from the hands of the wicked; preserve me from violent men, who have purposed to trip up my feet.*

• **Joy**

Ps. 140:6-7: *I said to the Lord, "Thou art my God; give ear, O Lord, to the voice of my supplications. O God the Lord, the strength of my salvation, Thou hast covered my head in the day of battle."*

• **Confidence**

Ps. 140:12-13: *I know that the Lord will maintain the cause of the afflicted, and justice for the poor. Surely the righteous will give thanks to Thy name; the upright will dwell in Thy presence.*

• **Anxiety**

Ps. 141:1: *O Lord, I call upon Thee; hasten to me! Give ear to my voice when I call to Thee!*

As you express yourself honestly to the Lord, remember to listen to Him, too. His Spirit will remind you of passages of Scripture and prompt you to think about the Lord and His desires for you. Focus on His character, His promises and His commands so that you can understand how He wants you to respond to your circumstances.

Be Honest with Others

After you have expressed your emotions to God, you will need to be appropriately honest with the person who hurt or offended you. But you don't need to tell him everything you have thought about him! That should be reserved for the time when you pour out your heart to the Lord.

What should you say? The answer comes from another question: What will help that person? The goal of expressing yourself is to benefit the other person. Loving confrontation can be a stepping stone for that person's growth and maturity, and ultimately, it can strengthen your relationship with him.

Think about that person's maturity level and his ability to apply what you would say. A reproof that would be digestible to a mature person may devastate a weaker one. You will need God's wisdom to know how much to say, and just as importantly, how much not to say. Solomon wrote: *A prudent man conceals knowledge, but the heart of fools proclaims folly* (Prov. 12:23). A wise man won't tell everything he knows, but a fool will tell everything, no matter how much it hurts someone else.

On rare occasions, the best thing to tell the other person is nothing. Do you remember Chris, the young pastor we described at the beginning of this chapter? What would be appropriate for him to say to his parents? After careful consideration, we realized that his parents wouldn't understand Chris, no matter how carefully he expressed himself. He decided to say nothing to them about his hurt. He also determined to act lovingly toward them even though he would no longer bow to their manipulative condemnation. His new attitude and actions may bring greater condemnation from them, or more positively, questions about his changed life. The latter situation, Chris decided, would provide for a more teachable moment.

Getting in touch with repressed emotions may seem almost unbearable at times, but continued repression is not the solution to one's pain and anger.

When a person contracts a terminal disease like cancer, he usually goes through several stages of emotional responses. Elisabeth Kübler-Ross described these stages in her very helpful book, *On Death and Dying.* Those with severe emotional trauma go through similar stages, including: denial, bargaining, anger, grief and acceptance.

Many of us who have experienced neglect, abuse or manipulation either suppress our pain and pretend it isn't there, or blame ourselves, assuming that our problems are of our own making.

When we do finally confront our problems and our repressed emotions begin to flow, we often try to bargain with God or with the person who has hurt us. We ask, in effect, *How can I get that person to love me? What can I do to be accepted? I'll change! I'll do anything!*

Sooner or later, we realize that bargaining won't work. We haven't been able to win that person's approval in the past, and we can't win it now. We may then experience deep anger toward the one who has hurt us. At that point, we should express our anger fully to God. This stage of anger may last for several months.

A period of grief often follows the experience and expression of anger. A life has been damaged. The past cannot be relived. A sense of loss over what never was or what might have been leads to the experience of grief. Grieving is healthy and positive, even if it doesn't feel good. Once it has been fully experienced, one finds relief and acceptance. Life can go on.

This process doesn't happen overnight. Some people may take a prolonged period of time just to uncork their emotions and move from denial to the anger stage. The time frame isn't as important as the process itself. Be patient and expect the process to take its course. If you try to hurry, you'll be disappointed and possibly will experience even more pain as a result of your unrealistic expectations. But if you are patient, you will be able to work through the messy and painful emotions, and God will provide you with healing and hope.

No matter how painful they may be, we need to be honest about our emotions. Used wisely, such transparency will lend itself to healing—in our lives and in the lives of others.

Chapter 17

Rivers in the Desert

Pat Springle

When you think about your relationships with your parents, what thoughts and emotions emerge: pain or thankfulness, cursing or blessing or some combination of these feelings? If you experience pain when you think of your parents, has it occurred to you that God can use even the most neglectful or abusive parents to produce strengths in your life? God's words to the prophet Isaiah are as relevant to our circumstances today as they were to the Israelites then:

> *Behold, I will do something new, Now it will spring forth; will you not be aware of it? I will even make a roadway in the wilderness, rivers in the desert.*
>
> Is. 43:19

No, the pain of being unloved, unaccepted and unprotected as a child is not God's design for the family, but He can use even our most trying difficulties to produce good. Many of us find comfort in Rom. 8:28:

> *And we know that God causes all things to work together for good to those who love God, to those who are called according to His purpose.*

We need to apply this promise to our most sensitive of situations: our relationships with our parents.

Before we look at the various strengths that God can build through the ordeal of a painful childhood, we need to again ask the question, *Why? Why did God let this happen in my life? Couldn't a loving God have given me nurturing, affirming parents?*

The role suffering plays in one's life is a complex and delicate issue. We need to understand that our sovereign God has allowed (not caused) evil in the world. Let's examine three causes of suffering: the fallen nature of man, the consequences of sin and the Lord's work of pruning for greater fruitfulness.

When Adam and Eve sinned, man's perfection ceased. Mankind and all of creation fell from perfect union with God. When a person enters this world, he enters a system that is dominated by the prince of evil. . .

> . . . *in which you formerly walked according to the course of this world, according to the prince of the power of the air, of the spirit that is now working in the sons of disobedience.*
>
> Eph. 2:2

Apart from Christ, mankind is subject to the unrestrained passions and pains of sin. Children, unfortunately, suffer greatly from this predicament. Too often, God's plan for the family to model His love and power is effectively nullified.

The cross of Christ enables fallen man to be reconciled to God, but it is not His intent that we be extricated from this fallen world. It is our responsibility and privilege to represent Him to others who are fallen and desperately in need of His grace. Even as we do so, however, we are still affected by the fallen and evil forces in the world. Even many Christian parents fail to represent the true character of God to their children. Instead of protecting and providing a godly example, they model the same selfishness, possessiveness or neglect that their heathen neighbors do.

The consequences of personal sin cause a great deal of suffering. Galations 6:7-8 states:

> *Do not be deceived, God is not mocked; for whatever a man sows, this he will also reap.*

For the one who sows to his own flesh shall from the flesh reap corruption, but the one who sows to the Spirit shall from the Spirit reap eternal life.

On television, we see happy endings at the end of almost every program, no matter how grave the characters' problems may be. This provides a very misleading picture of real life. These shows don't describe the tremendous, prolonged pain of adultery, alcoholism, selfishness, jealousy and hatred. That wouldn't sell detergent! The truth is that these sins destroy families, create deep bitterness and crush the lives of those who are most vulnerable: the children.

A third cause of suffering (and we could list several others) is pruning. This kind of suffering differs from the other two because it does not result from sin, but from honoring Christ. Christ used the metaphor of a vineyard to describe this phenomenon:

Every branch in Me that does not bear fruit, He takes away; and every branch that bears fruit, He prunes it, that it may bear more fruit.
John 15:2

I am the vine, you are the branches; he who abides in Me, and I in him, he bears much fruit; for apart from Me you can do nothing.
John 15:5

If we are serious about honoring Christ, we will bear fruit. And if we bear fruit, Christ says that He will prune us so that we can bear even more fruit. His purpose in this action is very positive, but it is painful!

Whether the cause of suffering is sin or fruitfulness, God can use our pain for good. Even when the pain is inflicted by a family member and the hurt is excruciating, God still can use it for good.

Joseph's brothers wanted to murder their upstart little brother (Gen. 37:18-20), but two of the twelve, Reuben and Judah, persuaded the others not to kill him (Gen. 37:21-22, 26-27). So his brothers sold him as a slave. After many years, and as a result of divine intervention, Joseph rose to prominence in Egypt. He became the prime minister under the Egyptian pharaoh.

His father and his brothers experienced a severe famine in Canaan and went to Egypt to buy food. When they came to Joseph, he could have had them executed on the spot, but he didn't. Joseph believed that God had a purpose for allowing him to suffer bitter rejection and brutal treatment by his own brothers. Instead of cursing them, he said to them:

> *"And as for you, you meant evil against me, but God meant it for good in order to bring about this present result, to preserve many people alive.*
>
> *"So therefore, do not be afraid; I will provide for you and your little ones." So he comforted them and spoke kindly to them.*
>
> Gen. 50:20-21

Joseph did not see himself as a victim of injustice (even though he was!). He saw himself as an extension of God's care for his family—even though they had wanted to murder him. He believed that God had a purpose for his suffering, and this sense of purpose enabled him to see himself as a servant of God instead of as a victim.

Perhaps you have been a victim of neglect, abuse or manipulation by your parents or family members. Do you see yourself only as a victim? Or do you see that God has a higher purpose, and that you can participate in that purpose as an extension of His love and power?

A "victim mentality" limits our focus to our own pain and needs. Believing that God has a higher purpose enables us to take our eyes off of ourselves so that we can serve Him and help others. Our pain probably won't evaporate as we focus on God's purposes, but we will have a new sense of contentment when we realize that God can turn even our greatest pain or weakness into strength (2 Cor. 12:9-10).

The Lord can and will use your past to develop strengths in your life. Because of your difficulties, you will be able to understand people and help others more. Let's examine these strengths.

Compassion for Others

Have you ever been really hurting; become desperate enough to tell someone because you needed his help, and had him look at you strangely and say, "What's the matter with you? Why don't you just trust the Lord?" That helped a lot, didn't it!?!

Simplistic answers don't cut it for hurting people. But how does a person develop understanding and compassion? Usually by experiencing pain himself. Our ability to comfort others is more or less proportional to the degree that we have experienced comfort in our own times of pain. Paul wrote to the Corinthian believers:

> *Blessed be the God and Father of our Lord Jesus Christ, the Father of mercies and God of all comfort;*
> *who comforts us in all our affliction so that we may be able to comfort those who are in any affliction with the comfort with which we ourselves are comforted by God.*
> *For just as the sufferings of Christ are ours in abundance, so also our comfort is abundant through Christ.*
>
> 2 Cor. 1:3-5

A woman in our church, Mary, recently experienced the pain of her father's death. At the funeral was an array of expensive floral arrangements, and she received many sympathy cards, but she said that one note meant more to her than any other. It was from a friend whose mother had died of cancer several months before. She wrote of how her emotions and sense of stability had been fractured. And she wrote about the comfort she had received. She didn't give advice. She didn't preach. She just let Mary know that she understood. That was the greatest comfort.

If you have experienced the pain of neglect, abuse or manipulation, you will be able to understand and comfort others who are experiencing the same kind of pain in their families. God can use you deeply and profoundly in the lives of others.

Dependence on the Lord

When the prophet Samuel came to Jesse's house, he invited Jesse and his sons to a ceremonial sacrifice (1 Samuel 16). It was an intense and exciting moment in Jesse's family. *Why has the prophet come to our home?* they undoubtedly wondered.

Samuel had been directed by the Lord to go to Jesse's home so that he could anoint a new king of Israel. "Bring your sons to me," Samuel instructed. One by one, Jesse's seven sons passed in front of the prophet, but the Lord said to Samuel, "No, not this one. . . not this one. . . not this one." There was no one left.

"Are these all of your sons?" Samuel asked.

Jesse replied, "There remains yet the youngest, and behold, he is tending the sheep."

Samuel ordered Jesse to bring David to him, and the Lord instructed, "Arise, anoint him; for this is he." David was to become the king of Israel, but his father didn't even count him among his own sons! Samuel had instructed Jesse to bring all of his sons to him, but Jesse had left David out in the field with the sheep. He was a reject in the eyes of his father.

His brothers, too, ridiculed David. (After all, that's how their father treated him.) When David took provisions to his brothers while they were in Saul's army, the eldest, Eliab, replied:

> . . . *Why have you come down? And with whom have you left those few sheep in the wilderness? I know your insolence and the wickedness of your heart; for you have come down in order to see the battle.*
>
> 1 Sam. 17:28

Rejected by his father and scorned by his brothers, David spent many lonely nights watching the sheep. A deeply sensitive young man, he needed to be accepted. He needed to be understood. No one else cared about him—no one else but the Lord. So day after day and night after night, alone with the Lord while tending sheep, David developed a close, rich relationship with God. His psalms reflect a depth of intimacy, honesty and understanding probably unparalleled in history. Yet we may fail to recognize the crucible that developed this intimacy and dependence: rejection. David had no where else to turn, so he turned to the Lord.

Somehow David recognized that God was not like his father. Maybe David memorized the Scriptures and realized that God is loving, kind and powerful instead of harsh, demeaning and neglectful like Jesse was. David's understanding of the contrast between the Lord and his father enabled him to experience the love and power of God's presence.

Perhaps you have experienced rejection. Perhaps you have no one else to depend on but God. He is faithful and kind and powerful. You can depend on Him even if you can depend on no one else.

Perception

Children need love and acceptance to experience stability. Without these provisions, they have to fend for themselves. Some try to do so by building emotional walls. *"If I can keep from getting close to people, then I won't get hurt,"* they surmise.

Others develop a different defense mechanism. They become acutely aware of the mood and intentions of those around them, and then change their behavior to win approval. Their "antennae" are always up, analyzing every word, expression and action. *Does that look mean that she's upset with me? Why did he raise his voice? His words say that he cares about me, but the tone of his voice tells me that he's faking it. What can I say to get her to like me?* It's a cat-and-mouse game, and the children are the poor mice.

This ability to "read" others is a tremendous strength, even if learned through great anguish and painful introspection. Bill is a friend of mine who is the most perceptive person I know. His parents fought a lot when he was young. They were so involved in their own selfishness and bitterness that they often neglected him. His defense was to try to please them in every way he could so that they would notice him and approve of him. He learned to read their every mood.

Bill can sense the attitudes of others long before most people can. I often ask him how he thinks other people in the church are doing. I may sense that something isn't quite right, but Bill usually has it pinpointed, described and illustrated with several examples. He is so perceptive that I sometimes walk into his office and jokingly say, "Hi, Bill, how am I doing?" His sense of perception is a great strength, but it was through pain that he acquired it.

Have you learned to "read" others because you felt that you had to respond perfectly as a child to gain approval? Perception is a wonderful strength to have.

Reflective

Some people respond to perceived rejection by becoming very cautious. These people are characterized by the thought, *I have to be right before I act.* This fear of failure and rejection can paralyze, but it can also have the positive result of developing an ability to reflect. This strength is similar to that of perception, but centers more on ideas, problems and issues than on people.

Patty is a friend of mine who has learned to analyze issues to a great degree. She often will ask a series of questions that no one else even thinks to ask. She likes to have her bases covered to avoid mistakes.

Some of us are risk-takers, blindly rushing ahead without being willing (or able) to take a hard look at the facts. We need someone like Patty who is more cautious and willing to ask the hard questions.

Are you a cautious person? Do you analyze problems well? Are you so cautious that you are afraid to make a decision even when all your questions have been answered? Or is your reflection a strength that enables you to ask questions, get solutions and press on with a high degree of success?

Effectiveness

Lyle is from an alcoholic family. He received very little attention when he was growing up, and what attention he did receive was often condemnation. Like anyone else, he developed a defense mechanism to blunt the pain. His defense mechanism was to excel in school and sports. He was driven to do well because he thought that good grades and involvement in athletics would earn him the respect and approval he longed for.

No matter how well he performed (he was an honor student and an all-star in three sports), he still felt like an outcast from his family. When he made ninety-five on his exams, his mother would ask him why he didn't make a hundred. When he went four for four on his baseball team, it still wasn't enough to win his parents' approval.

When Lyle graduated from college, he focused his finely-tuned skills on the business world. Soon he became a vice-president, the best employee in the company. He made a lot of money, married a beautiful girl and continued to advance in his career. *Maybe if I get to the next position,* he reasoned, *then they'll approve of me.* But they didn't.

Some people, like Lyle, have learned how to focus their attention and abilities to accomplish almost any given task. Are you exceptionally effective, but feel like nothing you do is ever quite good enough? Have you experienced the unconditional love and acceptance of God so that your drive to be effective can be channeled for His glory?

When we are in the midst of the agony of rejection, it is often difficult to see the strengths that God is building in us. We just want relief! Yet God is there, building and developing strengths in us that will enable us to honor Him and help others. It may encourage you to remember that no matter how difficult your past has been, God has a divine purpose for you, and He will use those very difficulties to develop depth, character and skills so that you can have a great impact on other people. He can produce hope from despair, compassion from pain, joy from bitterness and strength from weakness.

Chapter 18

Breaking the Cycle:
Modeling God's Character to Your Children

Pat Springle

A startling and disturbing dictum in the Bible is this: sin is reproduced in a family for four generations!

> And the Lord descended in the cloud and stood there with him as he called upon the name of the Lord.
> Then the Lord passed by in front of him and proclaimed, "The Lord, the Lord God, compassionate and gracious, slow to anger, and abounding in lovingkindness and truth;
> "who keeps lovingkindness for thousands, who forgives iniquity, transgression and sin; yet He will by no means leave the guilty unpunished, visiting the iniquity of fathers on the children and on the grandchildren to the third and fourth generations."
> And Moses made haste to bow low toward the earth and worship.
>
> Ex. 34:5-8

A father's sins—his bitterness, unbridled anger, neglect, abuse, passivity or manipulation—will be passed down to his children, his grandchildren and his great-grandchildren. This truth may seem harsh and cruel, but it is an accurate reflection of sin's terrible consequences.

Is this statement, given to Moses about 3500 years ago, still in effect today? I talked with a man, Steve, who described how his father very rarely showed affection for him:

"Dad was a driver. He worked long and hard, and he expected his children to do the same. If I didn't do something exactly the way he wanted it done—which was pretty often, though I really tried to do a good job—he'd let me have it. I can remember only one time that he put his hand on my shoulder when I was growing up. But he put his hand on my backside a few more times than that!"

"Did you ever spend much time with his father, your granddad?" I asked.

Steve responded instantly with a look of revelation: "You know, I did, and he was a crotchety old goat. He always seemed to have something to say about everybody, and it wasn't very complimentary! He even gave his grandchildren a pretty rough time."

Steve went on to say, "And I don't like to admit it, but I treat my children the same way my father treated me, the same way his father treated him. I hate it! And I feel so guilty about it!"

The sins of Steve's grandfather were being reproduced in his son, his grandson (Steve) and even his great-grandchildren.

Can this cycle be broken? Can the destruction and pain of reproduced sin be stopped? By the grace and power of God, yes, it can. Proverbs 28:13 describes the process necessary for doing so:

> *He who conceals his transgressions will not prosper, but he who*
> *confesses and forsakes them will find compassion.*

Most people conceal their transgressions either by denying that their actions are wrong, or by feeling so guilty for them that they can't face them. To break the cycle of sin, we must bring our transgressions out into the light of God's Word and confess them, confident of His forgiveness.

To confess means "to agree with." When we confess our sins, we agree with God that our attitude and/or actions are, indeed, sin. Sin is not relegated to only the more blatant varieties of wrongdoing: murder, rape and stealing. Sin is an attitude which says to God, *I want to run my own life. You go Your way; I'll go mine.* At its most fundamental level, sin is selfishness, and it can be expressed in many ways, subtle and blatant. When we confess to God, we also agree with Him that Christ's death is the complete payment for sin; therefore, we are completely forgiven.

After having agreed with God that we have sinned and that we are forgiven as a result of Christ's death on the cross, we must take a third step: to forsake that sin. *Forsake* means "to renounce, to leave altogether, to desert, to abandon." When we forsake a sin, we go to any length to reject a wrongful attitude or behavior and replace it with that which honors Christ.

Paul describes the process of rejecting sin and replacing it with godliness in his letter to the Ephesian believers:

> *But you did not learn Christ in this way,*
> *if indeed you have heard Him and have been taught in Him, just as*
> *truth is in Jesus,*
> *that, in reference to your former manner of life, you lay aside the*
> *old self, which is being corrupted in accordance with the lusts of deceit,*
> *and that you be renewed in the spirit of your mind,*
> *and put on the new self, which in the likeness of God has been*
> *created in righteousness and holiness of the truth.*
>
> Eph. 4:20-24

He instructs us to *lay aside the old self, which is being corrupted in accordance with the lusts of deceit.* "Laying aside" is a parallel of confession. To lay something aside, you first have to recognize that it is there and that it is harmful to you and/or to others.

Being *renewed in the spirit of* [our] *minds* occurs as we reflect on the truth of the Scriptures—especially the deep implications of the Gospel—that we are deeply loved, completely forgiven, fully pleasing and totally accepted by God because of the cross of Christ.

Putting on the new self means making choices to spend time and effort doing those things that honor the Lord and encourage others.

This process doesn't occur by magic. Breaking a cycle of family sin doesn't happen by waving a wand or reading a verse, but through a combination of powerful, God-given forces: the Scriptures, the Holy Spirit, the body of believers and the human will.

The Scriptures are our only source of truth about God, about ourselves and about the process of restoration that God can perform in our lives. The Holy Spirit is the agent of change. Self-effort is not enough. Real, lasting growth in a person's life requires the transforming power of the Spirit of God. The body of Christ needs to model and affirm the truth of the Scriptures and the work of God's Spirit corporately and individually. And finally, God has given each of us a will so that *we* play a role in the process of change. It is our choice to depend either on ourselves or on Christ to produce change. It is our choice either to continue living out the reproduced sin pattern in our family history or to have the courage to begin acting in a way that honors Christ and helps our children, even when it seems that every fiber of our hearts and emotions is tugging at us to continue in a familiar but destructive cycle of behavior.

If all of these ingredients are in operation, then eventually and gradually, the transformation we long for will happen!

Yes, there is hope for change and restoration, even if you have failed miserably at modeling God's character to your children. There is hope in the prophet Joel's words:

> *And the threshing floors will be full of grain, and the vats will overflow with the new wine and oil.*
>
> *Then I will make up to you for the years that the swarming locust has eaten, the creeping locust, the stripping locust, and the gnawing locust, my great army which I sent among you.*
>
> *And you shall have plenty to eat and be satisfied, and praise the name of the Lord your God, who has dealt wondrously with you; then My people will never be put to shame.*

> Joel 2:24-26

We can apply this promise to our need of changing the way we treat our children: *I will make up to you for the years that the swarming locust has eaten.*

In his book, *You and Your Child*, Charles Swindoll wrote:

> *The locust of parental neglect and insensitivity may have taken its toll on your children's lives years ago. The swarming insects of indifference or ignorance or impatience or a host of other famines brought on by your failures ate away at your relationship with those precious children, resulting today in barrenness and perhaps even bitterness and resentment on their part.*
>
> *Now they are grown. You cannot relive those years. That's a fact. But God can renew them. That's a promise. That's hope!* [1]

Let's look at five principles that are stepping stones for learning to model the character of God to our children:

1. A changed self-concept
2. A changed purpose
3. Changed affections
4. A changed schedule
5. Changed actions

A Changed Self-Concept

As has been mentioned several times before, most of us try to gain our security and significance by performing to win the approval of others. This is a hopeless rat race because God has created us in such a way that only His love, forgiveness and acceptance can truly satisfy us.

We need to change the way we see ourselves. If we are driven to perform, we may use others to get what we need and then condemn them when they fail. If we seek the approval of others, we may alter our behavior to suit them without being ourselves at all. Or, we may use our approval as a tool to manipulate others to make us happy.

Robin is a young mother who quickly realized that her perception of herself radically affects how she treats her children. As she has become more and more convinced that God loves her unconditionally, she has become more patient and affectionate with her children.

A Changed Purpose

Our culture glorifies the triad of selfish purposes: success, pleasure and approval. Practically every commercial on television and every billboard and magazine ad tells us that a product or service will give us success, pleasure or the approval of others. Then we'll be really happy! (Hogwash!)

Dan Hayes, a traveling speaker for Campus Crusade for Christ, illustrates our fruitless pursuit of happiness with this dialogue:

Q: "What do most people want out of life?"
A: "They want the American dream: a nice car, a nice home, a nice job, a nice boat, nice vacations, nice neighbors, a nice husband or a nice wife, and nice children. They work like crazy to get these things, but after a while, they get bored with them."
Q: "Then what do they want?"
A: "They want a bigger car, a bigger house, a better job, better vacations, better neighbors, bigger and better children, and a better spouse. People are never satisfied with 'things'!"

In fact, God has made us so that these things *cannot* satisfy us. No matter how we pursue them, they leave us empty. Jeremiah wrote about the emptiness of pursuing selfish goals with the vain hope that they will satisfy us:

> *For My people have committed two evils: They have forsaken Me,*
> *the fountain of living waters, to hew for themselves cisterns, broken*
> *cisterns, that can hold no water.*
>
> Jer. 2:13

Most people never even think about their purpose in life. They just adopt whatever purpose is given to them by someone else. Many companies demand that their employees put the company at the top of their priority list. One electronic company in the Southwest told a friend of mine who interviewed with them: "If you come to work for us, we'll pay you well. You'll have excellent benefits. And in return, we'll expect you to eat, breathe, sleep and work for our company. If you work for us, we'll expect our company to come before anything else in your life." They wanted to own him, but he didn't want to be owned by anyone but Christ.

Our compelling purpose in life should be to honor Christ in everything we think, say and do. If our purpose is to seek after as much success, pleasure and approval as we can get, we will pass our selfishness on to our children (in the little time we have left with them). If our purpose is to honor Christ, we will use every opportunity to model and teach God's character and truth to our children. They will be profoundly affected either way!

Changed Affections

The affections of some people have been numbed by years of withdrawal. The affections of others have been replaced by hatred, and their anger has a "hair trigger." Some avoid any intimacy with others because they are afraid of being hurt. Can our fear and sense of distance be overcome? Can anger be changed? Can we choose how we feel?

Well, yes and no. (How's that for a clear answer?) We should not try to change how we feel. If we try to deny or suppress negative emotions, they will only build and, sooner or later, cause either a depression or an explosion. We need to be honest about our emotions and *pour out our hearts to the Lord* (Ps. 62:8). We need to ask, *Why am I fearful? Why am I angry? What am I believing about God or about myself that is producing these emotions?* Then we can examine our thoughts and beliefs, and choose to change what we think about instead of trying to change how we feel. If we think properly about the Lord and about ourselves, and if these concepts are modeled to us by an affirming relative or friend, then our emotions will slowly change, too.

Although we cannot change our emotions from negative to positive, we can shift them from being destructively negative to being productively negative. Instead of anger, we can experience grief, especially in relation to the disobedience of our children. *The Search for Significance* includes this helpful insight: [2]

> *Our worth is totally secure in Christ, so our children's success or failure, cuteness or whining doesn't affect our value in the least. We need to see our children the way our heavenly Father sees us: deeply loved, completely forgiven, fully pleasing, and totally accepted. Then, when they disobey, our discipline will be like the Father's discipline of us: in love, not anger. If we approach our children with an attitude of*

grief rather than anger when they disobey, it will make a tremendous difference! What a difference it will make if we go to our children with the attitude and words, "It's sad that you disobeyed. It was harmful to you, and I love you so much that I don't want you to harm yourself. I will need to discipline you to help you remember not to do it again. Remember, the reason I am disciplining you is that I love you so much!" . . . instead of, "You've done it again, and I'll make sure you regret it! I wonder if you'll ever amount to anything!"

Many fathers work fifty-five to sixty hours a week, play golf on Saturday, sleep on Sunday and are involved in other outside activities. Their schedule doesn't allow for much time with their children.

Also, an increasing number of mothers are in the work force. Obviously, some of these are single parents who must work to support their families, but studies show that a large percentage of mothers who work simply want to gain more success, pleasure and approval through their jobs. Their purpose is self-centered. They want more. But what is more important: more possessions or an emotionally healthy family? The acquisition of things takes time and energy that could be devoted to nurturing and developing children. Helping children progress through the developmental stages of bonding, limits, adolescence and maturity requires concentrated attention and affection—but it is well worth it, both for the parents and their children.

To change your established schedule so that you have time to be with your children takes courage and planning. As you begin, be sure to schedule and protect your time. Don't let anything steal the precious moments you have allotted for interaction with your children and spouse.

Toward that end, many people I know have developed special family occasions which have become family traditions. These occasions give everyone something to look forward to, and in later years provide special memories to enjoy. One father makes chocolate chip pancakes or waffles for his wife and two children every Saturday morning. Another couple takes three hours every Sunday afternoon to spend with their three children. They take the phone off the hook and have a picnic (on the living room floor, if it's raining outside) and read books and play games together.

Family traditions can be weekly, monthly, seasonal or centered around holidays. A list of suggestions is found in the workbook section on pages 328 and 329. Look at these and think of some family traditions that are meaningful to you and your family.

Changed Actions

The four principles of change we've just examined focus on *why* and *when* you can model God's character to your children. This final principle centers on *what* to model. Good intentions aren't enough. Our children need affirmation through our words and our deeds.

In their award winning book, *The Blessing,* Gary Smalley and John Trent have examined the way that Isaac blessed his children.[3] We can follow the same example with our children. The elements of the blessing are:

- a meaningful touch
- a spoken message
- attaching high value to the one being blessed
- picturing a special future for the one being blessed, and
- an active commitment to fulfill the blessing

Let's explore each of these elements briefly:

- Touching someone can communicate warmth and a sense of intimacy. A hug, a pat on the shoulder or holding a person's hand tells a person that you care about him and accept him. A friend of mine, whose family typically avoided touching each other, determined to give his wife and children meaningful touches each day. He decided to try to touch each one ten times a day until it became a habit for him. Most of us don't have to go to such a mechanical extreme, but we would do well to have this kind of determination.

- A spoken message of affection and affirmation is also important. Condemnation and sarcasm are tremendously destructive. It has been estimated that it takes twenty positive messages to overcome every one that's negative. Some of us have experienced the reverse ratio: twenty negative to one positive! Simple statements have a powerful effect: "I love you." "You're a wonderful son." "You really did that well, honey."

• Attaching high value is another dimension of affirmation. When we communicate that we value a person, it shows him that he has a secure place in our eyes. One friend of mine tells his daughter, "If they lined up all the little girls in the whole world, do you know which one I would pick?"

She always smiles and says, "No, which one, Daddy?"

He waves his finger like he's in the process of deciding and then points to her and exclaims, "You! You're the one I'd pick!" That's communicating high value.

• Picturing a special future involves observing a child's strengths and abilities. One parent might say, after observing the drawings of his son, "You might become a great artist! You are so good at drawing monsters!" Or to a daughter, "You are so loving and kind, the Lord will use you in hundreds or thousands of people's lives some day!"

• Finally, we need to demonstrate an active commitment to fulfill the blessing. Taking time to observe children, and expending the physical and emotional energy to affirm them are important. But we also need to provide whatever is necessary to help our children develop and reach the "special future" we have described to them. Baseball practice, piano lessons, crayons and paper, or whatever else we provide for them communicates that we are actively committed to their welfare and development.

As we trust God to change our self-concepts, purposes, affections, schedules and actions, we will be able to model His character to our children more consistently, regardless of the modeling we received as children. Our children don't have to experience what many of us have. There is hope for change!

Chapter 19

Breaking the Cycle:
Responding to Your Parents

Jim Craddock

This chapter is difficult to write, but it is necessary. It is difficult because responding to one's parents in a godly way, especially if they have been abusive or neglectful, can be extremely painful. It is also difficult because everyone's situation is different. Many relationships are complex, and "cookie-cutter" answers often don't fit individual situations. But this chapter is necessary because our relationships with our parents are God-given. The Lord wants us to respond to them in a way that honors Him. To do that, we need His wisdom and strength.

Rick and I talked about his relationships with his parents. His father left when Rick was nine years old, and three years later, his parents divorced. His mother had to work to support him and his sister. When she got home each day, she was too tired to give the children much attention and affection. Unresolved bitterness toward her husband also sapped her energy for giving.

Throughout his childhood, Rick received no emotional support from his father and very little from his mother. After talking about how his family situation had affected his view of God and how he could change those misconceptions, our conversation eventually turned to how he could respond to his parents now.

Rick's expression became intense. He leaned forward in his chair and said, "It would be easier for me if they were dead!"

I responded carefully, "That may be true, Rick, but they aren't dead, and the

Lord can give you the wisdom and strength you need to respond to them properly now."

Some of us have had relatively good relationships with our parents all of our lives, and we need to make only some minor adjustments in our attitudes and actions toward them. But some of us need a major overhaul. Years of withdrawal from our parents or bitterness toward them will not be overcome in a day. Rather, we will need to apply God's Word diligently and follow His Spirit closely in order to learn how to respond properly to our parents.

Some of us have been so dominated by our parents that we feel they want us to say and do exactly what they want us to all the time. Otherwise, we will be criticized and rejected. If this is the case for you, you'll need to develop some objectivity in your relationships with your parents. You'll need to step out from under that domination (without stepping away entirely from your parents) and develop your own identity.

Some of us have coped with painful family relationships by going in the other direction. We have withdrawn, either emotionally or physically, to protect ourselves from the pain of parental neglect or disapproval. We need to pursue our relationships with our parents, and extend to them the love and forgiveness we have received from Christ.

In both the Old and New Testaments, the Scriptures direct us to honor our parents:

> *Honor your father and your mother, that your days may be prolonged in the land which the Lord your God gives you.*
>
> Ex. 20:12

> *Honor your father and mother (which is the first commandment with a promise), that it may be well with you, and that you may live long on the earth.*
>
> Eph. 6:2-3

What does it mean to *honor* one's parents? There are many misconceptions about this issue.

People who are very conscientious and overly responsible feel that if their parents aren't completely happy with everything they say and do, then they haven't honored their parents. But the burden of making other people happy is oppressive!

You are not responsible for making your parents happy. That is between them and the Lord. Their contentment and happiness should not rest on your shoulders. They need to depend on the Lord, not you, for their security and significance.

Although you are not responsible for your parents' happiness, you are responsible for developing your own separate identity and then extending your love to them. At that point, you should let them respond in any way they choose to respond. Sometimes they will appreciate what you say and do. Sometimes they won't, but you need to do what the Lord wants you to do whether they appreciate it or not.

A very helpful statement in *The Search for Significance* (McGee) gives objectivity and perspective to honoring our parents. As we develop our own identity and then seek to honor them, we should remember: *It would be nice if my father and my mother approved of me, but if they don't, I'm still deeply loved, completely forgiven, fully pleasing, and totally accepted by God.* [1] Remember, you are not responsible for their happiness, but you are responsible for acting in a way that pleases God. If your parents are happy with you, fine. If not, be content that you have obeyed and pleased God. After all, He is the Lord, and He deserves our primary affection and obedience.

Paul wrote that we can be bond-servants either to people or to God, but not to both:

> *For am I now seeking the favor of men, or of God? Or am I striving to please men? If I were still trying to please men, I would not be a bond-servant of Christ.*
>
> Gal. 1:10

We are responsible to treat our parents in a way that pleases the Lord. Our parents' response is up to them.

As we develop our own identity and learn how to express God's love and grace to our parents, they may well notice a difference in us, and they may not like it! If we have been withdrawn, they may not know how to handle our expressions of gratitude and acts of love. If we have been virtual puppets, doing anything and everything we can to make them happy, our new identities and healthy independence from them will likely threaten their domination of us. In that case, even our loving actions and words may be misunderstood because in their jaded, self-preoccupied view, they will see our new independence as dishonoring to them. Any change in the status quo can be disturbing to our parents; the transition to a new relationship with them is often awkward and sometimes painful.

Many people expect that treating their parents differently will cause their parents to change and treat them differently. That may happen after a while, but then again, it may not. In fact, no matter how much you change, your parents may not change at all! You can pray for their response. You can love them and accept them unconditionally. You can try to do everything perfectly (but, of course, nobody can do that), and they still may not change their behavior toward you. Don't fall into the trap of feeling that it's up to you to get them to change the way they evaluate and respond to you. That's bargaining. (See chapter 16.) They have their own free wills, and they make their own choices. Be content that you are doing all you know to do, learning by trial and error, depending on the Lord for His love and His strength, and let them respond. They may never change—but *you* can!

Let's take a look at some principles that will help you respond to your parents in a way that honors the Lord.

See Yourself As a Conqueror, Not a Victim

Some people have experienced extraordinarily tragic family situations. They have been emotionally and physically abused. They have been neglected or abandoned. They have been manipulated to accomplish their parents' selfish goals. If you haven't come from a family like this, it is hard to comprehend the anguish and trauma that such relationships can cause.

If a person has been hurt deeply by his or her parents, the normal response is either withdrawal to avoid pain or revenge to inflict pain (or some combination of these). Neither withdrawal nor revenge honors Christ. One of the greatest needs of a person who has severely repressed his emotions is to move from denial to honesty, and to begin to experience the hurt and anger that he has repressed. For a while, these people need to see themselves as victims of the neglect and abuse they have experienced.

Regardless of our backgrounds Christ can bring light out of darkness and purpose out of pain. He can give us hope and confidence because His grace is bigger than our pain. Because we are His children we can be conquerors instead of victims. Paul wrote to the believers in Rome about this perspective in the midst of his most severe difficulties.

> *Who shall separate us from the love of Christ? Shall tribulation,*
> *or distress, or persecution, or famine, or nakedness, or peril, or sword?*
> *...But in all these things we overwhelmingly conquer through Him*
> *who loved us.*

Rom. 8:35, 37

If we see ourselves as victims we will always be defensive, blaming others for the way we are. If we see ourselves as conquerors we will have a deep sense of both purpose and thankfulness, realizing that God uses difficulties to build character strengths in us. And He will use our difficulties to help us relate to the needs of others so that we can comfort them in times of need.

See Your Parents As People, Not Villains

Young children see their parents as gods. What they say is Truth. What they demand is Law. How they act is the Order of the Universe. Sooner or later, we realize that our parents aren't gods after all, and with that realization comes a conclusion. We either understand that they are more or less ordinary people, or we believe that they are villains who have maliciously hurt us.

The truth is: Very few parents intentionally hurt their children. The vast majority are simply living out their own heritage. They treat their children in the same way they have been treated by their own parents. Most of them, far from being evil villains, experience deep pains of guilt and shame because they know they aren't the parents they want to be.

Paula's mother was kind and gracious to most people, but she was a demanding tyrant to Paula. No matter how well Paula performed, it wasn't good enough for her mother, and nothing escaped her jaundiced eye: Paula's grades, her appearance, her friends, her activities—every facet of her life. Paula tried everything to please her mother, but constant disapproval and criticism had caused her to become passive and withdrawn.

When she later realized that she had been her mother's pawn all of her life, she became bitter and resented her mother. A few months later, Paula, still angry, traveled to visit her mother's parents who lived across the country. She hadn't seen them for a long time, but after only one day, she had a startling revelation. Her grandmother was a harsh and demanding woman. Her mother had never received genuine love and affirmation, only criticism and disapproval. Paula realized that her mother had treated her in the same way that she had been treated! Instantly, she understood that her mother was not the villain she had thought her to be. She was a person who had been hurt deeply all of her life by *her* mother's condemnation.

The pain Paula had felt from her mother's constant criticism remained, but her bitterness turned to grief as she understood that both she and her mother had never experienced the love they needed.

Our parents are not gods, but they aren't usually evil villains either. They are people who tend to treat us in the same way they have been treated. Many of them are deeply hurt themselves. They need our understanding and forgiveness, not our criticism and condemnation.

Develop a Healthy Sense of Independence

Some people base their whole identity on their parents' opinions of who they are. This is understandable for a child, but it is devastating for an adult. As people mature, they need to develop their own identities.

Lynda's father seemed to have a split personality. Most of the time, he was quiet and unassuming, even passive. But on occasion, he would explode in a profane fury. Lynda was deeply scarred by her father's mixed signals. She was fearful and insecure.

Her fear and insecurity didn't diminish as she grew older. She married and had children, but she cowered at the slightest change in her husband's tone of voice. She needed help.

When I asked her about her father, she could describe his behavior very accurately. But when I asked how she had felt when he was in a rage, she couldn't respond. "I. . . I'm not sure how I felt," she stammered.

"Did you feel afraid of him?"

"I don't know."

We were obviously getting nowhere fast, so I decided to be more objective.

"Lynda," I asked, "how would you feel if you saw a man in your neighborhood treat his daughter the way you were treated?"

"I'd be angry," she responded.

"You would?"

"Yes, I'd be really angry with him!" Now there was intensity in her eyes and voice.

"How would a normal little girl feel about a father like yours?"

"Well, I guess she'd be afraid of him. I guess she'd be very hurt and afraid." The lights began to come on in Lynda's mind. "I guess I'm just numb about my father."

Many of us can identify with Lynda's response to her father's behavior. Although we might be quick to agree that our parents have many faults, few of us would be able to name those faults and describe their affect on us. We tend to shut out the negative aspects of our parents' behavior toward us, not just because we love them, but because we have so much of our identity and security invested in who they are. What we might perceive as "loyalty" toward our parents is often a defense mechanism which protects us from seeing those behaviors that are disappointing and hurtful to us. The failure to establish this kind of objectivity (the ability to see both the good and the bad in our parents) prevents us from establishing a healthy sense of distance and independence from them. Instead, we focus on them and conduct ourselves according to their desires, hoping to secure their blessing and approval. Not only is this harmful to our human development, but it blocks our spiritual growth as well. After all, when we allow our world to revolve around our parents, we effectually serve them instead of Him.

I advised Lynda to think of her father as "that man in the neighborhood" for a while, until she could look at him and at herself more objectively. She allowed herself to feel normal emotions of hurt and anger as she thought about how she would feel if she saw him enraged at his daughter for no good reason. She was soon able to transfer those objective perceptions to her own father.

Gradually, as Lynda began to base her identity on the truths of God's Word instead of on the unreasonable fury of her unbalanced father, she was progressively able to develop a healthy sense of independence from him. This has been a long process, but it is making a world of difference to Lynda and her family.

Make Godly Choices

When one's primary goal in life is to bring honor to the Lord, the goal of his or her every activity and relationship is to honor Him. As a person begins to understand, believe and live by the truths of Christ's unconditional love and acceptance, he or she is then able to begin expressing that love and acceptance to others. In fact, it can be said that a person is able to express God's love, forgiveness and acceptance only in proportion to his experience of those qualities himself. We therefore need to drink deeply of these powerful truths so that our relationships can be characterized by them.

The apostles Paul and John flatly stated that our ability to love, forgive and accept others is based on our own experience:

> *The Samaritan woman therefore said to Him, "How is it that You, being a Jew, ask me for a drink since I am a Samaritan woman?" (For Jews have no dealings with Samaritans.)*
>
> *Jesus answered and said to her, "If you knew the gift of God, and who it is who says to you, 'Give Me a drink,' you would have asked Him, and He would have given you living water."*
>
> *She said to Him, "Sir, You have nothing to draw with and the well is deep; where then do You get that living water?"*
>
> John 4:9-11

> *. . . bearing with one another, and forgiving each other, whoever has a complaint against anyone; just as the Lord forgave you, so also should you.*
>
> Col. 3:13

> *Wherefore, accept one another, just as Christ also accepted us to the glory of God.*
>
> Rom. 15:7

Until we begin to develop our new identity in Christ, we have no choice but to simply try to defend ourselves as best we can and withdraw from or punish those who have hurt us. But when we realize that Christ is our protector, and that He is the complete source of our security and significance, then we can choose to act in a way that is good for us and others, and honoring to Him. We can take our attention off of ourselves, and put it on Christ and others because we are secure.

Sounds good, doesn't it? It is good, but the transition from self-defense and revenge to unconditionally accepting those who have hurt us deeply is awkward, long and difficult. Our emotions often go haywire. When our emotions tell us to fight back or hide, and the Scriptures tell us to believe the truth about ourselves and love others, we need to have the courage to live by the truth instead of our emotions. Many of us have been living by our emotions all of our lives; so the choice to live by the truth—in spite of our painful emotions—is difficult, indeed. But seeing our emotions objectively and knowing that they are often based on our old identity is at least half of the battle.

The transition may be difficult, and you may need the advice and encouragement of a friend or counselor to keep going in the midst of the battle, but realize that life is a series of choices. Will we choose to live by withdrawal and revenge or by the truth of the Scriptures and the power of God's Spirit?

After their parents have died, some people realize that they can choose to love, forgive and accept their parents, but it's too late; the potential for a reconciliation with their parents is gone. This can be very disappointing, but instead of letting this disappointment lead to bitterness, they can realize that God is sovereign. He is aware of the situation, and He doesn't demand anything that is beyond reason. Those whose parents have died can thank God for what they have learned about His character and share their newfound wisdom with those whose parents are still living. Then another family will have the potential for reconciliation.

Be Prepared

It may sound spiritual to believe that if you change, then your parents will automatically change, too. However, it took years (generations) for your family to develop certain behavior patterns, and it will probably take more than one conversation to rectify all of its wrongs and develop new habits of relating. It may even take years for you to change. And your parents may never change.

Be prepared for your communications with your parents. Don't expect them to change very quickly. They may, but they may not. Your new behavior may be threatening to them, and your desire for reconciliation may at first produce more bitterness.

Darren was from an alcoholic family. His father was neglectful and abusive. His mother was a perfectionist. Darren began to understand how he had been affected by his parents, and on one occasion he asked, "What should I tell my parents about what I'm learning?"

I asked, "What would happen if you told them?"

He answered, "They would be furious!"

"Then tell them only what would be positive and helpful to them and to your relationship with them."

Darren changed his game plan from telling his parents everything to planning his communication with them carefully.

Fortify yourself with the truth so that when you talk with your parents, you can remember that you are deeply loved, completely forgiven, fully pleasing and totally accepted by the Lord, no matter what they (or anyone else) think of you. Then you can make the hard but right choice to love, forgive and accept them, no matter what their response or your emotions might be.

Responding to parents can be very difficult. Don't be naive about the difficulties. Ask God for His wisdom and power, and be prepared.

Introduction

Your Parents and You Workbook

This workbook is divided into steps. Follow the directions given for each one. Here are some general suggestions:

1. Review chapters in the book.

Take time to review corresponding chapters of the book as you go through the steps; the chapters will offer fresh meaning as you work through them.

2. Write out your responses.

It's really important for you to use a pen or pencil with the workbook and actually complete the tasks assigned. If you have a habit of mentally answering questions on inventories instead of writing out the answers, break your habit! Studies show that you will profit five to eight times more if you write out your responses.

3. Follow each step's time frame.

Some of the steps only require a few minutes of your time to complete. Others are designed to be done over a number of days. All are designed to help you expand your awareness of God's character.

4. Don't rush through the material.

When you receive a new insight, stop to think and pray. Meditate on what you are learning. The goal is not to get through the material as quickly as you can, but to understand and apply what you learn. It is more important that you take time to reflect and absorb the content than it is for you to keep up some arbitrary pace.

Note: Some of these steps cover more or less the same ground in different ways. Though they may seem redundant to some people, most of us have a great need for objectivity. These steps, then, can provide more insight and perception by looking at the same issues from a variety of angles.

Step 1

The Nurturing Family:
A Biblical Model

Before we begin to analyze how we have been affected by our parents, it is helpful to get a clear picture of the kind of family God intended for each of us to have. This is not an ideal family, but a *real* family. An ideal family wouldn't have problems like arguments, misunderstandings, conflicts, hurt and anger. A family that is based on biblical principles and affections is one that does have those problems, but approaches them with honesty, and deals with them patiently and effectively.

First, we will study the responsibility of parents in this biblical model of the family; then we will examine the children's responsibility.

Parental Responsibilities

1. Paraphrase the following passages:
    a) Deut. 6:6-9

    _____

    _____

    _____

    b) Ps. 78:1-4

    _____

    _____

    _____

   c) Ps. 103:13

---

   d) Ps. 127:3-5

---

   e) Prov. 22:6

---

   f) Eph. 6:4

---

   g) Col. 3:21

---

2. Summarize: What are parents responsible to provide for their children?

The Child's Responsibility

3. Paraphrase these passages:

   a)   Eccl. 12:1

_____

_____

   b)   Ps. 119:9

_____

_____

   c)   Ps. 148:12-13

_____

_____

   d)   Prov. 1:8-9

_____

_____

   e)   Prov. 3:1-3

_____

_____

   f)   Prov. 8:32

_____

_____

   g)   Eph. 6:1-3 (also Ex. 20:12)

_____

_____

_____

   h)   Col. 3:20

_____

_____

4.   Summarize: How are children responsible to respond to their parents?

_____

_____

_____

_____

_____

_____

Obviously, it is much easier for a child to respond to his parents with honesty, respect and obedience if they are providing a loving and stable environment for him. However, even if the parents do not provide a nurturing home environment characterized by affirmation and instruction, children are still responsible for being obedient, respectful and honest with their parents.

You may wonder: *How have I been affected by neglectful or manipulative parents? How can I become healthy?* and *How does the Lord want me to respond to my parents now?* These questions are not easy to answer. The rest of this workbook is designed to help you begin to answer them.

Step 2

Stages of Development

Review chapters 5 and 6 in *Your Parents and You.*

Understanding our home environment and how we were affected by it can give us a lot of insight into both our past and present thoughts, feelings and behavior. It can also help us to see how we've progressed through the stages of development.

Can you identify the stages in which you seem to have grown significantly and those in which you haven't? Doing so will help you determine your progress (or blockage) in development. Map out your development by drawing a graph on the chart below:

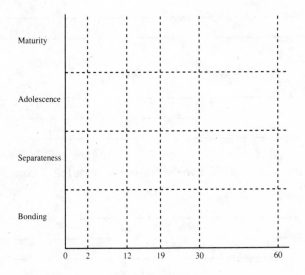

The following questions are designed to help you gain a better understanding of your progress through the stages of development. Complete each section of questions up to and including the stage you are in today. For example, if your development has been blocked in the separateness stage, then complete the bonding and separateness sections only.

Bonding

1. *a)* To what extent did you feel loved, valued and special to your parents when you were a child?

_____

_____

   b) Why did you feel that way? Be specific.

_____

_____

_____

2. *a)* To what extent do you feel loved, valued and special to people now?

_____

_____

   b) Why do you feel that way? Be specific.

_____

_____

_____

3. Describe some relationships you've had in which you felt loved and freed to be yourself.

_____

_____

_____

Limits

Indicate the degree to which you agree with the following statements by using the key below:

Not at all		Somewhat		Definitely
1	2	3	4	5

1. If people aren't happy, I need to do something to cheer them up.

1   2   3   4   5

Explain:

_____
_____
_____
_____

2. If someone needs something, I need to help him or her.

1   2   3   4   5

Explain:

_____
_____
_____
_____

3. If others are happy, I tend to be happy; if others are sad, I tend to be sad.

1   2   3   4   5

Explain:

_____
_____

_____
_____

4. When I say no, I usually feel guilty.

$$1 \qquad 2 \qquad 3 \qquad 4 \qquad 5$$

Explain:

_____
_____
_____
_____

5. I try to please others so they will approve of me.

$$1 \qquad 2 \qquad 3 \qquad 4 \qquad 5$$

Explain:

_____
_____
_____

6. I find it difficult to make decisions which affect other people.

$$1 \qquad 2 \qquad 3 \qquad 4 \qquad 5$$

Explain:

_____
_____
_____
_____

7. I make decisions impulsively, without reflecting on the consequences.

        1   2   3   4   5

Explain:

_____

_____

_____

_____

8. I often see people and situations as right or wrong, black or white.

        1   2   3   4   5

Explain:

_____

_____

_____

_____

9. I tend to be overly responsible.

        1   2   3   4   5

Explain:

_____

_____

_____

_____

10. I tend to be irresponsible or passive.

        1   2   3   4   5

Explain:

_____

_____

_____

_____

11. When I help people, I feel like a hero.

          1   2   3   4   5

Explain:

_____

_____

_____

_____

12. When I help people, I get angry with them for using me and not appreciating what I have done for them.

          1   2   3   4   5

Explain:

_____

_____

_____

Adolescence

1. An adult identity
    a) What are your strengths?

_____

_____

_____

b) What are your weaknesses?

_____

_____

_____

_____

c) How do you feel about yourself in light of your strengths?

_____

_____

_____

d) How do you feel about yourself in light of your weaknesses?

_____

_____

_____

2. Adult behavior
   a) Do you make choices easily? Why or why not?

_____

_____

_____

   b) How do you make choices? (What is your usual decision-making process?)

_____

_____

_____

   c) Do you see both good *and* bad in people and events, or do you only see good *or* bad? How can you tell?

_____

_____

_____

3. Adult goals

    a) What is really important to you? Why?

_____

_____

_____

_____

_____

_____

    b) How do you spend your time and money?

_____

_____

_____

_____

_____

    c) What do you want others to say about your life when you are seventy years old?

_____

_____

_____

4. Adult relationships

    a) How do you experience both intimacy and separateness in relationships?

_____

_____

_____

_____

    b) How do you usually handle conflict? Be specific.

_____

_____

_____

Maturity

1. How are you growing in . . .

    a)   your adult identity?

    b)   adult behavior?

    c)   adult goals?

    d)   adult relationships?

Step 3

Evaluating Your Relationships
with Your Parents

Step 3 is designed to help you evaluate your relationship with each of your parents as you were growing up. Beginning with your father on the following page, check the appropriate squares as you recall how he related to you when you were young.

Here's an example:

Characteristics	Always	Very often	Some-times	Hardly Ever	Never	Don't Know
Gentle			✔			
Stern	✔					
Loving			✔			
Aloof			✔			
Disapproving		✔				

After completing the evaluation of your relationship with your father, do the same exercises for your relationship with your mother.

WHEN I WAS A CHILD, MY FATHER WAS...

Characteristics	Always	Very often	Some-times	Hardly Ever	Never	Don't Know
Gentle						
Stern						
Loving						
Aloof						
Disapproving						
Distant						
Close and Intimate						
Kind						
Angry						
Caring						
Demanding						
Interested						
Disciplinal						
Gracious						
Harsh						
Wise						
Holy						
Leader						
Provident						
Trustworthy						
Joyful						
Forgiving						
Good						
Cherishing of Me						
Compassionate						
Impatient						
Unreasonable						
Strong						
Protective						
Passive						
Encouraging						
Sensitive						
Just						
Unpredictable						

Evaluation of Your Relationship with Your Father

1. What does this inventory tell you about your relationship with your father?

_____

_____

_____

_____

_____

_____

_____

2. *a)* If you were an objective observer of the type of relationship you have just described, how would you feel about the father?

_____

_____

_____

_____

_____

_____

_____

  b) About the child?

_____

_____

_____

_____

_____

_____

_____

3. *a)* How would you respond to the father? Be specific.

_____

_____

_____

_____

_____

_____

_____

   b) To the child?

_____

_____

_____

_____

_____

_____

Now complete the same exercise on the next page, this time to evaluate your relationship with your mother.

WHEN I WAS A CHILD, MY MOTHER WAS...

Characteristics	Always	Very often	Some-times	Hardly Ever	Never	Don't Know
Gentle						
Stern						
Loving						
Aloof						
Disapproving						
Distant						
Close and Intimate						
Kind						
Angry						
Caring						
Demanding						
Interested						
Disciplinal						
Gracious						
Harsh						
Wise						
Holy						
Leader						
Provident						
Trustworthy						
Joyful						
Forgiving						
Good						
Cherishing of Me						
Compassionate						
Impatient						
Unreasonable						
Strong						
Protective						
Passive						
Encouraging						
Sensitive						
Just						
Unpredictable						

Evaluation of Your Relationship with Your Mother

1. What does this inventory tell you about your relationship with your mother?

_____

_____

_____

_____

_____

_____

_____

_____

2. *a)* If you were an objective observer of the type of relationship you have just described, how would you feel about the mother?

_____

_____

_____

_____

_____

_____

_____

   b) About the child?

_____

_____

_____

_____

_____

_____

_____

3. *a)*   How would you respond to the mother? Be specific.

_____

_____

_____

_____

_____

_____

_____

_____

  b)   To the child?

_____

_____

_____

_____

_____

_____

_____

Step 4

Evaluating Your Relationship with God

This inventory is designed to help you evaluate your relationship with God. Because it is subjective, there are no right or wrong answers. Please follow the instructions carefully to ensure that the test reveals your actual feelings.

1. Answer openly and honestly. Don't respond from a theological knowledge of God, but from personal experience.

2. Don't describe what you believe your relationship with God ought to be, or what you hope it will be, but what it is right now.

3. Some people feel that God might be displeased if they give a negative answer. Nothing is further from the truth. He is pleased with our honesty. A foundation of transparency is required for spiritual growth.

4. Turn each characteristic into a question. For example: *To what degree do I really feel that God loves me? To what degree do I really feel that God understands me?*

5. Try to recall times of stress and difficulty, as well as normal situations, as you respond.

TO WHAT DEGREE DO I REALLY FEEL GOD IS...

Characteristics	Always	Very often	Some-times	Hardly Ever	Never	Don't Know
Gentle						
Stern						
Loving						
Aloof						
Disapproving						
Distant						
Close and Intimate						
Kind						
Angry						
Caring						
Demanding						
Interested						
Disciplinal						
Gracious						
Harsh						
Wise						
Holy						
Leader						
Provident						
Trustworthy						
Joyful						
Forgiving						
Good						
Cherishing of Me						
Compassionate						
Impatient						
Unreasonable						
Strong						
Protective						
Passive						
Encouraging						
Sensitive						
Just						
Unpredictable						

1. What does this exercise tell you about your relationship with God?

_____

_____

_____

_____

_____

_____

_____

_____

2. Are there any differences between what you know (theologically) and how you feel (emotionally) about Him? If so, what are they?

_____

_____

_____

_____

_____

_____

_____

_____

_____

Step 5

Your Parents' Influence on Your Perception of God

How has your relationship with your parents influenced your perception of your heavenly Father? To get a comparison, transfer all the check marks you made for your *father* on page 192 to the *shaded columns* on page 204. Use a check mark for this category.

When you have completed this, transfer the check marks you made on page 200, which relate to your relationship with God. To make them more obvious, use an "✗" for this category. Put them in the *white columns* in the appropriate places.

Example:

Characteristics	Always	Very often	Some-times	Hardly Ever	Never	Don't Know
Gentle		✗	✔			
Stern	✔	✗				
Loving		✗	✔			
Aloof		✔		✗		
Disapproving			✔			

After completing the comparison of your father to your heavenly Father, do the same exercises to compare your perceptions of your mother to those of your heavenly Father.

204

Instructions: Transfer all check marks from page 192 to the SHADED columns. Transfer all check marks from page 200 to the WHITE columns.

Characteristics	Always	Very often	Some-times	Hardly Ever	Never	Don't Know
Gentle						
Stern						
Loving						
Aloof						
Disapproving						
Distant						
Close and Intimate						
Kind						
Angry						
Caring						
Demanding						
Interested						
Disciplinal						
Gracious						
Harsh						
Wise						
Holy						
Leader						
Provident						
Trustworthy						
Joyful						
Forgiving						
Good						
Cherishing of Me						
Compassionate						
Impatient						
Unreasonable						
Strong						
Protective						
Passive						
Encouraging						
Sensitive						
Just						
Unpredictable						

What Did You Learn?

1. Which characteristics are the same for both your father and your heavenly
    Father?

    _____

    _____

    _____

    _____

    _____

    _____

    _____

2. Which characteristics are quite different (two or more boxes away from each
    other)?

    _____

    _____

    _____

    _____

    _____

    _____

    _____

3. What patterns (if any) do you see?

    _____

    _____

    _____

    _____

    _____

    _____

    _____

    _____

4. Write a summary paragraph about how your perception of God has been shaped by your relationship with your father:

Your Mother's Influence on Your Perception of God

How has your *mother* influenced your perception of your heavenly Father? To get a comparison, transfer all the check marks you made for your mother on page 195 to the *shaded columns* on page 208. Use a check mark for this category.

When you have completed this, transfer the check marks you made on page 200, which relate to your relationship with God. To make them more obvious, use an "✗" for this category. Put them in the *white columns* in the appropriate places.

Example:

Characteristics	Always	Very often	Some-times	Hardly Ever	Never	Don't Know
Gentle		✗	✔			
Stern	✔	✗				
Loving		✗	✔			
Aloof		✔		✗		
Disapproving			✔			

Instructions: Transfer all check marks from page 195 to the SHADED columns. Transfer all check marks from page 200 to the WHITE columns.

Characteristics	Always	Very often	Some-times	Hardly Ever	Never	Don't Know
Gentle						
Stern						
Loving						
Aloof						
Disapproving						
Distant						
Close and Intimate						
Kind						
Angry						
Caring						
Demanding						
Interested						
Disciplinal						
Gracious						
Harsh						
Wise						
Holy						
Leader						
Provident						
Trustworthy						
Joyful						
Forgiving						
Good						
Cherishing of Me						
Compassionate						
Impatient						
Unreasonable						
Strong						
Protective						
Passive						
Encouraging						
Sensitive						
Just						
Unpredictable						

What Did You Learn?

1. Which characteristics are the same for both your mother and your heavenly Father?

_____

_____

_____

_____

_____

_____

_____

_____

2. Which characteristics are quite different (two or more boxes away from each other)?

_____

_____

_____

_____

_____

_____

_____

3. What patterns (if any) do you see?

_____

_____

_____

_____

_____

_____

_____

_____

4. Write a summary paragraph about how your perception of God has been shaped by your relationship with your mother:

_____

_____

_____

_____

_____

_____

_____

_____

_____

_____

_____

_____

_____

_____

_____

_____

_____

_____

Step 6

Analyzing Your Family

This exercise will help you remember what your family relationships were like as you were growing up, and will help you see how you have been affected by them. Check the appropriate box (or write your answers where indicated) in response to the following questions:

1. How would you describe your parents' marriage?
   ❑ Unhappy   ❑ Poor   ❑ Good   ❑ Happy

2. Would you describe your home life as:
   ❑ Unhappy   ❑ Poor   ❑ Good   ❑ Happy

3. Would you describe your father as:
   ❑ Passive   ❑ Gregarious   ❑ Angry   ❑ Sad
   ❑ Manipulative   ❑ Strong   ❑ Gentle   ❑ Harsh
   ❑ Loving   ❑ Other

4. Did your father take time to play with you and your brothers and/or sisters?
   ❑ Yes   ❑ No

5. Was your father. . .
    ❑ Dictatorial   ❑ Indifferent   ❑ Interested in you
    ❑ Open   ❑ Tender   ❑ Protective

6. How important was TV to your father?
    ❑ Addicted to it
    ❑ Occasional viewer
    ❑ Seldom/Never watched

7. Are you afraid of becoming like your father?
    ❑ Yes   ❑ No
    Explain:

    _____

    _____

    _____

    _____

    _____

    _____

8. Would you describe your mother as:
    ❑ Passive   ❑ Gregarious   ❑ Angry   ❑ Sad
    ❑ Manipulative   ❑ Strong   ❑ Gentle   ❑ Harsh
    ❑ Loving   ❑ Other

9. Did your mother take time to play with you and your brothers and/or
    sisters?
    ❑ Yes   ❑ No

10. Was your mother. . .
    ❑ Dictatorial   ❑ Indifferent   ❑ Interested in you
    ❑ Open   ❑ Tender   ❑ Protective

11. How important was TV to your mother?
    ❏ Addicted to it
    ❏ Occasional viewer
    ❏ Seldom/Never watched

12. Are you afraid of becoming like your mother?
    ❏ Yes   ❏ No
    Explain:

    _____

    _____

    _____

    _____

    _____

    _____

13. What did you most enjoy doing as a child in a family setting?

    _____

    _____

    _____

    _____

    _____

14. Did your father and mother argue. . .
    ❏ Frequently   ❏ Seldom   ❏ Never

15. *a)* Would you classify your parents' economic status as. . .
    ❏ upper class   ❏ middle class   ❏ lower class

    b) What impact did their status have on you?

    _____

    _____

    _____

    _____

_____

_____

16. Are your parents living now?
    Mother: ❏ Yes   ❏ No
    Father: ❏ Yes   ❏ No

17. *a)* Describe your relationship with your father:

_____

_____

_____

_____

_____

_____

    b) . . . with your mother:

_____

_____

_____

_____

_____

_____

18. *a)* Did your father demonstrate affection toward your mother?
    ❏ Yes   ❏ No

    If so, how? If not, why not?

_____

_____

_____

_____

_____

b) Did your mother demonstrate affection toward your father?

❑ Yes ❑ No

If so, how? If not, why not?

_____

_____

_____

_____

_____

_____

19. Are you close to your brothers and sisters?

❑ Yes ❑ No

Explain:

_____

_____

_____

_____

_____

20. *a)* Were you teased as a child?

❑ Yes ❑ No

b) If so, about what?

_____

_____

_____

_____

_____

c) Who teased you the most?

_____

_____

_____

d) What was your emotional response?

_____

_____

_____

_____

21. *a)* Were you ever abused sexually as a child by anyone in your family? Did anyone in your family ever look at you lustfully, tease you, touch you or engage you in any type of behavior which exposed you to his or her sexuality?

❑ Yes ❑ No

b) Did anyone else abuse you by exposing you to adult sexual behavior during your childhood?

❑ Yes ❑ No

c) If you answered yes to either of the above questions, how has childhood sexual abuse affected you and your relationships with others, including God?

_____

_____

_____

_____

_____

_____

_____

_____

_____

_____

_____

22. *a)*   To your knowledge, was either of your parents sexually abused as a child?
❑ Yes   ❑ No

b)   If so, how has this affected you and your relationships with others, including God?

_____

_____

_____

_____

_____

_____

_____

_____

_____

_____

23. *a)*   Did you ever try to manipulate your parents to get attention or special treatment?
❑ Yes   ❑ No

b)   If so, how?

_____

_____

_____

24. *a)*   Did your parents agree with each other on how to discipline you?
❑ Yes   ❑ No

b)   Describe how you were disciplined as a child:

_____

_____

_____

25. *a)* Did you ever have any serious illness as a child?

❑ Yes   ❑ No

b) If so, how did this affect you and your relationships with your parents and siblings?

_____

_____

_____

_____

_____

_____

25. Was there anything about you for which your parents communicated consistent disapproval? If so, what? Why?

_____

_____

_____

_____

_____

_____

26. *a)* Are there any periods of your life you cannot remember?

❑ Yes   ❑ No

b) If so, can you identify those periods and any significant events that occurred just before or after them?

_____

_____

_____

_____

_____

27. *a)* Which parent did you most enjoy being with as a child?

❏ Father   ❏ Mother

b) Why?

_____

_____

_____

_____

28. Has this exercise prompted any personal feelings about your home life? If so, describe them:

_____

_____

_____

_____

_____

_____

_____

_____

Observations and Analysis

Imagine that you are a consultant in family relationships. You have just reviewed the answers written in step 6, and have been asked to give an impartial analysis to your professional colleagues about this family. Write out your conclusions, using a separate piece of paper if necessary.

29. What are the strengths of this family?

_____

_____

_____

_____

_____

_____

_____

30. What are some of the difficulties of this family?

_____

_____

_____

_____

_____

_____

_____

31. Describe the relationship of the husband and wife:

_____

_____

_____

_____

_____

_____

_____

_____

32. Describe the father's relationship with each child:

_____

_____

_____

_____

_____

_____

_____

_____

33. Describe the mother's relationship with each child:

_____

_____

_____

_____

_____

_____

_____

34. How was the character of God modeled by these parents?

_____

_____

_____

_____

_____

_____

35. How did these parents distort God's character?

_____

_____

_____

_____

_____

_____

Step 7

The Names of God

The more we understand God's character, the more we will trust Him. The various names of God given throughout the Bible reveal a specific aspect of His character. Though today's translations usually don't use these descriptive names, it is helpful for us to study them so that we can apply specific characteristics of God to our specific needs. This step is designed to facilitate that study.

Chapter 12 lists and describes God's different names. Read through that chapter again and write a definition for each of God's names in the spaces provided in this step. Then describe a circumstance in your life (present, past or future) when each name and characteristic would help you with an application for today.

For example:

ELOHIM
Definition: unlimited strength, energy, might and power; to make a covenant.
Circumstances: *When I entered salvation, I realized that God had promised to forgive me and make me His child if I would accept Christ's death as the payment for my sins. I realized that my faith could be based on His promise.*
Application: *I need the Lord to give me strength to relate to my boss in a way that honors Him. He has promised to provide the wisdom and strength I need.*

ELOHIM

Definition: _____

_____

Circumstances: _____

_____

_____

_____

_____

_____

Application: _____

_____

JEHOVAH

Definition: _____

_____

Circumstances: _____

_____

_____

_____

_____

_____

Application: _____

_____

ADONAI

Definition: _____

_____

Circumstances: _____

_____

_____

_____

_____

_____

Application: _____

_____

EL SHADDAI

Definition: _____

_____

Circumstances: _____

_____

_____

_____

_____

_____

Application: _____

_____

EL ELYON

Definition: _____

_____

Circumstances: _____

_____

_____

_____

_____

_____

Application: _____

_____

EL OLAM

Definition: _____

_____

Circumstances: _____

_____

_____

_____

_____

_____

Application: _____

_____

EL ROI

Definition: _____

_____

Circumstances: _____

_____

_____

_____

_____

_____

Application: _____

_____

JEHOVAH-JIREH

Definition: _____

_____

Circumstances: _____

_____

_____

_____

_____

_____

Application: _____

_____

JEHOVAH-NISSI

Definition: _____

_____

Circumstances: _____

_____

_____

_____

_____

_____

Application: _____

_____

JEHOVAH-TSIDKENU

Definition: _____

_____

Circumstances: _____

_____

_____

_____

_____

_____

Application: _____

_____

JEHOVAH-RAAH

Definition: _____
_____

Circumstances: _____
_____
_____
_____
_____
_____

Application: _____
_____

JEHOVAH-RAPHA

Definition: _____
_____

Circumstances: _____
_____
_____
_____
_____
_____

Application: _____
_____

JEHOVAH-SHALOM

Definition: _____
_____

Circumstances: _____
_____
_____

_____
_____
_____

Application: _____

JEHOVAH-SABBAOTH

Definition: _____
_____

Circumstances: _____

_____
_____
_____
_____
_____

Application: _____
_____

JEHOVAH-SHAMMAH

Definition: _____
_____

Circumstances: _____

_____
_____
_____
_____
_____

Application: _____
_____

Which of God's names is most meaningful to you? _____

Why? _____
_____
_____
_____
_____
_____
_____
_____

How will you apply that name to your circumstances today?

_____
_____
_____
_____
_____
_____
_____
_____

It will be helpful for you to use these names for God as you pray.

Step 8

In addition to providing the different names of God, many passages of Scripture highlight certain aspects of our relationship with Him. Psalm 139 is a perfect example. This psalm describes God's character in a number of ways. Studying it can help you understand how His omniscience, omnipresence and omnipotence apply to you and your circumstances. (Some people underline passages of Scripture that are particularly meaningful to them. This is a good habit because it reinforces what they are learning. Why not use your pencil and your Bible as you study this psalm?)

We will examine a few verses of this psalm at a time. Then we will ask questions to promote reflection and application.

God Knows Me Thoroughly

Verses 1-4 (NIV): *O Lord, you have searched me and you know me. You know when I sit and when I rise; you perceive my thoughts from afar. You discern my going out and my lying down; you are familiar with all my ways. Before a word is on my tongue you know it completely, O Lord.*

1. God always knows everything about you. You can keep no secrets from Him,
    yet He loves you unconditionally! How does this make you feel?

    _____

    _____

2. In what ways does God's omniscience give you courage and strength?

    _____

    _____

    _____

    _____

    _____

He Protects Me

   Verses 5-6 (NIV): *You hem me in—behind and before; you have laid
   your hand upon me. Such knowledge is too wonderful for me, too lofty
   for me to attain.*

1. God's perfect knowledge about you enables Him to protect you (to hem you in).
    From what do you need His protection?

    _____

    _____

    _____

    _____

    _____

2. Is it difficult for you to understand the Lord's omniscience? Why or why not?

    _____

    _____

    _____

    _____

He Is Always Present

Verses 7-12 (NIV): *Where can I go from your Spirit? Where can I flee from your presence? If I go up to the heavens, you are there; if I make my bed in the depths [Hebrew Sheol], you are there. If I rise on the wings of the dawn, if I settle on the far side of the sea, even there your hand will guide me, your right hand will hold me fast. If I say, "Surely the darkness will hide me and the light become night around me," even the darkness will not be dark to you; the night will shine like the day, for darkness is as light to you.*

3. The most important assurance to one who has strayed is that he is not lost! How close is God to you?

_____

4. How close does He seem to be?

_____

_____

5. How far can you get from Him?

_____

He Is a Sovereign Creator

Verses 13-15 (NIV): *For you created my inmost being; you knit me together in my mother's womb. I praise you because I am fearfully and wonderfully made; your works are wonderful, I know that full well. My frame was not hidden from you when I was made in the secret place. When I was woven together in the depths of the earth. . . .*

6. Who is responsible for the creation of your body?

_____

7. a) Can you rejoice that you look exactly the way the Father wants you to look?

_____

b)   If so, why?

_____

_____

_____

_____

_____

c)   If not, why not?

_____

_____

_____

_____

_____

d)   How do you normally respond to your appearance?

_____

_____

_____

_____

_____

e)   How does your perception of your appearance affect your self-image?

_____

_____

_____

_____

_____

8.   Do you consider (or worry) about what other people think of your appearance? Why or why not?

_____

_____

_____

_____

9. How could this psalm help free you from the fear of what others think of you?

_____

_____

_____

_____

God Has a Plan for You

Verse 16 (NIV): *Your eyes saw my unformed body. All the days ordained for me were written in your book before one of them came to be.*

10. Describe any comfort you gain from knowing that God has a plan for your life:

_____

_____

_____

11. List as many obvious aspects of God's plan for your life as you can think of.

Examples:

- *He wants me to have a relationship with Him through His Son, Jesus Christ* (John 3:16-18).
- *He wants to provide for my welfare, and give me a future and a hope* (Jer. 29:11).
- *He wants to give me things that will be good for me* (Matt. 7:7-11).

_____

_____

_____

_____

_____

_____

_____

God Is Constant and Consistent

Verses 17-18 (NIV): *How precious to me are your thoughts, O God! How vast is the sum of them! Were I to count them, they would outnumber the grains of sand. When I awake, I am still with you.*

12. The Lord is infinite and He is thinking about you all the time! How does that fact comfort and encourage you?

_____

_____

_____

_____

_____

Our Response

Verses 23-24 (NIV): *Search me, O God, and know my heart; test me and know my anxious thoughts. See if there is any offensive way in me, and lead me in the way everlasting.*

Openness to God's correction and guidance is the way the psalmist responds to the secure position he has with God. You also can have a secure position with God through Jesus Christ, who died to pay for your sins and rose from the dead to give you new life.

13. Are you open to God's correction and guidance? Why or why not?

_____

_____

_____

Conclusion:

You have taken another step toward developing a special, distinct category for your relationship with God. In addition to knowing Him by His name, you're becoming familiar with His ways. That's just a start! Think of how many years and experiences it took for you to create a category for earthly fathers. A strong and accurate understanding of your heavenly Father will require prayer and study, as well as time and experience with Him.

Step 9

Children of God

Being a child of God is the greatest privilege anyone can experience, yet we often use the term flippantly, without reflecting on what it means. This step is designed to help you reflect on the truths of your identity as God's child.

The Basis of Our Relationship with Him

Look at each of the following passages and describe what was true of you before you became a child of God and what is true of you now as God's child.

1. Col. 1:19-22

> *For it was the Father's good pleasure for all the fulness to dwell in Him,*
>
> *and through Him to reconcile all things to Himself, having made peace through the blood of His cross; through Him, I say, whether things on earth or things in heaven.*
>
> *And although you were formerly alienated and hostile in mind, engaged in evil deeds,*
>
> *yet He has now reconciled you in His fleshly body through death, in order to present you before Him holy and blameless and beyond reproach. . . .*

a) Before:

_____

_____

_____

b) Now:

_____

_____

_____

2.   Rom. 5:6-11

  For while we were still helpless, at the right time Christ died for the ungodly.

  For one will hardly die for a righteous man; though perhaps for the good man someone would dare even to die.

  But God demonstrates His own love toward us, in that while we were yet sinners, Christ died for us.

  Much more then, having now been justified by His blood, we shall be saved from the wrath of God through Him.

  For if while we were enemies, we were reconciled to God through the death of His Son, much more, having been reconciled, we shall be saved by His life.

  And not only this, but we also exult in God through our Lord Jesus Christ, through whom we have now received the reconciliation.

a) Before:

_____

_____

_____

b) Now:

_____

_____

3.   Titus 3:3-7

> *For we also once were foolish ourselves, disobedient, deceived, enslaved to various lusts and pleasures, spending our life in malice and envy, hateful, hating one another.*
>
> *But when the kindness of God our Savior and His love for mankind appeared,*
>
> *He saved us, not on the basis of deeds which we have done in righteousness, but according to His mercy, by the washing of regeneration and renewing by the Holy Spirit,*
>
> *whom He poured out upon us richly through Jesus Christ our Savior,*
>
> *that being justified by His grace we might be made heirs according to the hope of eternal life.*

a)   Before:

_____

_____

_____

b)   Now:

_____

_____

_____

The Nature of Our Relationship with Him

Paraphrase each passage, then describe God's role in the relationship and our response to Him.

4.   Rom. 8:14-17

> *For all who are being led by the Spirit of God, these are sons of God.*
>
> *For you have not received a spirit of slavery leading to fear again, but you have received a spirit of adoption as sons by which we cry out, "Abba! Father!"*

The Spirit Himself bears witness with our spirit that we are children of God,

and if children, heirs also, heirs of God and fellow heirs with Christ, if indeed we suffer with Him in order that we may also be glorified with Him.

a) Paraphrase:

_____

_____

_____

_____

_____

b) God's Role:

_____

_____

_____

c) Our Response:

_____

_____

_____

5.   1 John 3:1-3

See how great a love the Father has bestowed upon us, that we should be called children of God; and such we are. For this reason the world does not know us, because it did not know Him.

Beloved, now we are children of God, and it has not appeared as yet what we shall be. We know that, when He appears, we shall be like Him, because we shall see Him just as He is.

And everyone who has this hope fixed on Him purifies himself, just as He is pure.

a) Paraphrase:

_____

_____

_____

_____

_____

b) God's Role:

_____

_____

_____

c) Our Response:

_____

_____

_____

6. Matt. 7:7-11

> *Ask, and it shall be given to you; seek, and you shall find; knock, and it shall be opened to you.*
>
> *For everyone who asks receives, and he who seeks finds, and to him who knocks it shall be opened.*
>
> *Or what man is there among you, when his son shall ask him for a loaf, will give him a stone?*
>
> *Or if he shall ask for a fish, he will not give him a snake, will he?*
>
> *If you then, being evil, know how to give good gifts to your children, how much more shall your Father who is in heaven give what is good to those who ask Him!*

a) Paraphrase:

_____

_____

_____

_____

b)   God's Role:

_____

_____

_____

c)   Our Response:

_____

_____

_____

7.   Eph. 2:11-22

Therefore remember, that formerly you, the Gentiles in the flesh, who are called "Uncircumcision" by the so-called "Circumcision," which is performed in the flesh by human hands—

remember that you were at that time separate from Christ, excluded from the commonwealth of Israel, and strangers to the covenants of promise, having no hope and without God in the world.

But now in Christ Jesus you who formerly were far off have been brought near by the blood of Christ.

For He Himself is our peace, who made both groups into one, and broke down the barrier of the dividing wall,

by abolishing in His flesh the enmity, which is the Law of commandments contained in ordinances, that in Himself He might make the two into one new man, thus establishing peace,

and might reconcile them both in one body to God through the cross, by it having put to death the enmity.

And He came and preached peace to you who were far away, and peace to those who were near;

for through Him we both have our access in one Spirit to the Father.

So then you are no longer strangers and aliens, but you are fellow citizens with the saints, and are of God's household,

having been built upon the foundation of the apostles and prophets, Christ Jesus Himself being the corner stone,

*in whom the whole building, being fitted together is growing into
a holy temple in the Lord;*

*in whom you also are being built together into a dwelling of God
in the Spirit.*

a) Paraphrase:

_____
_____
_____
_____
_____
_____
_____
_____
_____

b) God's Role:

_____
_____
_____

c) Our Response:

_____
_____
_____

Conclusion

8. Write a summary paragraph about God's role in your relationship with Him.
   What has He accomplished? How does He feel and act toward you?

_____
_____
_____
_____

_____

_____

_____

_____

9. How have you perceived God in the past?

_____

_____

_____

_____

_____

10. Has this study begun to change this perception? If so, how?

_____

_____

_____

_____

_____

_____

11. How can you respond to the Lord more appropriately this week? Be specific.

_____

_____

_____

_____

_____

_____

_____

_____

Step 10

Characteristics of Christ and Our Relationship with Him

How can we know what God is like? How can we begin to comprehend the immensity of His love, forgiveness and power so that we can actually experience His grace, compassion and supernatural strength in all of our circumstances? By understanding and applying the truth of God's Word!

The Scriptures are our guide for living. They communicate clearly and powerfully mankind's predicament and the Lord's solution. Each of us needs to develop strong, biblical convictions about the nature of God so that we base our attitudes and actions on His constant love and power instead of on the fickle behavior and approval of others.

This study is designed to help you develop a better understanding of Christ's character through Scripture. To help you think through each passage and consider what it means, we want you to paraphrase the passages in the space provided. Remember the goal is not to "fill in the blanks," but to reflect on the powerful truth of God's Word. That takes time. Be thorough with this exercise. You may want to complete one characteristic per day until you finish the study. That will give you more time to think both about the meaning of each passage and how you can apply it in your daily experience.

On the following pages are eight characteristics of Christ and how we relate to Him. Take plenty of time to reflect on these passages as you paraphrase them.

Purpose

When Adam sinned, he brought both the burden and the penalty of sin upon all mankind. As a result, man is by nature rebellious against God, separated from Him and deserving of His wrath.

> *Or do you think lightly of the riches of His kindness and forbearance and patience, not knowing that the kindness of God leads you to repentance?*
>
> *But because of your stubbornness and unrepentant heart you are storing up wrath for yourself in the day of wrath and revelation of the righteous judgment of God. . . .*
>
> Rom. 2:4-5

Paraphrase:

_____

_____

_____

_____

> *And you were dead in your trespasses and sins,*
>
> *in which you formerly walked according to the course of this world, according to the prince of the power of the air, of the spirit that is now working in the sons of disobedience.*
>
> *Among them we too all formerly lived in the lusts of our flesh, indulging the desires of the flesh and of the mind, and were by nature children of wrath, even as the rest.*
>
> Eph. 2:1-3

Paraphrase:

_____

_____

But God, who created man for fellowship with Him, also created a plan whereby we can be united with Him. He sent His Son to die in our place, and through Christ's death, averted His wrath toward us and made a provision for us to enjoy an eternal relationship with Him.

Christ's purpose, then, was to glorify the Father by accomplishing the work He was sent to do:

> *And this is eternal life, that they may know Thee, the only true God, and Jesus Christ whom Thou hast sent.*
> *I glorified Thee on the earth, having accomplished the work which Thou hast given Me to do.*
>
> John 17:3-4

Paraphrase:

_____

_____

> *For Christ also died for sins once for all, the just for the unjust, in order that he might bring us to God. . . .*
>
> 1 Pet. 3:18

Paraphrase:

_____

_____

> *For the grace of God has appeared, bringing salvation to all men,*
> *instructing us to deny ungodliness and worldly desires and to live sensibly, righteously and godly in the present age,*
> *looking for the blessed hope and appearing of the glory of our great God and Savior, Christ Jesus;*
> *who gave Himself for us, that He might redeem us from every lawless deed and purify for Himself a people for His own possession, zealous for good deeds.*
>
> Titus 2:11-14

Paraphrase:

_____

_____

_____

    As we experience Christ's grace and love, our purposes will increasingly reflect our privilege and calling to know Him, love Him and serve Him as His ambassadors.

> *But when the Pharisees heard that He had put the Sadducees to silence, they gathered themselves together.*
> *And one of them, a lawyer, asked Him a question, testing Him,*
> *"Teacher, which is the great commandment in the Law?"*
> *And He said to him, "'You shall love the Lord your God with all your heart, and with all your soul, and with all your mind.'*
> *"This is the great and foremost commandment.*
> *"And a second is like it, 'You shall love your neighbor as yourself.'*
> *"On these two commandments depend the whole Law and the Prophets."*
>
> Matt. 22:34-40

Paraphrase:

_____

_____

_____

_____

> *But whatever things were gain to me, those things I have counted as loss for the sake of Christ.*
> *More than that, I count all things to be loss in view of the surpassing value of knowing Christ Jesus my Lord, for whom I have suffered the loss of all things, and count them but rubbish in order that I may gain Christ,*
> *and may be found in Him, not having a righteousness of my own*

derived from the Law, but that which is through faith in Christ, the righteousness which comes from God on the basis of faith,

that I may know Him, and the power of His resurrection and the fellowship of His sufferings, being conformed to His death. . . .

                                     Phil. 3:7-10

Paraphrase:

_____

_____

_____

_____

Now all these things are from God, who reconciled us to Himself through Christ, and gave us the ministry of reconciliation,

namely, that God was in Christ reconciling the world to Himself, not counting their trespasses against them, and He has committed to us the word of reconciliation.

Therefore, we are ambassadors for Christ, as though God were entreating through us; we beg you on behalf of Christ, be reconciled to God.

He made Him who knew no sin to be sin on our behalf, that we might become the righteousness of God in Him.

                                     2 Cor. 5:18-21

Paraphrase:

_____

_____

_____

_____

For the love of Christ controls us, having concluded this, that one died for all, therefore all died;

and He died for all, that they who live should no longer live for themselves, but for Him who died and rose again on their behalf.

                                     2 Cor. 5:14-15

Paraphrase:

_____

_____

_____

_____

> *Therefore also we have as our ambition, whether at home or absent, to be pleasing to Him.*
>
> 2 Cor. 5:9

Paraphrase:

_____

_____

_____

> *For we are His workmanship, created in Christ Jesus for good works, which God prepared beforehand, that we should walk in them.*
>
> Eph. 2:10

Paraphrase:

_____

_____

_____

> *And Jesus came up and spoke to them, saying, "All authority has been given to Me in heaven and on earth.*
>
> *"Go therefore and make disciples of all the nations, baptizing them in the name of the Father and the Son and the Holy Spirit,*
>
> *teaching them to observe all that I commanded you; and lo, I am with you always, even to the end of the age."*
>
> Matt. 28:18-20

Paraphrase:

_____

_____

_____

Unconditional love

Sacrificing His only Son's life on our behalf is overwhelming evidence of God's love for us.

> By this the love of God was manifested in us, that God has sent His only begotten Son into the world so that we might live through Him.
> In this is love, not that we loved God, but that He loved us and sent His Son to be the propitiation for our sins.
>
> 1 John 4:9-10

Paraphrase:

_____

_____

_____

> For God so loved the world, that He gave His only begotten Son, that whoever believes in Him should not perish, but have eternal life.
> For God did not send the Son into the world to judge the world, but that the world should be saved through Him.
> He who believes in Him is not judged; he who does not believe has been judged already, because he has not believed in the name of the only begotten Son of God.
>
> John 3:16-18

Paraphrase:

_____

_____

_____

_____

But God, being rich in mercy, because of His great love with which He loved us,

even when we were dead in our transgressions, made us alive together with Christ (by grace you have been saved),

and raised us up with Him, and seated us with Him in the heavenly places, in Christ Jesus,

in order that in the ages to come He might show the surpassing riches of His grace in kindness toward us in Christ Jesus.

For by grace you have been saved through faith; and that not of yourselves, it is the gift of God;

not as a result of works, that no one should boast.

Eph. 2:4-9

Paraphrase:

_____

_____

_____

Now may our Lord Jesus Christ Himself and God our Father, who has loved us and given us eternal comfort and good hope by grace,

comfort and strengthen your hearts in every good work and word.

2 Thess. 2:16-17

Paraphrase:

_____

_____

For I am convinced that neither death, nor life, nor angels, nor principalities, nor things present, nor things to come, nor powers,

nor height, nor depth, nor any other created thing, shall be able to separate us from the love of God, which is in Christ Jesus our Lord.

Rom. 8:38-39

Paraphrase:

_____

_____

_____

    As we grasp the truth of God's unconditional love, we are able to love others unconditionally.

Complete forgiveness

    Our sins separated us from God.

> *What then? Are we better than they? Not at all; for we have already charged that both Jews and Greeks are all under sin;*
> *as it is written, "There is none righteous, not even one;*
> *there is none who understands, there is none who seeks for God;*
> *all have turned aside, together they have become useless; there is none who does good, there is not even one."*
> *"Their throat is an open grave, with their tongues they keep deceiving," "The poison of asps is under their lips";*
> *"Whose mouth is full of cursing and bitterness";*
> *"Their feet are swift to shed blood,*
> *destruction and misery are in their paths,*
> *and the path of peace have they not known."*
> *"There is no fear of God before their eyes."*
> *Now we know that whatever the Law says, it speaks to those who are under the Law, that every mouth may be closed, and all the world may become accountable to God;*
> *because by the works of the Law no flesh will be justified in His sight; for through the Law comes the knowledge of sin.*
>
> Rom. 3:9-20

Paraphrase:

_____

_____

_____

_____

_____

But Christ's death completely paid our debt of sin so that we are completely forgiven.

> *And when you were dead in your transgressions and the uncircumcision of your flesh, He made you alive together with Him, having forgiven us all our transgressions,*
>
> *having canceled out the certificate of debt consisting of decrees against us and which was hostile to us; and He has taken it out of the way, having nailed it to the cross.*
>
> Col. 2:13-14

Paraphrase:

_____

_____

_____

> *For while we were still helpless, at the right time Christ died for the ungodly.*
>
> *For one will hardly die for a righteous man; though perhaps for the good man someone would dare even to die.*
>
> *But God demonstrates His own love toward us, in that while we were yet sinners, Christ died for us.*
>
> *Much more then, having now been justified by His blood, we shall be saved from the wrath of God through Him.*
>
> *For if while we were enemies, we were reconciled to God through the death of His Son, much more, having been reconciled, we shall be saved by His life.*
>
> *And not only this, but we also exult in God through our Lord Jesus Christ, through whom we have now received the reconciliation.*
>
> Rom. 5:6-11

Paraphrase:

_____

_____

_____

_____

*In Him we have redemption through His blood, the forgiveness of
our trespasses, according to the riches of His grace. . . .*

Eph. 1:7

Paraphrase:

_____

_____

And you were dead in your trespasses and sins,

*in which you formerly walked according to the course of this world,
according to the prince of the power of the air, of the spirit that is now
working in the sons of disobedience.*

*Among them we too all formerly lived in the lusts of our flesh,
indulging the desires of the flesh and of the mind, and were by nature
children of wrath, even as the rest.*

*But God, being rich in mercy, because of His great love with which
He loved us,*

*even when we were dead in our transgressions, made us alive
together with Christ (by grace you have been saved),*

*and raised us up with Him, and seated us with Him in the heavenly
places, in Christ Jesus,*

*in order that in the ages to come He might show the surpassing
riches of His grace in kindness toward us in Christ Jesus.*

*For by grace you have been saved through faith; and that not of
yourselves, it is the gift of God;*

not as a result of works, that no one should boast.

*For we are His workmanship, created in Christ Jesus for good
works, which God prepared beforehand, that we should walk in them.*

Eph. 2:1-10

Paraphrase:

_____

_____

_____

_____

> *. . . for all have sinned and fall short of the glory of God,*
> *being justified as a gift by His grace through the redemption which*
> *is in Christ Jesus. . . .*
>
> Rom. 3:23-24

Paraphrase:

_____

_____

_____

> *Now to the one who works, his wage is not reckoned as a favor, but*
> *as what is due.*
> *But to the one who does not work, but believes in Him who justifies*
> *the ungodly, his faith is reckoned as righteousness. . . .*
>
> Rom. 4:4-5

Paraphrase:

_____

_____

_____

Because we are forgiven by God, we can forgive others.

> *. . . bearing with one another, and forgiving each other, whoever*
> *has a complaint against anyone; just as the Lord forgave you, so also*
> *should you.*
>
> Col. 3:13

Paraphrase:

_____

_____

Then Peter came and said to Him, "Lord, how often shall my brother sin against me and I forgive him? Up to seven times?"

Jesus said to him, "I do not say to you, up to seven times, but up to seventy times seven.

"For this reason the kingdom of heaven may be compared to a certain king who wished to settle accounts with his slaves.

"And when he had begun to settle them, there was brought to him one who owed him ten thousand talents.

"But since he did not have the means to repay, his lord commanded him to be sold, along with his wife and children and all that he had, and repayment to be made.

"The slave therefore falling down, prostrated himself before him, saying, 'Have patience with me, and I will repay you everything.'

"And the lord of that slave felt compassion and released him and forgave him the debt.

"But that slave went out and found one of his fellow slaves who owed him a hundred denarii; and he seized him and began to choke him, saying, 'Pay back what you owe.'

"So his fellow slave fell down and began to entreat him, saying, 'Have patience with me and I will repay you.'

"He was unwilling however, but went and threw him in prison until he should pay back what was owed.

"So when his fellow slaves saw what had happened, they were deeply grieved and came and reported to their lord all that had happened.

"Then summoning him, his lord said to him, 'You wicked slave, I forgave you all that debt because you entreated me.

"Should you not also have had mercy on your fellow slave, even as I had mercy on you?'

"And his lord, moved with anger, handed him over to the torturers until he should repay all that was owed him.

"So shall My heavenly Father also do to you, if each of you does not forgive his brother from your heart."

Matt. 18:21-35

Paraphrase:

_____

_____

_____

_____

_____

_____

Total acceptance

Because of our sins, we were enemies of God.

For if while we were enemies, we were reconciled to God through the death of His Son, much more, having been reconciled, we shall be saved by His life.

Rom. 5:10

Paraphrase:

_____

_____

_____

Christ's payment for our sins took away the barrier between Him and us so that we are now His beloved children and His beloved friends.

For you have not received a spirit of slavery leading to fear again, but you have received a spirit of adoption as sons by which we cry out, "Abba! Father!"

The Spirit Himself bears witness with our spirit that we are children of God,

and if children, heirs also, heirs of God and fellow heirs with Christ, if indeed we suffer with Him in order that we may also be glorified with Him.

Rom. 8:15-17

Paraphrase:

_____

_____

_____

. . . in order that He might redeem those who were under the Law, that we might receive the adoption as sons.

And because you are sons, God has sent forth the Spirit of His Son into our hearts, crying, "Abba! Father!"

Therefore you are no longer a slave, but a son; and if a son, then an heir through God.

Gal. 4:5-7

Paraphrase:

_____

_____

_____

For it was the Father's good pleasure for all the fulness to dwell in Him,

and through Him to reconcile all things to Himself, having made peace through the blood of His cross; through Him, I say, whether things on earth or things in heaven.

And although you were formerly alienated and hostile in mind, engaged in evil deeds, yet He has now reconciled you in His fleshly body through death, in order to present you before Him holy and blameless and beyond reproach. . . .

Col. 1:19-22

Paraphrase:

_____

_____

_____

_____

. . . I in them, and Thou in Me, that they may be perfected in unity, that the world may know that Thou didst send Me, and didst love them, even as Thou didst love Me.

Father, I desire that they also, whom Thou hast given Me, be with Me where I am, in order that they may behold My glory, which Thou hast given Me; for Thou didst love Me before the foundation of the world.

John 17:23-24

Paraphrase:

_____

_____

_____

Jesus said to her, "Stop clinging to Me, for I have not yet ascended to the Father; but go to My brethren, and say to them, 'I ascend to My Father and your Father, and My God and your God.'"

John 20:17

Paraphrase:

_____

_____

_____

Because we are totally accepted by God, we can accept others unconditionally.

> *Wherefore, accept one another, just as Christ also accepted us to the glory of God.*
>
> Rom. 15:7

Paraphrase:

_____

_____

Authority and power

Christ has infinite authority and power.

> *And He is the image of the invisible God, the first-born of all creation.*
>
> *For by Him all things were created, both in the heavens and on earth, visible and invisible, whether thrones or dominions or rulers or authorities—all things have been created by Him and for Him.*
>
> *And He is before all things, and in Him all things hold together.*
>
> *He is also the head of the body, the church; and He is the beginning, the first-born from the dead; so that He Himself might come to have first place in everything.*
>
> *For it was the Father's good pleasure for all the fulness to dwell in Him,*
>
> *and through Him to reconcile all things to Himself, having made peace through the blood of His cross; through Him, I say, whether things on earth or things in heaven.*
>
> Col. 1:15-20

Paraphrase:

_____

_____

_____

_____

_____

When He had disarmed the rulers and authorities, He made a public display of them, having triumphed over them through Him.

Col. 2:15

Paraphrase:

_____

_____

I pray that the eyes of your heart may be enlightened, so that you may know what is the hope of His calling, what are the riches of the glory of His inheritance in the saints,

and what is the surpassing greatness of His power toward us who believe. These are in accordance with the working of the strength of His might

which He brought about in Christ, when He raised Him from the dead, and seated Him at His right hand in the heavenly places,

far above all rule and authority and power and dominion, and every name that is named, not only in this age, but also in the one to come.

And He put all things in subjection under His feet, and gave Him as head over all things to the church,

which is His body, the fulness of Him who fills all in all.

Eph. 1:18-23

Paraphrase:

_____

_____

_____

_____

I planted, Apollos watered, but God was causing the growth.

So then neither the one who plants nor the one who waters is anything, but God who causes the growth.

1 Cor. 3:6-7

Paraphrase:

_____

_____

And such confidence we have through Christ toward God.

Not that we are adequate in ourselves to consider anything as coming from ourselves, but our adequacy is from God,

who also made us adequate as servants of a new covenant, not of the letter, but of the Spirit; for the letter kills, but the Spirit gives life.

2 Cor. 3:4-6

Paraphrase:

_____

_____

_____

Finally, be strong in the Lord, and in the strength of His might.

Put on the full armor of God, that you may be able to stand firm against the schemes of the devil.

For our struggle is not against flesh and blood, but against the rulers, against the powers, against the world forces of this darkness, against the spiritual forces of wickedness in the heavenly places.

Therefore, take up the full armor of God, that you may be able to resist in the evil day, and having done everything, to stand firm.

Stand firm therefore, having girded your loins with truth, and having put on the breastplate of righteousness, and having shod your feet with the preparation of the gospel of peace;

in addition to all, taking up the shield of faith with which you will be able to extinguish all the flaming missiles of the evil one.

And take the helmet of salvation, and the sword of the Spirit, which is the word of God.

With all prayer and petition pray at all times in the Spirit, and with this in view, be on the alert with all perseverance and petition for all the saints,

and pray on my behalf, that utterance may be given to me in the opening of my mouth, to make known with boldness the mystery of the gospel,

for which I am an ambassador in chains; that in proclaiming it I may speak boldly, as I ought to speak.

Eph. 6:10-20

Paraphrase:

_____

_____

_____

_____

_____

_____

Hope

There is no hope of forgiveness and reconciliation to God apart from Christ.

. . . remember that you were at that time separate from Christ, excluded from the commonwealth of Israel, and strangers to the covenants of promise, having no hope and without God in the world.

Eph. 2:12

Paraphrase:

_____

_____

Christ's love, forgiveness and power give us hope for new life.

This hope we have as an anchor of the soul, a hope both sure and steadfast and one which enters within the veil. . . .

Heb. 6:19

Paraphrase:

_____

_____

Blessed be the God and Father of our Lord Jesus Christ, who according to His great mercy has caused us to be born again to a living hope through the resurrection of Jesus Christ from the dead. . . .

1 Pet. 1:3

Paraphrase:

_____

_____

_____

. . . that being justified by His grace we might be made heirs according to the hope of eternal life.

Titus 3:7

Paraphrase:

_____

_____

And not only this, but we also exult in our tribulations, knowing that tribulation brings about perseverance;

and perseverance, proven character; and proven character, hope;

and hope does not disappoint, because the love of God has been poured out within our hearts through the Holy Spirit who was given to us.

Rom. 5:3-5

Paraphrase:

_____

_____

_____

_____

> *And we know that God causes all things to work together for good to those who love God, to those who are called according to His purpose.*
>
> Rom. 8:28

Paraphrase:

_____

_____

_____

Faithfulness

Christ is always faithful to do what He has promised.

> *No temptation has overtaken you but such as is common to man; and God is faithful, who will not allow you to be tempted beyond what you are able, but with the temptation will provide the way of escape also, that you may be able to endure it.*
>
> 1 Cor. 10:13

Paraphrase:

_____

_____

_____

> *Faithful is He who calls you, and He also will bring it to pass.*
>
> 1 Thess. 5:24

Paraphrase:

_____

_____

Let us hold fast the confession of our hope without wavering, for He who promised is faithful. . . .

Heb. 10:23

Paraphrase:

_____

_____

Woe to you, scribes and Pharisees, hypocrites! For you tithe mint and dill and cummin, and have neglected the weightier provisions of the law: justice and mercy and faithfulness; but these are the things you should have done without neglecting the others.

Matt. 23:23

Paraphrase:

_____

_____

_____

It is a trustworthy statement: For if we died with Him, we shall also live with Him;

If we endure, we shall also reign with Him; If we deny Him, He also will deny us;

If we are faithless, He remains faithful; for He cannot deny Himself.

2 Tim. 2:11-13

Paraphrase:

_____

_____

_____

Wisdom

The Lord has all knowledge and all wisdom. He knows what is best for us, and He will give us wisdom to know how we can honor Him in every situation.

> *But if any of you lacks wisdom, let him ask of God, who gives to all men generously and without reproach, and it will be given to him.*
> *But let him ask in faith without any doubting, for the one who doubts is like the surf of the sea driven and tossed by the wind.*
>
> James 1:5-6

Paraphrase:

_____

_____

_____

> *The Son of Man came eating and drinking, and they say, "Behold, a gluttonous man and a drunkard, a friend of tax-gatherers and sinners!" Yet wisdom is vindicated by her deeds.*
>
> Matt. 11:19

Paraphrase:

_____

_____

> *And when I came to you, brethren, I did not come with superiority of speech or of wisdom, proclaiming to you the testimony of God.*
> *For I determined to know nothing among you except Jesus Christ, and Him crucified.*
> *And I was with you in weakness and in fear and in much trembling.*
> *And my message and my preaching were not in persuasive words of wisdom, but in demonstration of the Spirit and of power,*
> *that your faith should not rest on the wisdom of men, but on the power of God.*
>
> 1 Cor. 2:1-5

Paraphrase:

_____

_____

_____

> *For our proud confidence is this, the testimony of our conscience, that in holiness and godly sincerity, not in fleshly wisdom but in the grace of God, we have conducted ourselves in the world, and especially toward you.*
>
> 2 Cor. 1:12

Paraphrase:

_____

_____

_____

> *Therefore be careful how you walk, not as unwise men, but as wise, making the most of your time, because the days are evil.*
>
> *So then do not be foolish, but understand what the will of the Lord is.*
>
> *And do not get drunk with wine, for that is dissipation, but be filled with the Spirit,*
>
> *speaking to one another in psalms and hymns and spiritual songs, singing and making melody with your heart to the Lord;*
>
> *always giving thanks for all things in the name of our Lord Jesus Christ to God, even the Father;*
>
> *and be subject to one another in the fear of Christ.*
>
> Eph. 5:15-21

Paraphrase:

_____

_____

_____

_____

Which passage in each section has been most meaningful to you? List the passage and describe why it is so meaningful. Also describe how you can apply the truth of that passage in your life.

Purpose

_____

_____

_____

_____

_____

_____

Unconditional love

_____

_____

_____

_____

_____

Complete forgiveness

_____

_____

_____

_____

_____

Total acceptance

_____
_____
_____
_____
_____
_____
_____
_____

Authority and power

_____
_____
_____
_____
_____
_____
_____

Hope

_____
_____
_____
_____
_____
_____
_____

Faithfulness

_____
_____
_____
_____
_____
_____
_____
_____

Wisdom

_____
_____
_____
_____
_____
_____
_____
_____

Step 11

Motivations for Obedience

Our motivations for living in obedience to God are closely tied to how we perceive Him, just as a child's response to his parents is often determined by his view of them. If a child feels loved, accepted and protected, he will be more likely to respond to his parents with respect, love and joyful obedience. If, on the other hand, a child does not enjoy that kind of an environment, he will either rebel against his parents or try desperately to please them in an attempt to earn their love. This latter response is as unhealthy as rebellion.

As a person develops a more accurate concept of God and his identity as a child of God, his obedience to God will more often stem from proper motivations than from improper ones.

Before we examine proper and improper motivations for obedience in this step, we need to take a quick look at what it means to be under the heavenly Father's care. Paul wrote to the Christians in Rome:

> *For you have not received a spirit of slavery leading to fear again, but you have received a spirit of adoption as sons by which we cry out, "Abba! Father!"*

> Rom. 8:15

1. Imagine yourself as the slave of a cruel master. What would be some of your motivations to obey him?

_____

_____

_____

_____

_____

2. Now imagine yourself as the same slave under the ownership of a wealthy, kind and generous man who, having purchased you, then gives you your freedom. With this freedom, he also gives you a room in his mansion, his own clothes to wear and a seat next to him at his table for as long as you live. As a crowning gesture of his affection and commitment to you, he asks you to be one of his children. What would be some of your motivations to obey him?

_____

_____

_____

_____

3. Go back to step 5, "Your Parents' Influence on Your Perception of God." What are some characteristics of your father that you listed, both positive and negative?

_____

_____

_____

_____

4. Imagine that someone else had made this list of characteristics for his or her father. Would this person obey his or her father? (Try to be as objective as possible.)

    a) If so, explain why:

_____

_____

_____

b)   If not, explain why not:

_____

_____

_____

_____

The Lord is like the wealthy, kind and generous man who bought, freed and adopted the slave. His love for us and complete acceptance of us are based on grace, His unmerited favor, not on our ability to impress Him through our good deeds.

He is fully pleased with us as a result of Christ's death on our behalf. If this is true, then why should we desire to obey Him daily? In this step, will identify six biblical motivations for choosing to obey God rather than live in sin, rebellion and self-effort.[1] We will also examine some poor motivations for obeying God.

Six Reasons to Obey God

Christ's Love

When we experience love, we usually respond by seeking to express our love in return. Our obedience to God is an expression of our love for Him (John 14:15, 21), which comes from an understanding of what Christ has accomplished for us on the cross (2 Cor. 5:14-15). We love because He first loved us and clearly demonstrated His love for us at the cross (1 John 4:16-19).

This great motivating factor is missing in many of our lives because we don't really believe that God loves us unconditionally. We expect His love to be conditional, based on our ability to earn it.

Our experience of God's love is based on our perception. If we believe that He is demanding or aloof, we will not experience His love and tenderness. Instead, we will either be afraid of Him or angry with Him. Faulty perceptions of God often prompt us to rebel against Him.

Our image of God is the foundation for all of our motivations. As we grow in our understanding of His unconditional love and acceptance, we will increasingly want our lives to bring honor to the One who loves us so much.

1. *a)*   Does the love of Christ motivate you to obey Him? Why or why not?

_____

_____

_____

_____

Sin Is Destructive

Satan has effectively blinded man to the painful, damaging consequences of sin. The effects of sin are all around us, yet many continue to indulge in the pleasure-seeking and rampant self-centeredness that cause so much anguish and pain. Satan contradicted God in the Garden when he said, "You surely shall not die!" (Gen. 3:4). Sin is pleasant, but only for a season. Sooner or later, it will result in some form of destruction.

Sin is destructive in many ways. Emotionally, we can experience guilt and shame as well as the fears of failure and punishment. Mentally, we may experience painful flashbacks and expend enormous amounts of time and energy thinking about our sins and rationalizing our guilt. Physically, we may suffer psychosomatic disorders or a number of illnesses. Relationally, we can alienate ourselves from others. Spiritually, we grieve the Holy Spirit, lose our testimony and break our fellowship with God. The painful and destructive effects of sin are so profound that why we don't have an aversion to it is a mystery!

2. *a)*   Read the first chapter of Jonah. List the results of Jonah's choice of disobedience to God:

_____

_____

_____

_____

   b)   In what ways have you seen specific effects of a particular sin in your life?

_____

_____

_____

_____

c)   How can viewing sin as destructive be a motivation for obedience to God?

_____

_____

_____

_____

The Father's Discipline

Another purpose of the Holy Spirit is to convict us of sin. Conviction is a form of God's discipline, which serves as proof that we have become sons of God (Heb. 12:5-11). It warns us that we are making choices without regard to either God's truth or sin's consequences. If we choose to be unresponsive to the Holy Spirit, our heavenly Father will discipline us in love. Many people do not understand the difference between discipline and punishment. The following chart shows their profound contrasts:

	PUNISHMENT	DISCIPLINE
SOURCE:	God's Wrath	God's Love
PURPOSE:	To Avenge a Wrong	To Correct a Wrong
RELATIONAL RESULT:	Alienation	Reconciliation
PERSONAL RESULT:	Guilt	A Righteous Lifestyle
DIRECTED TOWARD:	Non-Believers	His Children

Jesus bore all the punishment we deserved on the cross; therefore, we no longer need to fear punishment from God for our sins. We should seek to do what is right so that our Father will not have to correct us through discipline, but when we are disciplined, we can remember that God is correcting us in love. His discipline leads us to righteous performance, which is a reflection of the righteousness of Christ.

3. *a)* Do you sometimes confuse God's correction with punishment? If so, why?

_____

_____

_____

  b) How can understanding God's discipline be a motivation for you to obey Him?

_____

_____

_____

God's Commands for Us Are Good

God's commands are given for two good purposes: to protect us from the destructiveness of sin, and to direct us in a life of joy and fruitfulness. We have a wrong perspective if we only view God's commands as restrictions in our lives. Instead we must realize that His commands are guidelines, given so that we might enjoy life to the fullest.

In addition, God's commands are holy, right and good. Therefore, since they have value in themselves, we should choose to obey God and follow His commands.

Avoid trying to keep God's commands by legalism and self-effort. That leads only to bitterness, condemnation and rigidity. The Holy Spirit will give you power, joy and creativity as you trust Him to fulfill the commands of God's Word through you.

4. *a)* Read Rom. 7:12 and 1 John 5:3. How are God's commands described?

_____

_____

_____

  b) Read Deut. 5:29; 6:24. What are some results of obeying God's commands?

_____

c)   How can viewing God's commands as good motivate you to obey them?

Our Obedience Will Be Rewarded

Our self-worth is not based on our performance and obedience; however, what we do (or don't do) has tremendous implications on the quality of our lives and our impact on others for Christ's sake. Disobedience results in spiritual poverty; a short-circuiting of intimate fellowship with the One who loves us so much that He died for us; confusion, guilt and frustration; and an absence of spiritual power and desire to see people won to Christ and become disciples. On the other hand, responding to the love, grace and power of Christ enables us to experience His love, joy and strength as we minister to others, endure difficulties and live for Him who has . . .*called us out of darkness into His marvelous light* (1 Pet. 2:9). We are completely loved, forgiven and accepted apart from our performance, but how we live is very important!

5.   *a)*   Read 1 Cor. 3:11-15; 2 Cor. 5:10; 1 John 4:17 and Rev. 20:11-15. According to these passages, unbelievers will be judged and condemned at the Great White Throne of Judgment for rejecting Christ. Though believers will be spared from this condemnation, we will stand before the Judgment Seat of Christ to have our deeds tested. Deeds done for the Lord will be honored, but deeds done for ourselves will be destroyed by fire. The Greek word to describe this judgment seat is the same word used to describe the platform on which an athlete stands to receive his wreath of victory for winning an event. The Judgment Seat is for the reward of good deeds, not for the punishment of sin.

The chart on the following page demonstrates some of the differences between the Judgment Seat of Christ and the Great White Throne of Judgment:

	JUDGMENT SEAT OF CHRIST	GREAT WHITE THRONE OF JUDGMENT
	(1 Cor. 3:11-15)	(Rev. 20:11-15)
WHO WILL APPEAR:	Christians	Non-Christians
WHAT WILL BE JUDGED:	Deeds	Deeds
PERSONAL RESULT:	Reward	Condemnation
ULTIMATE RESULT:	Used to honor Christ	Cast out of God's presence into the lake of fire

b)   Read 1 Cor. 9:24-27 and 2 Tim. 2:3-7; 4:7-8. How does receiving a reward become a motivation for obedience?

_____

_____

_____

Christ Is Worthy

Our most noble motivation for serving Christ is simply that He is worthy of our love and obedience. The apostle John recorded his vision of the Lord and his response to His glory:

> *After these things I looked, and behold, a door standing open in heaven, and the first voice which I had heard, like the sound of a trumpet speaking with me, said, "Come up here, and I will show you what must take place after these things."*
>
> *Immediately I was in the Spirit; and behold, a throne was standing in heaven, and One sitting on the throne.*
>
> *And He who was sitting was like a jasper stone and a sardius in appearance; and there was a rainbow around the throne, like an emerald in appearance.*
>
> *And around the throne were twenty-four thrones; and upon the thrones I saw twenty-four elders sitting, clothed in white garments, and golden crowns on their heads. . . .*

And when the living creatures give glory and honor and thanks to Him who sits on the throne, to Him who lives forever and ever,

the twenty-four elders will fall down before Him who sits on the throne, and will worship Him who lives forever and ever, and will cast their crowns before the throne, saying,

"Worthy art Thou, our Lord and our God, to receive glory and honor and power; for Thou didst create all things, and because of Thy will they existed, and were created."

Rev. 4:1-4, 9-11

Each time we choose to obey, we express the righteousness we have in Christ. Our performance, then, becomes a reflection of who we are in Him, and we draw on His power and wisdom so that we can honor Him.

6. *a)* Read 1 Cor. 3:16-17 and 1 Pet. 2:9. How are you described?

_____

_____

_____

b) What purposes for our lives do these passages suggest?

_____

_____

_____

_____

7. *a)* How much are you motivated by each of these six reasons to obey God? Reflect on these motivations and rate each on a scale of zero (no motivation to you at all) to ten (a persistent, conscious, compelling motivation):

_____ The love of Christ motivates us to obey Him.

_____ Sin is destructive.

_____ The Father will discipline us if we continue in a habit of sin.

_____ His commands for us are good.

_____ We will receive rewards for obedience.

_____ Christ is worthy of our obedience.

b)   Do any of these seem "purer" or "higher" to you? If so, which ones? Why?

_____

_____

_____

_____

c)   Which of these do you need to concentrate on? What can you do to further develop this motivation?

_____

_____

_____

_____

Improper Motivations for Obedience

Jesus repeatedly emphasized that His concern is not only what we do, but why we do it. The Pharisees obeyed many rules and regulations, but their hearts were far from the Lord. Motives are important! The following represent some poor motivations for obeying God and their possible results:

Someone May Find Out

Many people obey God because they are afraid of what others will think of them if they don't obey. Allen went on church visitation because he feared what his Sunday school class would think if he didn't. Barbara was married, but wanted to go out with a man at work. She didn't because of what others might think.

There are problems with determining behavior solely on the opinions of others. First, there are times when no one is watching. If the motive to refrain from sin is missing, we may indulge in it. A second problem is that our desire to disobey may eventually exceed the peer pressure to obey. Finally, once someone has found out we've sinned, we may no longer have a reason to obey.

8.   Is the "fear of someone finding out" a motivation for you to obey God? If it is, identify the specific sin you are trying to avoid; then go back over the six reasons to obey Him. Which of these proper motives seems to encourage you most in regard to your specific sin?

God Will Be Angry with Me

Some people obey God because they think He will get angry with them if they don't. We've already discussed the difference in God's discipline and punishment, but to reiterate, God disciplines us in love, not anger. His response to our sin is grief, not condemnation (Eph. 4:30).

Hank was afraid that God would "zap" him if he did anything wrong, so he performed for God. He lived each day in fear of God's anger. Predictably, his relationship with the Lord was cold and mechanical.

God doesn't want us to live in fear of His anger, but in response to His love. This produces joyful obedience instead of fear.

9. If you knew that God's response to your sin was grief instead of anger, would that affect your motivation to obey Him? Why or why not?

_____

_____

_____

I Couldn't Approve of Myself if I Didn't Obey

Some people obey God in an attempt to live up to certain standards they've set for themselves. Sadly, the idea of yielding their lives to a loving Lord is often far from their minds. They are only trying to live up to their own standards, and if they don't meet those standards, they feel ashamed. These people are primarily concerned with do's and don'ts. Instead of an intimate relationship with God, they see the Christian life as a ritual with the key emphasis on rules. If these people succeed in keeping the rules, they often become prideful. They may also tend to compare themselves with others, hoping to be accepted on the basis of being a little bit better than someone else.

Phillip was raised in a strict church family. He was taught that cursing is a terrible sin. All of Phillip's friends cursed, but he never did. He secretly thought that he was better than his friends. The issue with Phillip was never what God wanted or God's love for him. Instead it was his own compulsion to live up to his standards. Phillip needed to base his behavior on God and His Word, not on his own standards.

God gave us His commands out of love for us. We are protected and freed to enjoy life more fully as we obey Him.

10. *a)*   What things are you not doing because you couldn't stand yourself if you did them?

_____

_____

_____

_____

    b)   What are you doing to obey God with the motivation to meet your own standards?

_____

_____

_____

_____

I'll Obey to Be Blessed

God doesn't swap marbles. If our sole motive to obey is to be blessed, we are simply attempting to manipulate God. The underlying assumption is: *I've been good enough. . . bless me.* It's true that we will reap what we sow. It's true that obedience keeps us within God's plan for us. But our decision to obey should never be based solely on God's rewarding us.

Brian went to church so that God would bless his business, not because he wanted to worship God. Cheryl chose not to spread gossip about Diane because she had told God that she wouldn't tell anybody about Diane if He would get her the promotion she wanted.

11. *a)*   Do you try to make deals with God? Why or why not?

_____

_____

_____

b) We will never be totally freed of improper motives until we're with the Lord, but what is the process of changing improper motives to godly motives?

_____

_____

_____

c) How can the Holy Spirit help you in this process?

_____

_____

Christ has freed us from the bondage of sin so that we can respond to Him in obedience. We have discussed six biblical reasons to be involved in good works:

1. The love of Christ motivates us to obey Him.
2. Sin is destructive.
3. The Father will discipline us.
4. His commands for us are good.
5. We will receive rewards.
6. Obedience is an opportunity to honor God.

There are times when our feelings seem to get in the way of our obedience. We may want to indulge in some particular sin, or we may be afraid of failure or what someone might think of us. We may be selfish or maybe just tired. But the Lord never said pleasant emotions were a prerequisite for following Him. He said, "If anyone wishes to come after Me, let him deny himself *(and the 'right' to pleasant emotions),* and take up his cross daily, and follow Me" (Luke 9:23). This doesn't mean we should deny our emotions, whether they are positive or negative. We should express them fully to the Lord, telling Him how we feel, and then act in faith on His Word. But spiritual growth, character development and Christian service should not be held hostage by our emotions. God has given each of us a will, and we can choose to honor the Lord in spite of our feelings.

In different situations, we will draw upon different motivations for obedience. Sometimes we will need to be reminded of the destructiveness of sin in order to choose righteousness. At other times we will be truly overwhelmed by God's love and want to honor Him. Either way, it is our underlying motive which determines if our actions are done to honor God or to selfishly make us more acceptable to Him, to others or ourselves.

12. *a)*   Are your emotions prompting you to postpone obedience in any area of your life? If yes, what area(s)?

_____

_____

_____

  b)   What steps of action do you need to take to obey the Lord?

_____

_____

_____

_____

As you become more aware of correct motives for obedience, and as you begin to identify improper motivations in your life, you may think, *I've never done anything purely for the Lord in my whole life!* You may feel a sense of pain and remorse for your inappropriate motives. But try not to demean yourself for your past attitudes. . .they are common to all of us. Instead realize that the Lord wants you to make godly choices today so that you can enjoy the benefits of those decisions in the future. Then ask the Holy Spirit to help you develop a sense of intensity about these choices, as Paul wrote, . . .*we have as our ambition. . . to be pleasing to Him* (2 Cor. 5:9).

Realize, too, that because your motives are a reflection of what you believe, they will change as your belief system changes. Considering and applying God's truth consistently will have a profound and far-reaching impact on your motives. As you reject Satan's lies, you will be *transformed by the renewing of your mind. . .* (Rom. 12:2). You will have an increasing desire to honor the One who loves you and purchased you by His own blood.

So, as an act of your will, choose to honor the Lord no matter what your emotions tell you, and consistently learn and apply the truths of God's Word so that these truths begin to pervade your thoughts.

Your motives won't become totally pure until you see the Lord face to face (1 John 3:2), but the more you grow in your understanding of Him and relationship with Him, the more you will desire to honor Him with your love, loyalty and obedience.

Step 12

Overcoming Emotional Roadblocks

"Why do I act this way?"

"Why can't I ever feel secure and happy?"

"I feel numb. I know I should feel angry or happy or sad, but I just feel numb."

"Why am I so volatile?"

"Why do I give in so readily? I am so easily manipulated!"

"I treat my children the same way my parents treated me—and I hate it!"

These and many other questions and statements are expressions of profound desperation. Many of us have developed strong defense mechanisms to block emotional pain and to win the approval of others. Some of us are driven to succeed. Some of us have only selective memories. Some of us have become emotionally numb, or sullen and depressed, and some of us are withdrawn from others. Some of us seem to be even-tempered most of the time, but occasionally we explode in anger. Any of these emotional roadblocks can prevent us from enjoying intimacy with God and others.

To overcome these roadblocks, we need to go to their source: the events that caused us pain. Then we can experience the hurt, feel the anger, grieve over our loss and accept the Lord's grace even in the midst of our pain. This process does not yield instantaneous results. The procedure can be long, but it does result in hope and healing.

In chapter 16, "What Do I Do with My Emotions?" we looked at the stages a person goes through as he comes to grips with emotional trauma. Let's review those stages.

Denial: A defense mechanism which is demonstrated by an inability or unwilling-ness to recognize one's problems. Those in denial tend to rationalize conflicts and justify either their own behavior or someone else's. They also will attempt to avoid painful emotions by suppression, diversion and/or withdrawal.

Bargaining: Our first response to the reality of any hurt, neglect and condemnation we've experienced is usually bargaining. We try to make a deal: *What can I do to get him to love me?* But the bargaining stage still lacks objectivity.

Bargaining may be triggered by an initial awareness of hurt and anger, but because it usually precedes a deeper awareness of those emotions, bargaining is in effect sandwiched between pain and anger. (The entire process, as you may recall, doesn't follow a rigid schedule. People tend to drift back and forth over these stages as they continue to gain new insights.)

Anger: When a person begins to feel the pain he has suppressed (often for many years), he usually becomes very angry. His anger may be directed toward God or toward the one(s) who hurt him, including himself.

Grief: After a time of anger, the person's indignation abates and a sense of loss prevails. He realizes that he has lost the chance to have a happy childhood, a close relationship with his parents or some other important and meaningful experience in life. He experiences deep sorrow over the qualities of life he has never had—qualities like love, intimacy and security.

Acceptance: Sooner or later, the process of grieving for these losses is over, and though the person may have periods of anger and grief from time to time, he can accept the concept that a loving and sovereign God has a perfect plan for his life. Now he can begin to experience the intimacy and warmth of God and other people previously blocked by his defense mechanism(s).

Step 12 is an introduction to the process described above. For many people, it is a pivotal step which may provide the framework for the healing they so desperately need from the Lord.

Before you begin to apply the principles that will help you through these stages, there are some additional ideas that can aid you:

1.   Don't rush the process. It will take more than an hour or a day to dig through the defense mechanisms you have erected over the years. You may have suppressed hurt and anger for twenty, thirty, forty years or more. Don't expect too much too soon. Take time to reflect and to experience the hurt and anger you have suppressed. Then, take time to feel sorrow in the grief process. You will experience a gradual healing throughout these stages. The entire process may well take months (or even years!), but it is worth it.

2.   Throughout the process, you will become aware of a growing sense of objectivity. Defense mechanisms may protect us from pain, but they blind us to the truth. Some people will realize that they experienced guilt (instead of hurt) when their parents shouted at them. These people felt responsible for their parents' happiness, and when their parents weren't happy, they believed it was their fault. Some people will realize that, apart from divine intervention, their parents will never love and affirm them, no matter how hard they try to please them. Such objectivity often brings with it a new sense of identity. The truth is a tool for breaking one's bondage to parental approval and for beginning to develop a healthy sense of independence.

3.   As you begin to experience and express your new identity, it is quite possible that your parents and siblings may not like it at all. As long as you play your role in the family, they are in control. Your new identity may pose a threat to their control, and they may respond with more condemnation and manipulation than ever! Be prepared for more conflict, not less.

4.   Many of us may associate grieving with the loss of a loved one at death. However, the death of a child's identity through neglect, manipulation or condemnation is a very real loss, even though there is no actual corpse to prove it. Still, grieving over this kind of loss is unusual because it is intangible, and because you may have to continue relating to the person(s) who caused the hurt. These subsequent experiences of grief will slowly diminish if going through the stages is initially a deep, profound and cathartic process.

5.   Learning to respond with a new identity (especially to those who have hurt you deeply) is much like learning to ride a bicycle. No six year old can get off of his tricycle, hop onto a 26" ten-speed and ride around the neighborhood success-fully. A person learns to ride a bike by trying... and falling... and trying again, going a little farther. . . and falling again. Turns and hills present new challenges. . . and new falls.

Be realistic about your progress. Don't expect perfection! Responding within the framework of a new identity is at first as awkward and scary as it is to get on a bike for the first time. After a while, and after a lot of practice, it gets easier.

6.   Be prepared for the battle ahead by fortifying your mind and heart with the encouragement of the Scriptures. Chapter 12 and step 7, "The Names of God," step 9, "Children of God" and step 10, "Characteristics of Christ" will help you learn what's true about the Lord and your new identity. Take time to study, reflect and memorize. It will be well worth the trouble!

7.   The process of overcoming denial and experiencing hurt, anger and grief is a painful ordeal. A loving and faithful friend can help you endure it. There will be times when you will need a fresh perspective, some objective wisdom, strong encouragement or a warm hug of reassurance. Find someone who understands what you're going through and who will be a true friend to you.

DENIAL

The first several steps in this workbook are designed to help you overcome denial by understanding how your parents have related to each other, how they have related to you and how they have affected your concept of God.

Perhaps these exercises have already awakened some of your repressed emotions. The next section will help you go through yet another step in this process.

BARGAINING

As you have become aware of the pain of your past, how have you tried to get your parents to give you the love and acceptance you have wanted? What have you said or done to win their approval?

_____

_____

_____

_____

_____

_____

Dealing with Previous Hurt and Anger

To complete this exercise, you'll need to find a quiet place where you won't be disturbed. Ask the Lord to remind you of specific instances in your past, particularly in your childhood, when you experienced hurt, anger or guilt because of your parents. Some of these events will probably come to mind very quickly, but others may not. You may have a lull of twenty to thirty minutes or even several days before the Lord reminds you of an instance or two, and then another period of time before you remember another one. Make a list of these events until your memory's "well has run dry."

List and briefly describe those events below and on the following pages. (Use additional sheets of paper if necessary.)

1. _____

_____

_____

2. _____

_____

_____

3. _____

_____

_____

4. _____

_____

_____

5. _____
   _____
   _____

6. _____
   _____
   _____

7. _____
   _____
   _____

8. _____
   _____
   _____

9. _____
   _____
   _____

10. _____
    _____
    _____

11. _____
    _____
    _____

12. _____
    _____
    _____

13. _____
    _____
    _____

14. _____
   _____
   _____

15. _____
   _____
   _____

Now go back and describe these events in more detail. For example:

1. *Event:*
   My mother made me wear a new dress to school. It didn't fit. I felt ugly and the other girls laughed at me.

My feelings then:
   I was humiliated and felt ashamed. I was angry with my mother.

My actions:
   I tried to avoid people all day. I went to the restroom to cry. I didn't say anything to my mother because she would have laughed at me and then she would have been mad at me.

What a healthy response would have been:
   I think most little girls could have told their mothers that they didn't want to wear a dress that no longer fit properly because the other girls would laugh at them. Their mothers would respond by being reasonable and loving. They wouldn't demand that they wear a dress like that.

How I feel about the event and people involved now:
   I am really mad at my mother. She wasn't reasonable or loving. She only wanted her way. She didn't care about my feelings at all.

Lie(s) I've been believing (see chart on pp. 126-127):
   Those who fail are unworthy of love and deserve to be blamed and condemned. Fear of punishment.

God's truth (see chart on pp. 126-127):

Christ satisfied God's wrath by His death on the cross; therefore, I am deeply loved by God. As I experience God's love and forgiveness in my life, I will be able to extend His love and forgiveness to others, including my mother.

Steps I need to take now:

I need to forgive my mother. I also need to be more honest in my relationships with others; therefore, it would be wise for me to seek relationships with people who value and affirm honesty.

2. *Event:*

I was hit in the head with a baseball bat, and my forehead bled a lot, but I refused to cry because my father never let me cry about anything.

My feelings then:

I was afraid that I might have a concussion or that I would pass out, but I was also afraid that if I cried, everyone would think I was a wimp.

My actions:

My friends tried to get me to go home, but I stayed in the game even though blood got in my eyes and all over my uniform.

What a healthy response would have been:

I would have cried and my father would have taken me home to comfort me and put a bandage on the cut.

How I feel about the event and people involved now:

I'm hurt. My father was always tough with me. He never cried, and he wouldn't let me cry. Now I don't feel emotions very much. I've blocked my feelings all my life.

Lie(s) I've been believing (see chart on pp. 126-127):

I must meet certain standards to feel good about myself. I must be approved by certain others to feel good about myself.

God's truth (see chart on pp. 126-127):

It would be nice to have the approval of others, but even if I don't, I'm fully pleasing to God and am totally accepted by Him despite my performance. Therefore, I can be vulnerable with God, and can afford to take the risk of being rejected by others.

Steps I need to take now:

I need to forgive my father. I also need to ask God to help me experience my emotions so that I can have healthier relationships.

As you go through this exercise, remember to relive the event, but this time don't suppress the emotions or try to change them. Express them fully to the Lord (Ps. 62:8).

1. *Event:*

_____

_____

_____

_____

   a) My feelings then:

_____

_____

_____

   b) My actions:

_____

_____

_____

   c) What a healthy response would have been:

_____

_____

_____

d) How I feel about the event and people involved now:

_____

_____

_____

e) Lie(s) I've been believing:

_____

_____

_____

f) God's truth:

_____

_____

_____

g) Steps I need to take now:

_____

_____

_____

2. *Event:*

_____

_____

_____

a) My feelings then:

_____

_____

_____

b) My actions:

_____

_____

_____

c) What a healthy response would have been:

_____

_____

_____

d) How I feel about the event and people involved now:

_____

_____

_____

e) Lie(s) I've been believing:

_____

_____

_____

f) God's truth:

_____

_____

_____

g) Steps I need to take now:

_____

_____

_____

3. *Event:*

_____

_____

_____

a) My feelings then:

_____

_____

_____

b) My actions:

_____

_____

_____

c) What a healthy response would have been:

_____

_____

_____

d) How I feel about the event and people involved now:

_____

_____

_____

e) Lie(s) I've been believing:

_____

_____

_____

f) God's truth:

_____

_____

_____

g) Steps I need to take now:

_____

_____

_____

4. *Event:*

_____

_____

_____

a) My feelings then:

_____
_____
_____

b) My actions:

_____
_____
_____

c) What a healthy response would have been:

_____
_____
_____

d) How I feel about the event and people involved now:

_____
_____
_____

e) Lie(s) I've been believing:

_____
_____
_____

f) God's truth:

_____
_____
_____

g) Steps I need to take now:

_____
_____
_____

5. *Event:*

_____

_____

_____

a) My feelings then:

_____

_____

_____

b) My actions:

_____

_____

_____

c) What a healthy response would have been:

_____

_____

_____

d) How I feel about the event and people involved now:

_____

_____

_____

e) Lie(s) I've been believing:

_____

_____

_____

f) God's truth:

_____

_____

_____

g) Steps I need to take now:

_____

_____

_____

6. *Event:*

_____

_____

_____

a) My feelings then:

_____

_____

_____

b) My actions:

_____

_____

_____

c) What a healthy response would have been:

_____

_____

_____

d) How I feel about the event and people involved now:

_____

_____

_____

e) Lie(s) I've been believing:

_____

_____

_____

f) God's truth:

_____

_____

_____

g) Steps I need to take now:

_____

_____

_____

7. *Event:*

_____

_____

_____

a) My feelings then:

_____

_____

_____

b) My actions:

_____

_____

_____

c) What a healthy response would have been:

_____

_____

_____

d) How I feel about the event and people involved now:

_____

_____

_____

e)   Lie(s) I've been believing:

_____

_____

_____

f)   God's truth:

_____

_____

_____

g)   Steps I need to take now:

_____

_____

_____

8.   *Event:*

_____

_____

_____

a)   My feelings then:

_____

_____

_____

b)   My actions:

_____

_____

_____

c)   What a healthy response would have been:

_____

_____

_____

   d)   How I feel about the event and people involved now:

_____

_____

_____

   e)   Lie(s) I've been believing:

_____

_____

_____

   f)   God's truth:

_____

_____

_____

   g)   Steps I need to take now:

_____

_____

_____

9. *Event:*

_____

_____

_____

   a)   My feelings then:

_____

_____

_____

   b)   My actions:

_____

_____

_____

c) What a healthy response would have been:

_____

_____

_____

d) How I feel about the event and people involved now:

_____

_____

_____

e) Lie(s) I've been believing:

_____

_____

_____

f) God's truth:

_____

_____

_____

g) Steps I need to take now:

_____

_____

_____

10. *Event:*

_____

_____

_____

a) My feelings then:

_____

_____

_____

b) My actions:

_____

_____

_____

c) What a healthy response would have been:

_____

_____

_____

d) How I feel about the event and people involved now:

_____

_____

_____

e) Lie(s) I've been believing:

_____

_____

_____

f) God's truth:

_____

_____

_____

g) Steps I need to take now:

_____

_____

_____

11. *Event:*

_____

_____

_____

a) My feelings then:

_____

_____

_____

b) My actions:

_____

_____

_____

c) What a healthy response would have been:

_____

_____

_____

d) How I feel about the event and people involved now:

_____

_____

_____

e) Lie(s) I've been believing:

_____

_____

_____

f) God's truth:

_____

_____

_____

g) Steps I need to take now:

_____

_____

_____

12. *Event:*

_____

_____

_____

   a)   My feelings then:

_____

_____

_____

   b)   My actions:

_____

_____

_____

   c)   What a healthy response would have been:

_____

_____

_____

   d)   How I feel about the event and people involved now:

_____

_____

_____

   e)   Lie(s) I've been believing:

_____

_____

_____

   f)   God's truth:

_____

_____

_____

g)   Steps I need to take now:

_____

_____

_____

13. *Event:*

_____

_____

_____

a)   My feelings then:

_____

_____

_____

b)   My actions:

_____

_____

_____

c)   What a healthy response would have been:

_____

_____

_____

d)   How I feel about the event and people involved now:

_____

_____

_____

e)   Lie(s) I've been believing:

_____

_____

_____

f) God's truth:

_____

_____

_____

g) Steps I need to take now:

_____

_____

_____

14. *Event:*

_____

_____

_____

a) My feelings then:

_____

_____

_____

b) My actions:

_____

_____

_____

c) What a healthy response would have been:

_____

_____

_____

d) How I feel about the event and people involved now:

_____

_____

_____

e)   Lie(s) I've been believing:

_____

_____

_____

f)   God's truth:

_____

_____

_____

g)   Steps I need to take now:

_____

_____

_____

15. *Event:*

_____

_____

_____

a)   My feelings then:

_____

_____

_____

b)   My actions:

_____

_____

_____

c)   What a healthy response would have been:

_____

_____

_____

d)   How I feel about the event and people involved now:

_____

_____

_____

e)   Lie(s) I've been believing:

_____

_____

_____

f)   God's truth:

_____

_____

_____

g)   Steps I need to take now:

_____

_____

_____

GRIEF

After several weeks or months of experiencing and expressing repressed hurt and anger, you will begin to grieve. Look at each of the events that you described on pages 297-314, and answer the following questions using additional paper as needed:

1.   What did you lose?

_____

_____

_____

2.   What would a child in a healthier situation have had that you didn't have?

_____

_____

3. What do you wish you had received from your parents?

_____

_____

_____

4. How has your view of God been affected by your parents?

_____

_____

_____

_____

5. How have your relationships been affected?

_____

_____

_____

_____

_____

6. How have your self-concept, identity and confidence been affected?

_____

_____

_____

_____

7. How do you feel about what you have lost?

_____

_____

_____

ACCEPTANCE

As you continue to experience feelings of hurt, anger and grief, you will begin to see that you can have a relationship with God that is warm, intimate and powerful. You also will begin to see that God can build strength in your life through pain.

1. How has your concept of God changed as you have gone through this process?

    _____

    _____

    _____

2. What strengths has God built into your life through your painful family experiences? (See chapter 17, "Rivers in the Desert.")

    _____

    _____

    _____

3. How might God use these strengths to help you and others?

    _____

    _____

    _____

4. What do you need to know, feel and do when your parents and siblings don't understand your new identity, attitude, independence or actions?

    _____

    _____

    _____

    _____

    _____

    _____

    _____

    _____

    _____

    _____

Step 13

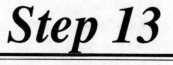

Forgiving Others

The following exercises are based on chapter 9, and are designed to help you understand biblical principles of forgiveness and apply them to your relationships with others: [1]

1. Read Matt. 18:21-35.

   a) How great was the debt of the king's servant?

   _____

   _____

   b) Was it possible for him ever to repay it?

   _____

2. *a)* Likewise, before you trusted Christ, how great was your debt to God?

   _____

   _____

   b) Was it possible for you ever to repay it?

   _____

3. *a)* What did the servant ask for?

   _____

b)   What did the king grant him?

_____

4.   Why was the king's servant so harsh with his fellow servant over such a small debt?

_____

_____

5.   Read Luke 7:36-50 (especially verse 47) and compare it with the parable in Matt. 18:21-35. What is the foundation for being able to love and forgive others?

_____

_____

6.   Read Eph. 4:32 and Col. 3:12-13.

a)   To what degree are we to forgive others?

_____

b)   Describe how God has forgiven you:

_____

_____

7.   Name some of the effects people experience when they fail to forgive (their attitudes toward others, their opinion of themselves, the quality of their relationships, etc.):

_____

_____

_____

_____

_____

8. Do you see any of the answers to question 7 in your life? In your attitudes toward others? Toward yourself? If so, describe them:

_____

_____

_____

_____

9. Is there any particular sin for which you haven't experienced God's forgiveness?

_____

_____

List ten things for which you are glad God in Christ has forgiven you. This will prime you to be willing to forgive all other offenders.

1. _____   6. _____
2. _____   7. _____
3. _____   8. _____
4. _____   9. _____
5. _____   10. _____

The exercise on the following pages will help you recognize any lack of forgiveness in your life and enable you to begin to forgive freely, as God in Christ has forgiven you.

1. Offense: List in some detail several events which caused you pain.

2. Persons to Be Forgiven: List all who participated in the offense.

3. Reasons for Failing to Forgive: Go through the list of reasons for not forgiving on the next page, noting in the exercise the ones that apply.

4. Act of Forgiveness: Choose to forgive, remembering the complete forgiveness you have in Christ.

At the conclusion of the exercise, use the prayer below (or use your own) as an exercise of faith for each offense.

Summary of Reasons for Not Forgiving

1. *The offense was too great.*
2. *He (she) won't accept responsibility for the offense.*
3. *He (she) isn't truly sorry.*
4. *He (she) never asked to be forgiven.*
5. *He (she) will do it again.*
6. *He (she) did it again.*
7. *I don't like him (her).*
8. *He (she) did it deliberately.*
9. *If I forgive the offense, I'll have to treat the offender well.*
10. *Someone has to punish him (her).*
11. *Something keeps me from forgiving.*
12. *I'll be a hypocrite if I forgive, because I don't feel like forgiving.*
13. *I'll forgive, but I won't ever forget.*
14. *I have forgiven a lesser offense after excusing the real offense.*

Dear Lord,

I forgive _____ *for*

_____ *(offense) on the basis*

that God has freely forgiven me and commanded me to forgive others. I have the capacity to do this because Christ has completely forgiven me. I do not excuse this person's offense in any way, nor do I use any excuse for not extending forgiveness. Thank You, Lord Jesus, for enabling me to forgive.

I also confess that I have sinned by using the following excuses for not forgiving:

_____   _____

_____   _____

_____   _____

_____   _____

_____   _____
_____   _____
_____   _____
_____   _____
_____   _____
_____   _____
_____   _____
_____   _____
_____   _____
_____   _____
_____   _____
_____   _____
_____   _____
_____   _____

Step 14

Breaking the Cycle:
Modeling God's Character to Your Children

To the degree that we understand and experience God's love, forgiveness and power, we will be able to express these characteristics and model them to our children.

The following step is designed to help you model the character of God to your children. (If you don't have children, you may want to apply what you learn in this step to your other family members, roommate or friends.)

1. Read Ex. 34:5-8. Is it fair for God to allow sin to be reproduced in our families? Why or why not?

_____

_____

_____

_____

2. Read Eph. 4:20-24. How does the process described here apply to modeling God's character to your children? Be specific.

_____

_____

_____

_____

3. Read Joel 2:24-26. Does this passage give you hope about your relationships
    with your children? Why or why not?

    _____

    _____

    _____

4. *a)* Describe your self-concept. What do you think of yourself? What is the
    basis of your self-worth?

    _____

    _____

    _____

    _____

    b) What difference would it make in your life and in your relationships with
    your children if your self-concept were based on the unconditional love of God
    instead of on your performance and the opinions of others?

    _____

    _____

    _____

5. *a)* What is your purpose in life? If a friend were to observe your attitude and
    activities, what would he say is your purpose in life?

    _____

    _____

    _____

    b) Does your purpose need to be changed or modified in some way? If so,
    how?

    _____

    _____

    _____

6. *a)* How would being thankful for your children affect your relationships with
    them?

    _____

_____

_____

b)   How would responding to their disobedience in grief instead of anger affect your relationship with them?

_____

_____

_____

7.   What physical and/or emotional stage of development (Bonding, Limits, Adolescence, Maturity) do you think each of your children is in? Why do you think so?

Child's Age	Physical Stage of Development	Emotional Stage of Development
_____	_____	_____
_____	_____	_____
_____	_____	_____
_____	_____	_____

8.   What are some specific steps you can take to help each child progress in his or her stage of development? (You may want to review chapter 7.)

_____

_____

_____

_____

9.   Using the form on the following page, write out your schedule of an "average week."

a) How much time do you spend working, sleeping, preparing, being with your spouse, with your children, in Bible study and prayer, doing chores around the house, watching TV, doing hobbies, etc.?

_____

_____

_____

	MORNING	AFTERNOON	EVENING
SUN.			
MON.			
TUES.			
WED.			
THURS.			
FRI.			
SAT.			

b)   How much time do you spend each week giving undivided attention to your children?

_____

_____

_____

_____

c)   Do you need to change your schedule to spend more time with them? If so, what specific changes will you make?

_____

_____

_____

_____

10. What actions will you take to model the character of God to your children? How will you express:

a)   a meaningful touch?

_____

_____

_____

_____

b)   a spoken message?

_____

_____

_____

_____

c)   high value to the one being blessed?

_____

_____

_____

d) a special future for the one being blessed?

_____

_____

_____

_____

e) an active commitment to fulfill the blessing?

_____

_____

_____

_____

11. Look at the following list of family traditions.[1] What do your children enjoy doing? What can you do together? What traditions do you already have? What traditions will you begin?

Christmas Traditions

Birthday Box for Baby Jesus

Make this the most beautiful present under the tree. Have a Bible in the box with the Christmas story marked. Open this present first, and begin gift-giving time by reading the Christmas story.

Decorate Your Children's Doors

Put wrapping paper and a big bow on each door. Then place a gift tag on it that says something like this: "Meagan, you are God's gift to our family, and God's gift to you is Jesus."

Give Coupons to Family Members

These are gifts of time and can be special ways to tell others how much we love them.

Valentine's Day Traditions

Baked Valentines

Bake a cake in a heart-shaped pan. Write Bible verses that speak of love on small strips of paper. Fold them up and wrap them in a small square of foil. Place as many verses as you would like in the batter before baking. After serving the cake, let whoever finds the pieces of foil open them up and read the verses to the group.

Valentine's Day Dinner

Have a candlelight dinner for your children. You can also choose a specific country for the theme of this special time together. Serve the appropriate ethnic food. Talk about God's love and how we need to take His love to the world. Pray together after giving everyone a specific prayer request for that country.

Easter Traditions

Celebrate with a Romanian Custom

In Romania, an Easter tradition for Christians is to place red eggs on the dinner table (one in front of each person). Before the meal, each person picks up his egg. The person at the head of the table starts by turning to the person on his right and saying, "He is risen." That person responds by saying "He is risen, indeed," and then turns to the person on his right and repeats the process until the message has gone around the table.

Passover Meal

You can obtain information about the Passover meal from the book, *Hebrew Christian Passover Haggadah,* by Arnold G. Frucktenbrus, c/o Beth Bar Shalom Fellowship, 460 Sylvan Avenue, P.O. Box 1331, Englewood Cliff, New Jersey, 07632.

Birthdays

VIP Chair

Decorate a special chair for the birthday person. If it is for your child, tell the story of his/her birth and how much he/she was wanted.

Celebrate "Spiritual Birthdays"

For children, give Christian books, tapes, games, etc.

Thanksgiving

Talk about the people you are especially thankful for. Write them a letter and express your feelings for them.

Read the story of the "Ten Lepers" at your Thanksgiving meal. Jesus healed ten of them and only one came back to thank Him. Talk about their lack of thankfulness.

Weekly

Have a special breakfast on Saturday mornings: chocolate chip pancakes, waffles, etc.

Schedule a family fun night with games and snacks.

Have a family picnic on Sunday afternoon that includes reading and games.

Daily

Read together before bedtime.

Conduct family devotions in the morning or evening.

Keep a chart of responsibilities for each person (based on age and ability) with treats for jobs well done.

Other

Canoeing, hiking, rafting, fishing

Working on hobbies together, building or making things together

Saving children's clothes or other heirlooms

Special celebrations of birthdays

Step 15

Breaking the Cycle:
Responding to Your Parents

This step is designed to help you respond to your parents in a way that honors the Lord and reflects His wisdom, love and power.

1. To summarize the first several steps in this workbook, describe your relationships with your parents when you were a child. How did they show affection? How did they discipline you? Did you feel loved and accepted? Why or why not?

_____

_____

_____

_____

_____

_____

_____

_____

_____

2. What does it mean to honor one's parents (Eph. 6:2-3)?

_____

_____

_____

_____

3. Do you feel responsible for making your parents happy? Why or why not?

_____

_____

4. **Principle 1: See yourself as a conqueror, not a victim.**
    a) Read Rom. 8:35, 37. Do you see yourself as a conqueror or as a victim in your relationships with your parents?

_____

_____

    b) What differences would it make if you saw yourself as a conqueror?

_____

_____

_____

_____

5. **Principle 2: See your parents as people, not villains.**
    a) Describe your father's relationships with his parents:

_____

_____

_____

_____

_____

    b) Describe your mother's relationships with her parents:

_____

_____

_____

_____

_____

_____

c) How does understanding your parents' families affect your attitude toward them?

_____

_____

_____

6. **Principle 3: Develop a healthy sense of independence.**
   a) What does it mean to have a "healthy independence" or sense of objectivity in your relationships with your parents?

_____

_____

   b) How would this help you?

_____

_____

7. **Principle 4: Make godly choices.**
   Paraphrase these passages:

> *By this the love of God was manifested in us, that God has sent His only begotten Son into the world so that we might live through Him.*
> *In this is love, not that we loved God, but that He loved us and sent His Son to be the propitiation for our sins.*
> *Beloved, if God so loved us, we also ought to love one another.*
> 1 John 4:9-11

Paraphrase:

_____

_____

_____

_____

> *. . . bearing with one another, and forgiving each other, whoever has a complaint against anyone; just as the Lord forgave you, so also should you.*
>
> Col. 3:13

Paraphrase:

_____

_____

_____

_____

> *Wherefore, accept one another, just as Christ also accepted us to the glory of God.*
>
> Rom. 15:7

Paraphrase:

_____

_____

9. List some ways you can communicate God's love, forgiveness and acceptance to your parents:

_____

_____

_____

_____

_____

_____

_____

10. **Principle 5: Be prepared.**

  a) What do you need to do to prepare yourself for your communications and interactions with your parents?

  _____

  _____

  _____

  _____

  b) What should you always do?

  _____

  _____

  _____

  c) What should you never do?

  _____

  _____

  _____

  _____

  d) What is wise to avoid?

  _____

  _____

  _____

  _____

  e) On what common ground can you build or rebuild your relationships with your parents?

  _____

  _____

  _____

  _____

  _____

Step 16

Christ Repairs Damaged Lives

Here is a plan you can use for the rest of your life. It will help you to use your problems to develop a deeper and richer relationship with God the Father through His Son.

1. *Before you continue, review chapter 15 and step 3.* Step 16 is built on the foundational truths explained in detail in chapter 15. Reread that chapter before continuing with this section.

2. *From step 3, select a negative characteristic you recognized in one of your parents which is now a characteristic of your life.* In the spaces below, briefly describe this characteristic:

_____

_____

_____

_____

   This particular characteristic probably carries with it a sense of pain for you. It has probably caused you a lot of concern in the past.

   a) Describe how you have responded to this characteristic in your parents:

_____

_____

_____

_____

_____

b)   How have you felt about this characteristic in yourself?

_____

_____

_____

c)   How have you acted?

_____

_____

_____

     Behind your response is one of Satan's lies. Which of those listed below relates to your response? Check the appropriate box or boxes:

❑   **The Fear of Failure:** *I must meet certain standards in order to feel good about myself.*

❑   **The Fear of Rejection:** *I must be approved by certain others to feel good about myself.*

❑   **The Fear of Being Punished:** *Those who fail (including me) are unworthy of love and deserve to be punished.*

❑   **The Feeling of Shame:** *I am what I am. I cannot change. I am hopeless.*

3.   *Use the truth of God's Word to confront these lies.* Step 10 lists eight characteristics of Christ. With each are Scriptures which describe these characteristics for you. These Scriptures reveal the character of your heavenly Father as demonstrated by the life and words of Jesus.

     In the last exercise, you selected a worry or fear you experience because of negative parental influences. Now look through the characteristics of Christ until you find the one which best relates to your fear or fears.

a) In the space below, write the characteristic of Christ you have selected:

_____

_____

b) Look up the Scriptures given with the above characteristic. Underline the ones in your Bible which you want to remember. (You may even decide to memorize some of them!)

c) Which particular verse (or verses) pertaining to this characteristic of Christ is most meaningful to you? Write it in the spaces below:

_____

_____

_____

_____

_____

_____

_____

_____

_____

d) Meditate on this Scripture. What does it teach you about your worth and your ability to overcome your fear?

_____

_____

_____

_____

_____

4. *a)* *Express yourself to the Lord, realizing your situation, rejecting the lies you may be believing and replacing those lies with the powerful truth of God's Word.* You may want to include some of the thoughts on the following page in your prayers:

Realize

Father, I need Your help. I feel angry (or hurt, or. . .) *because. . .* (Pour out your heart to the Lord [Ps. 62:8]).

Reject

Lord, I am experiencing the fear of rejection (or failure, or. . .).

Replace

Father, thank You for the truth of Your Word. (Select a passage from the preceding step that confronts the lie. Think and pray about how you can apply the truth of God's Word to your situation.)

Father, I claim Your peace and protection. You alone are my provider. You understand me completely and You care about me. Thank You that because of Christ's death to pay for my sins, I am deeply loved, completely forgiven, fully pleasing and totally accepted by You.

b) Recall some times that you've felt understood and comforted by the Lord:

_____

_____

_____

_____

_____

_____

_____

_____

Those times that I thought You were distant and insensitive, I was deceived. There is not one moment that You are not sensitive to every detail of my life.

Thank You, Lord, for understanding me, and providing for me. Your truth and Your Spirit are stronger than anything that can come into my life.

Sometimes when we reflect on God's character, our hurt and pain changes to joy rather quickly. At other times our feelings don't change so rapidly. Don't despair. Emotions are fickle. Continue to concentrate on the truth of God's Word, and put yourself in an environment where you can experience His love and acceptance, and see His character modeled by mature, honest believers. Growth takes time and fertile soil.

5. *Begin a twenty-day experiment with this pattern.* Take time each day for the next twenty days to discover the true nature of your heavenly Father by sharing your stresses with Him. (You will find some guidelines to help you with this in the following step.) You may wish to return to step 3 and choose additional characteristics from those you checked, or you may choose to complete the exercise using current situations.

   In either case, refer daily to the list of "Characteristics of Christ." As the next twenty days pass, you will begin to experience positive results from confronting every negative thought with the loving and powerful character of God.

   As you mature, your confidence in Him will give you a new way of dealing with stress. You will no longer be controlled by circumstances. Instead, you will be controlled by the Holy Spirit of God, and you will begin to discover the joy that comes from His control.

Step 17

A Twenty-Day Journal

For the next twenty days select a specific time and place to work on this step. Everything else of value in your life happens by being scheduled, doesn't it? You have a regular time to eat, to begin the workday, to rest, to watch television. Consider developing a habit in your scheduled activities which could permanently change your life by setting aside a specific time each day to spend with God and complete this exercise.

In this step you will be reflecting on God's character by using the "Characteristics of Christ" from step 10. Each time you catch yourself feeling anxious because of a situation, comment, thought, problem or relationship, take that condition to your meeting place. As the days pass, you will expose many thoughts that contradict the truth about God's character.

Below and on the following pages is an outline to guide you through this exercise. Twenty days from now, you will have a good start on developing a new pattern for living—one which we urge you to continue indefinitely.

1. *Realize:* Be objective about your stressful situation by writing it out.

2. *Reject:* Next, list the fear or fears triggered by it.

3. *Replace:* Review the characteristics of Christ and select one appropriate to your situation. Then select a passage of Scripture from page 345 which portrays that aspect of His character. Write out the Scripture which describes this characteristic.

4. Study the passage more specifically, perhaps using the method of observation, interpretation and application:

    • *Observation: Who* is portrayed in this passage? If there is a dialogue between persons, *what* are they saying? *What* are they doing? *When* are they saying or doing it? *Where* does the conversation/activity take place? *How* does the conversation/activity occur?

    • *Interpretation:* What does the passage mean? What biblical principles are portrayed in this passage about God, people, relationships, goals, behavior and responses?

    • *Application:* Ask yourself, *What does this mean to me? How can I specifically apply one or more of these principles today? ...this week? ...this year?* (Avoid trying to apply too much too soon, or you may become frustrated and give up on the process altogether.)

5. In prayer, affirm the application to your situation.

    On the following pages is a list of the passages you paraphrased in step 10. (Note: if you prefer going through a book of the Bible and looking for characteristics of Christ paragraph by paragraph, or if you want to work with some other passages of Scripture, feel free to do so.)

Purpose
Matt. 22:34-40
Matt. 28:18-20
John 17:3-4
Rom. 2:4-5
2 Cor. 5:9
2 Cor. 5:14-15
2 Cor. 5:18-21
Eph. 2:1-3
Eph. 2:10
Phil. 3:7-10
1 Pet. 3:18
Titus 2:11-14

Total Acceptance
John 17:23-24
John 20:17
Rom. 5:10
Rom. 8:15-17
Rom. 15:7
Gal. 4:5-7

Unconditional Love
John 3:16-17
Rom. 8:38-39
Eph. 2:4-9
2 Thess. 2:16-17
1 John 4:9-10

Complete Forgiveness
Matt. 18:21-35
Rom. 3:9-20
Rom. 3:23-24
Rom. 4:4-5
Rom. 5:6-11
Eph. 1:7
Eph. 2:1-10
Col. 2:13-14
Col. 3:13

Authority and Power
1 Cor. 3:6-7
2 Cor. 3:4-6
Eph. 1:18-22
Eph. 6:10-20
Col. 1:15-19
Col. 1: 19-22
Col. 2:15

Hope
Rom. 5:3-5
Rom. 8:28
Eph. 2:12
Titus 3:7
Heb. 6:19
1 Pet. 1:3

Wisdom
Matt. 11:19
1 Cor. 2:1-5
2 Cor. 1:12
Eph. 5:15-21
James 1:5-6

Faithfulness
Matt. 23:23
1 Cor. 10:13
1 Thess. 5:24
2 Tim. 2:11-13
Heb. 10:23

To complete this exercise, you may want to get a small notebook, or you may already have another way of keeping up with your study. Your entries on each page might look something like the following pages:

DAY ONE

Date:___/___/___

1. *Realize:* Describe your situation.

_____

_____

_____

_____

_____

2. *Reject:* Which of the four fears does this trigger for you?

   • **The Fear of Failure:** *I must meet certain standards in order to feel good about myself.*

   • **The Fear of Punishment:** *Those who fail (including me) are unworthy of love and deserve to be punished.*

   • **The Fear of Rejection:** *I must be approved by certain others to feel good about myself.*

   • **The Feeling of Shame:** *I am what I am. I cannot change. I am hopeless.*

3. *Replace*
   a) What characteristic of Christ helps overcome this fear?

• Purpose	• Authority and Power
• Unconditional Love	• Faithfulness
• Complete Forgiveness	• Hope
• Total Acceptance	• Wisdom

b)   From the characteristics above, which passage(s) from page 345 do you find most meaningful and encouraging for this particular situation? Write them out in the spaces below:

_____

_____

_____

_____

_____

_____

_____

_____

_____

_____

4.   What are your...

    a)   Observation(s)?

_____

_____

_____

    b)   Interpretation(s)?

_____

_____

_____

    c)   Application(s)?

_____

_____

_____

5.   Pray. Thank the Lord for the truth of His Word. Ask Him to help you apply His Word and experience His presence today.

Notes

Chapter 1

1. Burton L. White, *The First Three Years of Life,* rev. ed. (Englewood Cliffs, NJ: Prentice-Hall Press, 1985), p. 268.

Chapter 2

1. Jim Craddock, "The Absent-Father Syndrome" (Houston, TX: Rapha Publishing, 1986).

Chapter 5

1. Pat Springle, *Codependency,* 2nd ed. (Houston and Dallas, TX: Rapha Publishing/Word, Inc., 1990), pp. 192-193.

Chapter 9

1. Robert S. McGee, *The Search for Significance,* 2nd ed. (Houston and Dallas, TX: Rapha Publishing/Word, Inc., 1990), pp. 313-323, 325-328.

Chapter 10

1. John Newton, "Amazing Grace," stanzas 1-4, 1779. Tune by Virginia Harmony, 1831. Arranged by Edwin O. Excell, 1990. Source: *The Baptist Hymnal* (Nashville, TN: Convention Press, 1975).

Chapter 11

1. John R.W. Stott, *The Cross of Christ* (Downers Grove, IL: InterVarsity Press, 1986), pp. 193-194.

Chapter 14

1. McGee, *The Search for Significance*, pp. 122-123.

Chapter 18

1. Charles R. Swindoll, *You and Your Child* (Nashville, TN: Thomas Nelson Publishers, 1977), p. 158.

2. McGee, *The Search for Significance*, p. 303.

3. Gary Smalley and John Trent, *The Blessing* (Nashville, TN: Thomas Nelson Publishers, 1986), p. 24.

Chapter 19

1. McGee, *The Search for Significance*, pp. 292-293.

Step 11

1. McGee, *The Search for Significance*, pp. 55-60, 254-264, 269-271.

Step 13

1. McGee, *The Search for Significance*, pp. 320-323, 325-328.

Step 14

1. "Traditions" courtesy of Reneé McIntosh.